# OXFORD THEOLOGICAL MONOGRAPHS

*Oxford Theological Monographs*

———◆———

# TRINITY AND TEMPORALITY

## THE CHRISTIAN DOCTRINE OF GOD IN THE LIGHT OF PROCESS THEOLOGY AND THE THEOLOGY OF HOPE

JOHN J. O'DONNELL, S.J.

OXFORD UNIVERSITY PRESS

1983

1/1984
Phil.

Oxford University Press, Walton Street, Oxford OX2 6DP

London   Glasgow   New York   Toronto
Delhi   Bombay   Calcutta   Madras   Karachi
Kuala Lumpur   Singapore   Hong Kong   Tokyo
Nairobi   Dar es Salaam   Cape Town
Melbourne   Auckland
and associates in
Beirut   Berlin   Ibadan   Mexico City   Nicosia

Oxford is a trade mark of Oxford University Press

Published in the United States by
Oxford University Press, New York

© John J. O'Donnell, S. J., 1983

British Library Cataloguing in Publication Data

O'Donnell, John J.
Trinity and temporality.—(Oxford theological monographs)
1. Trinity
I. Title
231'.044   BT111.2
ISBN 0-19-826722-3

Library of Congress Cataloging in Publication Data
O'Donnell, John J. (John Joseph), 1944–
Trinity and temporality.
(Oxford theological monographs)
Bibliography: p.
Includes index.
1. God—History of doctrines.   2. Trinity—
History of doctrines.   3. Process theology.   4. Ogden,
Schubert Miles, 1928–        5. Moltmann, Jürgen.
I. Title.   II. Series.
BT98.O36   1983   231'.044   82-22550
ISBN 0-19-826722-3

Typeset by Oxprint Ltd, Oxford
Printed in Great Britain
at the University Press, Oxford
by Eric Buckley
Printer to the University

*To the brethren of Campion Hall, Oxford and of the Pfarrhaus of St. Pankratius, Tübingen-Bühl, without whose support and friendship this study could not have been completed.*

# PREFACE

THE seed for this study was first planted during a course on process theology with Professor Daniel Day Williams at Union Theological Seminary New York City in 1972. At that time I wrote an essay comparing the process view of eschatology with that of Karl Rahner. Professor Williams believed that such comparative studies were important for the dialogue of process theologians with those of other traditions.

The theme for the present study emerged with the publication of Jürgen Moltmann's *The Crucified God* several years later. With that book Moltmann's trinitarian orientation became clear. Although Moltmann saw a similarity between his thought and that of process theology in the mutual concern for the relation of God to time, he nevertheless believed that his understanding of the trinitarian God offered an alternative to the di-polar God of process theism. The nature of the similarities and differences between these two traditions in regard to the question of God and history, and more particularly in regard to the trinitarian question, is the central focus of the present study.

I would like to thank Professor John Macquarrie of Christ Church, Oxford for his supervision, advice, and generous bestowal of his time during the four years in which this book was written. I am also grateful to Professor Maurice Wiles, also of Christ Church, for his willingness to help, for his friendship, and for the stimulating theological discussions which he offered the postgraduate students in theology.

In addition I owe a special debt of gratitude to Professor Schubert Ogden of Southern Methodist University, Dallas, Texas and to Professor Jürgen Moltmann of Tübingen University, West Germany, who offered me every assistance I required to pursue my research. Without their help and the unpublished materials which they provided, this study could never have been completed.

Finally, I would like to offer a special word of thanks to Mrs Dorothy Heapy who so carefully prepared the manuscript for publication.

# CONTENTS

## *A note on translations*

In citing works which originally appeared in German, the author has used published English translations wherever available. Otherwise he has provided his own translations of the original German texts.

# I

# CONTEMPORARY ATHEISM AND CLASSICAL PHILOSOPHICAL THEISM

### i. *Introduction*

THEOLOGY, as the name itself indicates, is the study of God. Though this point may seem obvious, the number of subsidiary issues in which theology must perforce engage has often obscured theology's central task. We must agree then with Schubert Ogden when he proposes that theology today should once again take the problem of God as its focal theme. He notes, 'Rightly understood, the problem of God is not one among several others; it is the only problem there is. Hence all our thinking, on whatever theme and whether properly theological or not, is of some, at least indirect, relevance to clarifying and solving it.'[1]

The problem is particularly acute for Christian theology today, for the reality of God is not something one can simply take for granted. Given the critique of atheistic philosophies and secular world-views, Christianity cannot simply presuppose theistic belief and build its faith in Jesus Christ upon it. Rather, to some extent, the credibility of Jesus Christ and the credibility of faith in God stand or fall together. Thus, for example, Moltmann believes that one's ability to believe in God today is intimately linked to the problem of resurrection. But he asks: 'How can we believe today in a supernatural event such as the resurrection of the dead when we no longer know, feel or fear the almightiness of a God, without being dishonest to our intelligence and alienated from the suffering of our contemporaries?'[2] He concludes:

Earlier protests were made in the name of religion against belief in the crucified one and, for the sake of the gods, Christians were called

---

[1] Schubert M. Ogden, *The Reality of God and Other Essays* (London: SCM Press, 1967), p. 1.
[2] Jürgen Moltmann, *Hope and Planning* (London: SCM Press, 1971), p. 31.

'atheists'. Today, atheism shrugs its shoulders at Christians as the last people who believe in God. Earlier, the existence of God was accepted even without a Christ, a mediator and saviour. Christians did not doubt the existence of God either. Under the influence of Christian cultural history, however, conditions have been reversed, so that now belief in God is itself at stake in belief in Jesus. 'God' increasingly becomes the concern of faith itself and is no longer its universally demonstrable presupposition.[3]

Our concern in this chapter is to give some indication of how this cultural shift has taken place and what it entails. In short, I should want to argue that although there are great varieties of atheistic experience today, they can basically be reduced to two types, methodological atheism and protest atheism. The first argues that God must be rejected as a meaningless term, a reality unverifiable in principle because outside the scope of our experience. God is beyond anything we know or could know. The second type of atheism rejects God in the name of man. It either sees the divine and the human as necessarily opposed or rejects God in the name of the suffering of the world. It is interesting that both types of atheism have roots in the philosophy of David Hume, and we can conveniently begin there in order to grasp the shift that has taken place away from the medieval world-view to the typically Godless world-view of today.

## ii.   Hume's Methodology

In his study of David Hume's philosophy, Frederick Copleston observes, 'It is to Hume that modern empiricists look as the progenitor of the philosophy which they accept . . . Hume remains . . . the one outstanding philosopher up to the end of the eighteenth century who took empiricism seriously and who endeavoured to develop a consistent empiricist philsophy.'[4]

According to Hume's philosophy, all the contents of the mind are derived from experience. These contents are called perceptions which are of two types: impressions which are the immediate data of experience such as sensations, emotions, and passions, and ideas which are copies or faint images of impressions in thinking and reasoning.

[3] Ibid., p. 32.
[4] Frederick Copleston, *A History of Philosophy*, vol. v: Hobbes to Hume (Paramus, N. J., New York, Amsterdam, London, Toronto: The Newman Press, 1959), p. 258.

If one accepts this understanding of experience, one is thereby committed to a phenomenalistic account of human knowing, that is, one limited to appearances. This restriction is laden down with epistemological and metaphysical consequences. One can observe this very clearly, for example, in Hume's treatment of causality. For Hume, causality is nothing more than the generalization of an empirical experience based on the temporal priority and spatial contiguity of two events. The ordinary man observes the constant conjunction of A and B in repeated instances where A is contiguous with B and is prior to B, and he calls A the cause and B the effect. There is no necessary connection between these events. What I feel as a necessary connection, is derived from repeated observation of the connection. As Copleston puts it,

The propensity, caused by custom or association, to pass from one of the things which have been observed to be constantly conjoined to the other is the impression from which the idea of necessary connection is derived. That is to say, the propensity, produced by custom, is something given, an impression, and the idea of necessary connection is its reflection or image in consciousness.[5]

The implications of this account of the principle of causality for the doctrine of God are significant indeed. If we can only establish a causal relation where we observe constant conjunction, and we cannot observe God at all, we have no way to proceed from effect to cause. Hume admits that we have a strong natural tendency to affirm God as the cause of the order of the world but there is no cogent reason to do so. Thus in the *Dialogues Concerning Natural Religion*, Philo argues:

When two *species* of objects have always been observed to be conjoined together, I can *infer*, by custom, the existence of one wherever I *see* the existence of the other. And this I call an argument from experience. But how this argument can have place, where the objects, as in the present case, are single, individual, without parallel, or specific resemblance, may be difficult to explain. And will any man tell me with a serious countenance, that an orderly universe must arise from

[5] Ibid., p. 283.
[6] David Hume, *Dialogues Concerning Natural Religion*, ed. with an introduction by Norman Kemp Smith. 2nd edn., with supplement (London, Edinburgh, Paris, Melbourne, Toronto and New York: Thomas Nelson and Sons Ltd., 1947), pp. 149–50.

some thought and art, like the human, because we have experience of it? To ascertain this reasoning, it were requisite, that we had experience of the origin of worlds.[6]

Hume's philosophical principles then lead him to a worldview in which God is methodologically excluded from the outset. God is in principle beyond the limits of human knowing. What else could follow for a philosopher whose major epistemological treatise concludes with the following peroration:

When we run over libraries, persuaded of these principles, what havoc must we make? If we take in hand any volume; of divinity or school metaphysics, for instance; let us ask, Does it contain any abstract reasoning concerning quantity or number? No. Does it contain any experimental reasoning concerning matter of fact and existence? No. Commit it then to the flames: for it can contain nothing but sophistry and illusion.[7]

The conclusion to be drawn from this account of Hume's philosophy is that whereas the medievals had an understanding of experience that was radically open to the transcendent, those of us who stand in the tradition of Hume's empiricism are inclined to find the world a closed system.

Contemporary descendants of Hume such as A. J. Ayer rule out God-talk not just because they believe there is no rational basis for proving the existence of God but because they take the word 'God' to be literally meaningless. Ayer distinguishes his position from both atheism and agnosticism. An atheist holds that there are good reasons not to believe in the existence of God. An agnostic holds the existence of God to be a real possibility in which there is no good reason either to believe or disbelieve. Ayer, on the other hand, holds that all utterances about the nature of God are non-sensical.[8] According to his verification principle, the word 'God' cannot possibly have a referent and therefore theology is ruled out from the start on methodological grounds. In his preface to *Language, Truth and Logic*, Ayer seeks to deal the death-blow to theological language in the following argument. He writes:

[7] David Hume, *An Enquiry Concerning Human Understanding*, ed. L. A. Selby-Bigge (Oxford, 1894), p. 165.
[8] See A. J. Ayer, *Language, Truth and Logic* (2nd edn., London: Victor Gollancz, 1946), pp. 115–16.

To test whether a sentence expresses a genuine empirical hypothesis, I adopt what may be called a modified verification principle. For I require of an empirical hypothesis, not indeed that it should be conclusively verifiable, but that some possible sense-experience should be relevant to the determination of its truth or falsehood. If a putative proposition fails to satisfy this principle, and is not a tautology, then I hold that it is metaphysical, and that, being metaphysical, it is neither true nor false but literally senseless. It will be found that much of what ordinarily passes for philosophy is metaphysical according to this criterion, and, in particular, that it can not be significantly asserted that there is a non-empirical world of values, or that men have immortal souls, or that there is a transcendent God.[9]

This kind of empiricism has not only gained ground among philosophers but has even been accepted by some theologians as well. One notable example is the American death of God theologian Paul van Buren. In his book *The Secular Meaning of the Gospel* he writes, 'If the choice is between "God", however subtly hidden in oblique language, and the man Jesus of Nazareth, the empirically-minded, secular "believer" can only choose the latter, for he does not know what to do with theology. Analogical as well as literal language about God makes no sense to him.'[10]

For van Buren, then, Christian faith can only be a 'blik', a way of looking at reality which cannot be verified by empirical enquiry.[11] Such an a-rational approach to Christianity must detach all references to the transcendent God from the empirically verifiable history of Jesus of Nazareth. Van Buren's secular meaning of the gospel entails the acceptance of Jesus

[9] See Preface to the first edition, reprinted in the 2nd edn., p. 31.
[10] Paul van Buren, *The Secular Meaning of the Gospel* (London: SCM Press, 1963), p. 79.
[11] The term 'blik' is first proposed by R. M. Hare in response to Antony Flew's argument in his essay 'Theology and Falsification' that theism is not an explanation. While accepting this point, Hare argues that theism is a blik. By a blik Hare means a fundamental stance in perceiving the world. He provides the following example: 'A certain lunatic is convinced that all dons want to murder him. His friends introduce him to all the mildest and more respectable dons they can find, and after each of them has retired, they say, "You see, he doesn't really want to murder you; he spoke to you in a most cordial manner; surely you are convinced now?" But the lunatic replies, "Yes, but that was only his diabolical cunning: he's really plotting against me the whole time, like the rest of them; I know it I tell you." However many kindly dons are produced, the reaction is still the same.' *New Essays in Philosophical Theology* edd. Antony Flew and Alasdair Macintyre (London: SCM Press, 1955), pp. 99–100. For the entire discussion between Flew and Hare, see ibid., pp. 96–103.

without God. The language of Christian faith has no transcendent reference; it merely indicates that a man's blik is
functioning. It is clear that, whenever this type of narrow
empiricism is accepted, the task of theology is undermined. On
the basis of Hume's empiricism and Ayer's verification
principle it may be possible to develop a Christology, but
theology in the strict sense is impossible.

### iii   *Hume and the Problem of Evil*

Hume is not only the father of modern atheism because his
epistemological principles rule out God-talk on methodological
grounds. He also sets the stage for the contemporary theistic
debates[12] by arguing that whatever slim evidence can be
adduced for theistic belief is negated by the overwhelming force
of the presence of evil in the world.

Hume states his case in the context of his debate with the
advocates of the argument from design, so popular in the
eighteenth century. Put most succinctly, his challenge is this:
why is there any misery at all in the world it if is produced by an
all-powerful God who is benevolent toward us?

Philo, whom we may take to be a spokesman for Hume
himself, states the objection in this fashion in the *Dialogues
Concerning Natural Religion:*

And is it possible, Cleanthes, said Philo, that after all these reflections, and infinitely more, which might be suggested, you can still
persevere in your anthropomorphism, and assert the moral attributes
of the Deity, his justice, benevolence, mercy and rectitude, to be of the
same nature with these virtues in human creatures? His power we
allow infinite: Whatever he wills is executed: But neither man nor any
other animal are happy: Therefore he does not will their happiness.
His wisdom is infinite: He is never mistaken in choosing the means to
any end: But the course of nature tends not to human or animal
felicity: Therefore it is not established for that purpose. Through the
whole compass of human knowledge, there are no inferences more
certain and infallible than these. In what respect, then, do his benevolence and mercy resemble the benevolence and mercy of men?

[12] Thus, for example, toward the end of *Process and Reality*, in discussing his doctrine
of God, Whitehead observes: 'What follows is merely an attempt to add another
speaker to that masterpiece, Hume's *Dialogues Concerning Natural Religion*.' Alfred North
Whitehead, *Process and Reality. An Essay in Cosmology* (New York: Harper Torchbooks,
1960), p. 521.

Epicurus's old questions are yet unanswered. Is he willing to prevent evil, but not able? Then he is impotent. Is he able, but not willing? Then he is malevolent. Is he both able and willing? Whence then is evil?[13]

Hume's attack on the premises of theistic belief is thus twofold. The experience of the world offers no reason to ground it in a transcendent deity. In fact, if anything, the experience of our world, riddled as it is with evil and suffering, would more likely suggest atheism than theism, for surely an all-powerful, benevolent creator could not be responsible for the world as we know it. Hume's philosophy thus both leads to the methodological atheism of contemporary secularists and empiricists as well as to the protest atheisms of our time. Let us now turn to some varieties of protest atheism to see in more detail why they assert that belief in God is inimical to belief in man.

iv. *The Father of Protest Atheism: Ludwig Feuerbach*

The protest atheisms of the twentieth century are all variations on the theme first clearly enunciated by Feuerbach, that God and man must necessarily be opposed beings.

For Feuerbach, religion projects human qualities onto a being distinct from man. According to this analysis, however, man's consciousness of the infinite is merely the consciousness of the infinity of consciousness.

More interesting, however, than Feuerbach's theory of projection is his analysis of why man makes this projection in the first place. According to Feuerbach, the projections of religion are rooted in human wishes, fantasies, and needs. He says, 'The more empty life is, the fuller, the more concrete is God. The impoverishing of the real world and the enriching of God is one act. Only the poor man has a rich God.'[14]

From this it follows that religion necessarily alienates man. For it takes what is properly his own and gives it to another. Feuerbach writes,

God is not what man is and man is not what God is. God is the infinite being, man the finite; God is perfect, man is imperfect; God is eternal,

---

[13] Hume, *Dialogues Concerning Natural Religion*, p. 198.
[14] Ludwig Feuerbach, *The Essence of Christianity* (London, 1854), p. 73 as cited by Eugene Kamenka, *The Philosophy of Ludwig Feuerbach* (London: Routledge and Kegan Paul, 1970), p. 40.

man is temporal; God is almighty, man is powerless; God is holy, man is sinful. God and man are extremes: God is the absolutely positive, the essence of all realities, while man is the negative, the essence of all nothingness.[15]

Given these presuppositions, the only consequence for a humanist to draw is atheism. Feuerbach insists that his atheism is not merely a speculative matter. What is essentially at stake is nothing less than the affirmation or negation of man's humanity. He writes,

The question as to the existence or non-existence of God, the opposition between theism and atheism, belongs to the sixteenth and to the seventeenth centuries but not to the ninteenth. I deny God. But that means for me that I deny the negation of man. In place of the illusory, fantastic, heavenly position of man which in actual life necessarily leads to the degradation of man, I substitute the tangible, actual and consequently also the political and social position of mankind. The question concerning the existence or non-existence of God is for me nothing but the question concerning the existence or non-existence of man.[16]

Feuerbach's philosophy has, therefore, delineated one of the central problematics of contemporary theology. Can one defend belief in God only at the cost of the dehumanization of man, the next world only at the cost of this one, spirit only at the cost of body, transcendence only at the cost of immanence, the freedom of God only at the cost of human servility? To all these questions a resounding 'Yes' has been spoken by the leader of the twentieth century French existentialism, Jean-Paul Sartre, whose brand of existentialism has become synonymous with protest atheism. Let us now turn briefly to his critique of theism.

v.  *Atheism in the Name of Freedom*

Sartre is perhaps the clearest example in our century of a philosopher who chooses atheism for the sake of humanism. According to his philosophy, to believe in God is to reject human freedom, and to believe in freedom is to renounce God.

---

[15] Feuerbach, op. cit., p. 33 as cit. ibid., p. 52.
[16] Feuerbach, Preface to vol. i of his collected works in *Sämtliche Werke* (Stuttgart–Bad Constatt, 1960–4), II, pp. 410–11 as cit. ibid., p. 17.

In this sense his atheism is postulatory. Atheism is a premise of his system rather than the conclusion of an argument. Sartre's philosophy is based on the distinction between essence and existence. An essence is a being which has a fixed identity. Sartre refers to such a being as an *en-soi*. For example, if I carve a statue of marble, its essence is fixed. It is precisely the essence that I have given it. Man, however, is that being whose essence is not to have an essence. He is *pour-soi* or existence. In the etymological sense of existence (from the Latin *ex-sistere*), he stands outside of himself. He is a project to be created out of his own freedom.

According to Sartre, this implies that God does not exist. If God existed as creator, then he would bestow on man an essence and man would no longer be radically free. His destiny would be to realize the essence set for him by God. In his famous lecture *Existentialism as a Humanism*, Sartre explains his point in this way:

Atheistic existentialism, of which I am a representative, declares . . . that if God does not exist there is at least one being whose existence comes before its essence, a being which exists before it can be defined by any conception of it. That being is man, or as Heidegger has it, the human reality. What do we mean by saying that existence precedes essence? We mean that man first of all exists, encounters himself, surges up in the world—and defines himself afterwards. If man as the existentialist sees him is not definable, it is because to begin with he is nothing. He will not be anything until later, and then he will be what he makes of himself. Thus, there is no human nature, because there is no God to have a conception of it.[17]

Though this philosophy is an exaltation of freedom, it is also a philosophy that leaves man in anguish, for the freedom that is proclaimed is a totally groundless freedom. Man finds himself alone and without excuse. As Orestes says to Zeus in Sartre's play *The Flies*,

Suddenly, out of the blue, freedom crashed down on me, and swept me off my feet. Nature sprang back, my youth went with the wind, and I knew myself alone, utterly alone in the midst of this well-meaning little universe of yours. I was like a man who's lost his

---

[17] Jean-Paul Sartre, *Existentialism and Humanism*, trans. with an introduction by Philip Mairet (London: Eyre Methuen, 1973), pp. 27–8.

shadow. And there was nothing left in heaven, no Right or Wrong, nor anyone to give me orders.[18]

This reveals that there is a profound ambiguity in Sartre's understanding of the sacred. On the one hand Sartre wants to abolish God in the name of man. On the other hand, Sartre longs for a God because a God would relieve him of his anguish. A God would bestow on man an essence, an identity.

In his book *Sartre and the Sacred*, Thomas M. King analyses Sartre's studies of famous literary figures such as Genet, Baudelaire, and Flaubert. In all these analyses there is a similar phenomenon which King identifies as the phenomenon of the sacred. For Sartre the experience of the sacred occurs when the *pour-soi* finds itself reduced to an *en-soi*. This reduction is the fulfilment of the *pour-soi's* deepest desire, namely to find an identity. Every *pour-soi* ultimately longs to be God, i.e. the union of the *pour-soi* and the *en-soi*. This is an impossible wish-fulfilment but man is inescapably religious and so cannot rid himself of it. For this reason, Sartre calls his atheism 'a cruel and long-range affair'[19]

We can see more clearly what Sartre's phenomenology of the sacred involves if we look at his study of Genet. Speaking of Genet's childhood, he records a key incident which he relates to his understanding of the sacred. Let me quote from King's book cited above:

Genet tries to imitate the actions of adults, but this he cannot do for the child possesses nothing. He appropriates things. He does not really seek the object appropriated, he seeks to be like others because others are just and good. At times a vague anguish comes over the child. When no one is around he relieves his anguish by stealing. But though he steals, he still considers himself well-behaved and virtuous, for there is only one life that counts: the life one leads in the presence of adults.

One day when Genet is about ten years old, he is playing in the kitchen. Suddenly he becomes aware of his inner solitude, and he is seized with anxiety. To get relief he will appropriate. But this time someone is watching. An adult voice calls out, 'you are a thief'. This

[18] Jean-Paul Sartre, *The Flies*, trans. Stuart Gilbert (London: Hamish Hamilton, 1946), p. 96.
    [19] Jean-Paul Sartre, *The Words*, trans. Bernard Frechtman (New York: Fawcett Crest Book, 1966) p. 158 as cited by Thomas M. King, *Sartre and the Sacred* (Chicago: University of Chicago Press, 1974), p. 48.

moment divides Genet's life into two parts: before and after. Sartre
refers to the incident as a 'sacred drama' or as a 'liturgical drama'. In
this moment the unreflecting act of a child has been objectified, and
an unreflecting child has been fixed as an object. Genet learns what he
is objectively; he is a thief. His act is petrified and eternalized by the
gaze of the Just. He is a thief and will be a thief forever.[20]

This story is a vivid illustration of Sartre's ambivalence
regarding the sacred. There is a pathos in the story, for in the
stare of the Just, Genet's freedom is lost. He is reduced to an
object, an *en-soi*, in this case a thief. At the same time there is a
sense of joy and liberation. He knows who and what he is. His
anguish is over. He has an identity.

Every man according to Sartre has an analogous attitude
toward God. He wants both his own freedom and an excuse for
his being. He wants, in other words, to be God, the union of the
*en-soi* and the *pour-soi*. Since this union is ontologically impossible, the only authentic response is to reject God in the name of
freedom. Any other response would be an instance of what
Sartre calls bad faith. In the last analysis every man must say of
himself what Sartre confesses in *Being and Nothingness*. 'I carry
the weight of the world by myself alone without anything or any
person being able to lighten it'[21]

vi.   *The Problem of Suffering*

Of all the forms of protest atheism that have emerged in the
twentieth century, the one which carries the greatest conviction
is that which is rooted in the suffering and anguish of human
beings. If God exists, how can he remain silent and inactive in
the face of the suffering cries of men and women? Especially
disturbing is the question of the suffering of innocent children.
In the case of adults one could possibly argue that their
sufferings are divine punishments for their sins. Since this
argument is inapplicable to children, the problem of the justice
of God becomes acute. In the nineteenth century Dostoevsky
gave brilliant literary expression to this problem in *The Brothers
Karamazov*. In a chapter entitled 'Rebellion' Ivan narrates the
story of a serf-boy who throws a stone which accidentally hurts

[20] King, op. cit., pp. 6–7.
[21] Jean-Paul Sartre, *Being and Nothingness*, trans., Hazel Barnes (New York:
Washington Square Press, 1966), p. 680 as cited by King, op. cit., p. 36.

the paw of a general's dog. In retribution, the general forces the child to run naked before a pack of blood-thirsty hounds. The boy is torn to pieces in front of his mother's eyes.

Ivan explains to his brother that there is no answer which one can make in the face of such overwhelming cruelty. He protests, 'I understand solidarity in sin among men. I understand solidarity in retribution, too; but there can be no such solidarity with children. And if it is really true that they must share responsibility for all their fathers' crimes, such a truth is not of this world and is beyond my comprehension.'[22] Ivan concludes that it is not God he cannot believe in but his world. If one must believe in a world in which children are tortured and killed and accept that world as God's world then Ivan prefers to withdraw from such a world. 'It's not God that I don't accept, Alyosha, only I most respectfully return Him the ticket.'[23]

In our own time Camus took up the same problem implicitly in his literature and explicitly in his philosophy. In his early philosophical career Camus had centred his attention on the problem of suicide. In *The Myth of Sisyphus* Camus addressed the question of the viability of life in an absurd world. He argued that in spite of life's radical meaninglessness, it was still worth living. In an absurd world in which man's desires are continually thwarted by the negations of the world, man can find a reason to live in protest itself. At this early stage of his career, Camus found a compelling symbol in Sisyphus' repeated efforts to carry his burden in the face of the inevitability of endless frustration.

In the middle of his career, however, Camus realized that his earlier response to the absurd was contradictory. If life is utterly meaningless, then it is equally a matter of indifference whether one becomes a rebel against death or a murderer. During this period Camus attempted to show that a rejection of suicide implies a rejection of all killing. In choosing to rebel against absurdity, one chooses the conditions of possibility of rebellion, namely solidarity with all living things. In the major philosophical work of this period, *The Rebel*, Camus writes

Man's solidarity is founded upon rebellion, and rebellion can only be

[22] Fyodor Mikhailovich Dostoevsky, *The Brothers Karamazov*, Everyman's Library Edition (London: J. M. Dent and Sons, 1942), Vol. i., p. 249.
[23] Ibid., p. 250.

justified by this solidarity. We then have authority to say that any type of rebellion which claims the right to deny or destroy this solidarity simultaneously loses the right to be called rebellion and actually becomes an accomplice to murder. In the same way, this solidarity, except in so far as religion is concerned, only comes to life on the level of rebellion. And so the real drama of revolutionary thought is revealed. In order to exist, man must rebel, but rebellion must respect the limits that it discovers in itself—limits where minds meet, and in meeting, begin to exist.[24]

Camus is giving us more here than a philosophical doctrine. It is also an ethical imperative. At the end of *The Rebel*, he wrote somewhat autobiographically, 'Those who find no rest in God or in history are condemned to live for those who, like themselves, cannot live: in fact, for the humiliated.'[25] And in a talk to the Dominicans of Latour-Maubourg, he said, 'I share with you the same revulsion from evil. But I do not share your hope and I continue to struggle against this universe in which children suffer and die.'[26]

In the same period in which Camus wrote *The Rebel*, he gave literary expression to his philosophy in his novel *The Plague*. There are at least three major contrasting figures who represent various human reactions to the plague that sweeps through Oran.

The first is that of the Jesuit priest, Father Paneloux. When the plague first strikes Oran, he preaches a fiery sermon in which he proclaims the plague as a divine visitation for the sins of the city. Such a glib response, however, is shattered when he personally witnesses the agonizing death of M. Othon's small son. He knows that all such explanations are proved empty in the face of such suffering. He is moved to preach another sermon in which he argues that a Christian is confronted with a radical choice. Either he must accept everything or reject everything. An all or nothing response is demanded. He frankly admits that in the case of the innocent suffering of children he is left totally without argument or reason. For his own part he

[24] Albert Camus, *The Rebel*, trans. Anthony Bower (London: Hamish Hamilton, 1953), p. 27.
[25] Ibid., p. 271.
[26] Albert Camus, *Resistance, Rebellion, and Death*, trans. with an introduction by Justin O'Brien (London: Hamish Hamilton, 1961), p. 50.

must cling to the crucifix and the image of the suffering Christ and resolutely bear even the agony of a child's death.

No such response is possible either for Tarrou or Dr Rieux, both atheists. Tarrou's life has been changed by the experience of witnessing an execution. Since that time he knows that the only possible response to the suffering of the world is to side with the victim. He has resolved 'to have no truck with anything which, directly or indirectly, for good reasons or for bad, brings death to anyone, or justifies others putting him to death.'[27] For Tarrou we are all guilty of murder to some degree. The goal of life is to reduce the scale of killing. He strives in this way to become a saint without God.

The difference between Tarrou and Rieux is that Rieux's goal is simply to become a man. Sainthood is too lofty an ideal. As a doctor, Rieux simply devotes himself to that which has to be done. According to Rieux, no one really believes in an omnipotent God. If he did, he would let God take care of human misery. At any rate, it is better for us to act if God doesn't exist, so that we can enter into the struggle against sickness and death. Like Ivan in *The Brothers Karamazov* he refuses to believe that a God of love could allow the suffering of innocent children. And so he rejects Paneloux's faith. ' "No, Father," he says, "I've a very different idea of love. And until my dying day I shall refuse to love a scheme of things in which children are put to torture." '[28]

In speaking of the suffering of the innocent, especially the suffering of children, we have been speaking in a somewhat theoretical fashion. But for our own century this problem has become terrifyingly real in the experience of the holocaust and the slaughter of six million Jews. One of the most moving autobiographical accounts of such suffering is that of Elie Wiesel, a boy of fifteen at the time of his incarceration in Auschwitz. In his testimonial, appropriately entitled *Night*, he relates the story of the hanging of a young child in the camp.

The SS hanged two Jewish men and a youth in front of the whole camp. The men died quickly, but the death throes of the youth lasted for half an hour. 'Where is God? Where is he?' someone asked behind

[27] Albert Camus, *The Plague*, trans. Stuart Gilbert (Penguin Books, 1960), p. 207.
[28] Ibid., p. 178.

me. As the youth still hung in torment in the noose after a long time, I heard the man call again, 'Where is God now?' And I heard a voice in myself answer: 'Where is he? He is here. He is hanging there on the gallows . . .'[29]

For Wiesel and for may other Jews, the experience of Auschwitz could only mean the death of God. Recalling his first night in the camp, he writes, 'Never shall I forget those moments which murdered my God and my soul and turned my dreams to dust.'[30]

Richard L. Rubenstein has become one of the leading spokesmen for those Jews who find it impossible to believe in the God of history after Auschwitz. He writes, 'If there is a God of history, He is the ultimate author of Auschwitz. I am willing to believe in God the Holy Nothingness who is our source and final destiny, but never again in a God of history.'[31]

In the experience of the death camps, theism meets a defiant challenge. If God is the ultimate actor in the drama of history, how could he keep silence as six million Jews were slaughtered? Traditional Jewish theology interpreted the major catastrophes of Israelite history as divine punishment. Modern Jews like Wiesel and Rubenstein find such an interpretation outrageous. Thus they abandon the God of history as a protest in the name of man. For Rubenstein, at least, this implies a tragic vision of human destiny, for man is left utterly alone in an unfeeling cosmos. Yet the choice is clear: either God is lord of the death camps or Holy Nothingness is man's ultimate origin and end. Given that choice, Rubenstein resolutely accepts the latter.

If Rubenstein is an example of a Jew who has become an atheist for the sake of solidarity with human suffering, he has found an ally in a brother Christian, Thomas Altizer, who has become an atheist for the same reason. Like Rubenstein he finds the idea of an omnipotent deity intolerable. In his book *The Gospel of Christian Atheism*, Altizer writes, 'Blake ingeniously sensed that the God of deism and the God of orthodoxy are

[29] My synopsis of the account is cited from Jürgen Moltmann, *The Experiment Hope*, ed. and trans. with a foreword by M. Douglas Meeks (Philadelphia: Fortress Press, 1975), p. 73. For the full account see Elie Wiesel, *Night, Dawn, The Accident: Three Tales* (London: Robson Books, 1974), pp. 71–2.

[30] Wiesel, op. cit., p. 43.

[31] Richard L. Rubenstein, *After Auschwitz, Radical Theology and Contemporary Judaism* (Indianapolis: Bobbs-Merrill, 1966), p. 204.

identical, for both banish the redemptive God from the world, and in positing God as either impassive source of cosmic order or the tyrannical despot of history, arrive at a common conception of a distant and alien God.'[32] For Altizer the only way in which one can truly identify with man is to refuse to accept such a God. Therefore in place of the God of deism and orthodoxy he substitutes a new understanding of God as self-negating, self-emptying, self-annihilating process. The God of theism truly emptied himself in the incarnation and he died once and for all on the cross. The transcendent God disappeared forever in the experience of the crucifixion but in this event the transcendent God became immanent spirit, a spirit of reconciliation which works for the liberation of man from all oppressive servitude. Charles Bent summarizes Altizer's new gospel of Christian atheism in this way, 'With the death of God in Christ, the ultimate and transcendent source of all human repression and alienation has been completely abolished. The result is that man is now free to pursue full human integrity, maturity and autonomy within the framework of a wholly radical immanence, in union with a totally immanent God who is now present in every human hand and face.'[33]

This brief survey of some varieties of contemporary protest atheism leaves us apparently with a dilemma: either we accept a commitment to humanism without God or we accept the traditional God with the necessity of abandoning man. The choice seems to be between the death of God and the death of man.

The question arises, however, whether this dilemma is not insoluble because of a false concept of God. The protest atheists whom we have considered are united in rejecting the God of classical philosophical theism. But is this the only God there is? Is this the God of Christian faith? Has not Altizer rightly seen that the event of the cross forces us to re-think our idea of God? The latter part of this chapter seeks to follow up this suggestion by investigating some of the problems inherent in the classical theistic understanding of God.

---

[32] Thomas J. J. Altizer, *The Gospel of Christian Atheism* (London: Collins, 1967), p. 91.
[33] Charles N. Bent, *The Death of God Movement* (New York: Paulist Press, 1967), p. 197.

vii. *The Failure of Classical Philosophical Theism*

There is a measure of consensus today that a great number of the difficulties experienced by contemporary atheists are due to the problems inherent in classical philosophical theism itself. In other words, given the concept of God elaborated by the classical theistic tradition, it was inevitable that we should end up in the cul-de-sac of contemporary atheism.

The chief indictments brought against the classical tradition are twofold. The first is the charge that the concept of God developed by classical philosophical theism is metaphysically incoherent. According to this concept God is absolute, unchanging, a-temporal, without potentiality, and totally unrelated to the world.

St. Thomas, for example, teaches that the concept of God's perfection is incompatible with the notion of mutability. In the *Summa Theologiae*, he argues that God is altogether unchangeable 'because anything in change acquires something through its change, attaining something previously not attained. Now God, being limitless and embracing within himself the whole fullness of perfection of all existence, cannot acquire anything, nor can he move out towards something previously not attained. So one cannot in any way associate him with change.'[34]

When St. Thomas draws out the full implications of this doctrine in regard to the question of God's relatedness to the world, he consistently maintains that God does not have a real relation to his creation. Real relations can only exist between two beings that mutually affect one another. But God's relation to the world is in St. Thomas's doctrine a mixed relation, that is, the world is related to God but God is not related to the world. Thomas illustrates this doctrine by appealing to an example of Aristotle. According to Aristotle some things are said to be relative not because they are related to others but because others are related to them. One side of a pillar is said to be the right side because it is said to be at somebody's right hand. The relation of being on the right is real in the man but not in the pillar.

---

[34] *Summa Theologiae* Ia, q. 9, art. 1 (Latin text and English translation, Blackfriars, in conjunction with Eyre and Spottiswoode, London and McGraw Hill, New York, 1964).

The same understanding of relation could be applied ana-
logously to God's relation to the world. St. Thomas says:

> It is clear that being related to God is a reality in creatures, but being
> related to creatures is not a reality in God. . . . When we speak of his
> relation to creatures we can apply words implying temporal sequence
> and change in the creatures; just as we can say that the pillar has
> changed from being on my left to being on my right, not through any
> alteration in the pillar but simply because I have turned around.[35]

John Macquarrie has termed such an understanding of God
'monarchical'. He writes, 'On this view, God's transcendence
over and priority to the world has therefore been understood as
an asymmetrical relation. The world needs God, but God has
no need of the world; God affects the world, but the world does
not affect God; the world owes everything to God, but God is
not increased by the world.'[36]

At least three serious objections have been raised on metaphysical grounds against this conception of God. First, it has
been argued that a wholly necessary creation of a wholly con-
tigent world is a meaningless idea. Thus, for example, Schubert
Ogden observes

> Theologians usually tell us that God creates the world freely, as the
> contingent or non-necessary world our experience discloses it to be.
> This assertion is also made necessary because it offers the only really
> credible construction of the account of creation in Holy Scripture. At
> the same time, because of their fixed commitment to the assumptions
> of classical metaphysics, theologians usually tell us that God's act of
> creation is one with his eternal essence, which is in every respect
> necessary, exclusive of all contingency. Hence, if we take them at their
> word, giving full weight to both of their assertions, we at once find
> ourselves in the hopeless contradiction of a wholly necessary creation
> of a wholly contingent world.[37]

---

[35] S. T. Ia, q. 13, art. 7.

[36] John Macquarrie, Thinking About God (London: SCM Press, 1975), p. 111.

[37] Schubert Ogden, The Reality of God, p. 17. It must also be said, however, that
significant attempts have been made within the classical philosophical tradition itself
to defend its concept of God while at the same time trying to do justice to the kinds of
objections raised by Ogden. Thus for example, Walter Stokes, working from the
Augustinian concept of person as relation, develops the idea of God's freedom as
self-determination, self-relation, self-giving without coercion from any outside force. In
this sense one could say that God's act of creation is free and at the same time identical
with his essence. 'Is God Really Related to the World?' Proceedings of the American Catholic
Philosophical Association 39 (1965) 149.

A similar objection has been raised in regard to the divine knowledge. The classical philosophical tradition asserted that God knows his world without being metaphysically changed in the act of knowledge.[38] This certainly violates our ordinary understanding of the act of knowledge. A human subject cannot remain unaffected by what he knows. Is it possible that God could remain so? The objection can be formulated in this way.

Given the contingency of the world, or more specifically the fact that certain things have happened in or are true about the world that need not have happened or been true, must not the contents of the divine knowing be dependent—contingent—upon them? 'Thus God knows that a certain world exists which might not have existed; but surely had it not existed, he would not have known it to exist; hence he has knowledge which he might not have had.'[39]

The third objection concerns the divine willing. Again, let us note the two presuppositions of classical philosophical theism: 1. God's willing is his essence. 2. God's action in creation is free (i.e. he might have created a different world or none at all).[40] Commenting on these premises Hartshorne writes, 'Since the essence or self-identity of a being is the only one *that* being could have, it follows that if the essence is the willing, no different

[38] See *S. T.* Ia. q. 14.

[39] Colin Gunton, *Becoming and Being, The Doctrine of God in Charles Hartshorne and Karl Barth* (Oxford University Press, 1978), pp. 17–18. In this passage Gunton is citing Hartshorne's *Creative Synthesis and Philosophic Method* (London: SCM Press, 1970), p. 48. For vigorous defences of the classical position, see John H. Wright SJ, 'Divine Knowledge and Human Freedom,' *Theological Studies* 38, 3 (Sept. 1977) 450–77; W. Norris Clarke, 'A New look at the Immutability of God', in *God Knowable and Unknowable*, ed. Robert Roth SJ (New York: Fordham University Press, 1973), pp. 43–72. Wright argues that Hartshorne and process philosophers fail to understand the classical philosophical doctrine of divine knowledge because they lack a doctrine of creation. For Wright, the key to the classical doctrine lies in the fact that 'The conditions of the divine causality of existing creatures and the conditions of divine knowledge of those creatures are identical' (pp. 453–4). For Norris Clarke, the classicial understanding becomes intelligible when one adheres to St Thomas's doctrine of the distinction between real and intentional being. In the technical language of Aristotelian philosophy, God cannot change in knowing the world, because change would imply a transition to a higher level of perfection than he possessed before. This is impossible because what God knows, he knows by creating it. Since God is the full pletitude of being, what exists flows from this source. In God's knowing it he is not thereby increased. None the less his intentional consciousness is determined by the order of the world which he has created. Thus the contingent facts of our universe do determine the content of the divine knowledge. But this would not imply a change in the order of real being in the Aristotelian sense.

[40] See *S. T.* Ia, q. 19.

willing was possible for that being. If then, on the assumptions,
God willed to create this world, he could not but so have willed.
I am persuaded, after considerable discussion of the matter
with proponents of orthodox theory, that there is here sheer
contradiction, or words with no meaning at all.'[41]

Apart from the metaphysical objections which have been
raised against the classical philosophical concept of God, there
are the more serious religious objections. If, for example, love
implies a mutual reciprocity of persons, a vulnerability, if love
opens a space and allows the other to make a difference, then,
given the classical understanding of God, it is impossible to say
'God is love'. Thus Ogden writes,

The deep reason for a theological rejection of classical metaphysics is
not that such an outlook no longer commends itself to reasonable
men, important as it is that we should recognize that fact and face up
to its implications. No, the more profound reason is that such a
metaphysics never has allowed, and in principle, never could allow,
an appropriate theological explication of the central theme of
Wesley's evangelical witness, that God is love.[42]

This leads to the conclusion that our fundamental belief in
the worth of our lives and our effort to create a human world are
undermined. For if God is ultimately indifferent to our world
and unaffected by what we do, then what point is there in living
so as to glorify God? As Colin Gunton has observed, 'If God is
totally unrelated to the world, and, like the Epicurean gods, is
totally unaffected by its suffering, the value of the created order
is called into question, at least from the point of view of God. . . .
If the reality of God remains unchanged whatever we do, there
is really very little point in performing one act rather than
another.'[43]

In short, this view sets God and man over against one
another. God has everything, man has nothing. God has complete power over man but man has literally no power over God.
It is hardly surprising that this God comes to be seen more as a
threat to man's liberty than as its fulfilment, a God who reduces

[41] Charles Hartshorne, *Reality as Social Process, Studies in Metaphysics and Religion*
(Glencoe, Ill. and Boston: The Free Press and Beacon Press, 1953), pp. 198–9.
[42] Schubert Ogden, 'Love Unbounded: The Doctrine of God', *The Perkins School of
Theology Journal* 19, 3 (Spring 1966) p. 16.
[43] Gunton, op. cit., p. 20.

man's subjectivity to an object. And, in the face of the overwhelming presence of evil in our world, it hardly becomes
credible to believe in a God who maintains indifferent silence
while human flesh is consumed in the ovens of Auschwitz. To
quote Colin Gunton once again

The concept of a totally independent deity 'seems plainly an ideal-
isation of the tyrant–subject relationship . . .' Not only is it morally
repugnant but it contradicts basic insights of the Christian faith.
'How can anyone believe that being a follower of Jesus is like being an
imitator of Aristotle's divine Aristocrat, who is serenely indifferent to
the world's turmoils?'[44]

Therefore we may agree with Walter Kasper when he says of
the classical philosophical conception of God, 'Because he never
changes he can can never do anything, no life goes out from
him, he is dead. Nietzsche's "God is dead" is therefore only the
final implication of this form of Western metaphysics.'[45]

Are we then left at an impasse? If classical philosophical
theism leads inevitably to the cul-de-sac of contemporary
atheism, then our only alternative is to seek a revolution in our
concept of God. If we agree that the God of philosophical
theism is poor, as Jürgen Moltmann maintains, then we must
also agree with him that 'Without a revolution in the concept of
God, there is no revolutionary theology.'[46] Let us therefore now
turn to the question of the requirements necessary for a concept
of God adequate to meet the objections raised by the contemporary atheists we have examined in this chapter.

viii.  *Three Requirements for Religious Belief Today*

From the analysis of contemporary atheism which we have just
made and the difficulties of classical philosophical theism which
we have noted, we can conclude that at least three conditions
must be met if Christian faith in God is to be credible today.

First, Christian theology must be able to show that God-talk
is not meaningless as the Humean tradition of empiricism
asserts. As Schubert Ogden observes, the crucial question for

[44] Ibid., pp. 20–1.
[45] Walter Kasper, *Jesus the Christ*, trans. V. Green (London: Burns and Oates, 1976),
p. 82.
[46] See Jürgen Moltmann, *The Experiment Hope*, pp. 82–3.

theology today is not 'whether theology's witness to God is appropriate, but whether it is understandable'.[47] He goes on to assert that God-language will be understandable only when 'it meets the relevant conditions of meaning and truth universally established with human existence'.[48] This implies that part of theology's task today is a critique of the secularistic world-view presupposed by so many of our contemporaries.

Secondly, theology must make clear that, contrary to the presuppositions of many atheists today, God does not stand in opposition to genuine humanity but rather as the only authentic possibility of its fulfilment. Moltmann notes, 'In their struggle against each other, theism and atheism begin from the presupposition that God and man are fundamentally one being. Therefore what is ascribed to God must be taken from man and what is ascribed to man must have been taken from God.'[49] As we have seen above, for Moltmann the way out of this dilemma is a revolution in our concept of God. Agreeing with this basic programme, Schubert Ogden argues that theology must rethink its idea of God so that Christian faith can vindicate its most basic assumption, namely that it 'is not utterly alien to man . . . but rather is his own most proper possibility of existence, which can and should be understandable to him, provided it is so expressed as to take his situation into account'.[50] According to Ogden the most radical meaning of the Christian doctrine of creation and sin is that self, neighbour, and God are so inextricably linked together that it is as impossible to find one without finding all three as it is to lose one without losing all three. He writes,

The Scriptural point, in any case, is that, insofar as man's life is not centred in God, it is also not centred in himself or in the neighbour with and for whom he is given his existence. So far from being in any way opposed to one another, these three centres are so related that the loss of any is the loss of all, just as all are gained if any is gained.[51]

Borrowing from the tradition of German idealistic philos-

[47] Ogden, *The Reality of God*, p. 123.
[48] Schubert Ogden, 'What is Theology?', *Journal of Religion* 52 (1972), 25.
[49] Jürgen Moltmann, *The Crucified God, The Cross of Christ as the Foundation and Criticism of Christian Theology* (London: SCM Press, 1974), p. 249.
[50] Ogden, *The Reality of God*, p. 6.
[51] Schubert Ogden, 'Tillich's Theological Anthropology', III, p. 6 (unpublished).

ophy, Walter Kasper sets the task of theology as concern with 'the mystery of an unfathomable love, the very essence of which is to unite what is distinct while respecting the distinction; for love is, in an almost paradoxical way, the unity of two who, while remaining distinct and essentially free, nevertheless cannot exist the one without the other'.[52] Kasper's formulation we may take to be an appropriate formulation of the second requirement of religious belief which we have been discussing, namely the exigency to show that God and man are not contradictories but complementaries.

Finally, Christian theology must be able to formulate its doctrine of God in such a way that it takes account of the suffering of the world. If the classical philosophical theist argued from the finite world to the existence of an all-powerful transcendent God, the contemporary atheist argues from the experience of the same world to an ultimate nothingness. To quote Moltmann again,

Metaphysical atheism, too, takes the world as a mirror of the deity. But in the broken mirror of an unjust and absurd world of triumphant evil and suffering without reason and without end it does not see the countenance of a God, but only the grimace of absurdity and nothingness. Atheism too, draws a conclusion from the existence of a finite world as it is to its cause and its destiny, but there it finds no good and righteous God, but a capricious demon, a blind destiny, a damning law or an annihilating nothingness.[53]

For Moltmann, it is the question 'Why do I suffer?' which is the rock of atheism.[54] Classical philosophical theism's apathetic God could only intensify the question. A revolution in the concept of God will surely point in the direction of a God who participates in the suffering of his creation. And in fact with this suggestion we stand on the threshold of the specifically Christian experience of God and the symbol of his involvement in suffering, the cross of Jesus Christ.

ix. *The Christianization of the Concept of God*

The reflections which we have made in this chapter have led us

[52] Kasper, op. cit., p. 249.
[53] Moltmann, *The Crucified God*, pp. 219–20.
[54] Moltmann, *Hope and Planning*, p. 32.

to several conclusions. First, Christian theology must think its doctrine of God today in the light of the problems of modern atheism. Secondly, since the present atheistic situation is traceable at least in some measure to the concept of God prevalent in classical philosophical theism, the only way in which Christian theology can extricate itself from this impasse is by revolutionizing its doctrine of God.

I should want to argue that such a revolution most fundamentally entails thinking through the doctrine of God consistently and radically in the light of Jesus Christ. In other words, I am suggesting that classical philosophical theism failed to be Christian enough and imported ideas of God from an alien world rather than focusing its attention consistently on Jesus Christ, his life, death, and resurrection. As John Macquarrie puts it,

> Where we go wrong is that we bring along some ready-made idea of God, wherever we may have learned it, and then try to make Jesus Christ fit in with that idea of God . . . But if we take the idea of a revelation of God in Christ seriously, then we must be willing to have our understanding of God corrected and even revolutionized by what we learn in Jesus Christ.[55]

Such an approach may also have the advantage of suggesting possible solutions to the objections raised by atheists today. In the words of John Cobb, 'Perhaps by thinking of God in a more fully Christian way we will also find that we will reduce, or even remove, the force of the objections to faith in God on the part of those who have rejected it.'[56]

Now if these conclusions are justified, we have several indications of the way forward for Christian theology today. If we think of God not in terms of Aristotle's Unmoved Mover, but in terms of the God of Israel and Jesus Christ, then we must think of a God who goes out of himself, who acts in history, who is involved in the affairs of his people and even enters into contention with them. If then we are to revolutionize our concept of God, the critical question appears to be the relation of God to history and temporality. We need to bring God and

---

[55] John Macquarrie, *The Humility of God* (London: SCM Press, 1978), p. 60.
[56] John Cobb, *God and the World* (Philadelphia: The Westminster Press, 1969), pp. 24–5.

history into a more intimate relation than Greek thinking was willing to allow. Secondly, if we think of God in the light of Jesus Christ, we must not think in terms of mere monotheism. The Christian understanding of God is dominated by the trinitarian symbols of Father, Son, and Holy Spirit. As Moltmann has written,

The more one understands the whole event of the cross as an event of God, the more any simple idea of God falls apart. In epistemological terms it takes so to speak trinitarian form. One moves from the exterior of the mystery which is called 'God' to the interior, which is trinitarian. This is the 'revolution in the concept of God' which is manifested by the crucified Christ.[57]

These two suggestions establish the contours of our study, namely Trinity and temporality. I propose in the chapters which follow to look at the doctrine of God, both from its Christian origins and hence from a trinitarian perspective, and from the peculiar perspective of our secularistic age, namely the question of God and time. Nearly every school of theology in the twentieth century has addressed itself to this problem, but since 1960 at least two contemporary schools of theology have made the problem of God and time peculiarly their own. I am referring to the American process theologians and the German eschatological theologians. I have chosen them as the particular focus of this study. But before taking up our investigation of these two schools, I propose to turn briefly to the period of the Church Fathers, because it was during this period that the symbolic language of Jesus and the primitive community was developed into the intricate metaphysical doctrine which became the basis of all subsequent thinking about God in the Christian tradition, and which even today provides the framework for the passionate debates that centre on the question of the relation of God to temporal process.

[57] Moltmann, *The Crucified God*, p. 204.

# II

# THE EARLY CHRISTIAN DOCTRINE
# OF GOD IN THE LIGHT OF TODAY'S
# QUESTIONS

### i. *The Hermeneutical Question*

To speak of contemporary approaches to trinitarian theology, to seek to develop a contemporary Christian doctrine of God is inevitably to take a stand in regard to tradition. For the early Christian doctrine of God or the doctrine of the Trinity was worked out on the basis of Christian experience within the first four centuries of the church's life and reached a certain maturity by the fourth century in the writings of the Cappadocians in the East, and in the West by the fifth century in the writings of Augustine.

The burden of the present chapter is to examine the development of the early Christian doctrine of God in light of our present problematic. Or to put it another way, the present chapter is an effort in hermeneutics. We might bear in mind here the task of hermeneutical investigation as outlined by Piet Schoonenberg in his article 'Historicity and the Interpretation of Dogma'. He writes, 'The interpretation of a dogma is the "bridge" between the situation in which the dogma arose and the contemporary situation.'[1] Therefore the interpreter 'must correctly understand what is said in one language and accurately express that in the other language. Here it is not a question of grammatically different languages, but of languages of thought and feeling, and philosophical, cultural, scientific and pre-scientific pre-conceptions.'[2]

How are we to understand this 'bridge' between what has been said in the past and what must be said today if Christian

---

[1] Piet Schoonenberg, 'Historicity and the Interpretation of Dogma', *Theology Digest* 18 (1970) 133. This article is digested from 'Historiciteit en interpretatie van het dogma', *Tijdschrift voor Theologie* 8 (1968) 278–311.

[2] Ibid., p. 133.

faith is to be adequately expressed? Certainly it is inadequate merely to repeat past formulas. Speaking of the revelation of the Trinity in the New Testament, Franz Josef Schierse makes the point that under the guidance of the Holy Spirit the church in each age must take a genuine risk. Working from the original sources of faith, the church has the task of creating a new synthesis as it enters into a genuinely new dialogue with the Word of God.[3]

In what sense then is there continuity between what the Fathers of the church taught and what the church believes today? In his book *The Making of Christian Doctrine*, Maurice Wiles has made an interesting suggestion which may serve as a point of departure for our investigation in this chapter. He writes, 'True continuity with the age of the Fathers is to be sought not so much in the repetition of their doctrinal conclusions or even in the building upon them, but rather in the continuation of their doctrinal aims.'[4]

This principle rests on the conviction commonly held in the science of hermeneutics that dogmatic texts do not speak for themselves but rather must be seen as answers to questions. To understand the precise point of dogmatic definitions one must understand the precise question being asked at the time. Thus, for example, Thomas B. Ommen in his article 'The Hermeneutic of Dogma' lists as one hermeneutical principle the investigation of the intention of a given definition. The intended meaning, he suggests, 'usually emerges, in the case of dogma, in response to a question or set of questions, as an effort to express the true content of faith at a particular moment in history'.[5]

[3] See Franz Josef Schierse, 'Die neutestamentliche Trinitätsoffenbarung', *Mysterium Salutis, Grundriß heilsgeschichtlicher Dogmatik*, herausgegeben von Johannes Feiner und Magnus Löhrer. Band II. Die Heilsgeschichte vor Christus (Einsiedeln: Benziger Verlag, 1967), p. 129.

[4] Maurice Wiles, *The Making of Christian Doctrine, A Study in the Principles of Early Doctrinal Development* (Cambridge: Cambridge University Press, 1967), p. 173. Although I have reservations about Professor Wiles's reluctance to admit the need to build upon past doctrinal conclusions, I fully agree with the need to seek continuity with their fundamental aims.

[5] Thomas B. Ommen, 'The Hermeneutic of Dogma', *Theological Studies* 35,4 (Dec. 1974) 609. Writing in the same vein, Avery Dulles states the following hermeneutical principle: 'No doctrinal decision of the past directly solves a question that was not asked at the time.' *The Survival of Dogma* (Garden City, NY: Doubleday, 1971), p. 179. Similarly Piet Schoonenberg maintains, 'A theological–historical study should uncover the question to which the dogma was an answer.' Art. cit., p. 134.

Let us then begin our investigation of the early Christian doctrine of God with such questions as these: What questions emerged in the patristic period that led the Church Fathers to state the doctrine of God in the way they did? What problems were they attempting to resolve in formulating their doctrine of God? What fundamental aims did they seek to achieve? I suggest that at least four problem areas are critical to understanding the doctrinal formulations of the patristic doctrine of God. These are: God's absoluteness and relatedness, the relation of Jesus to the Father, the continuity between God's revelation in Jesus and his revelation in creation and in the history of Israel, the meaning of salvation in Christ. Let us investigate each of these in turn.

ii.   *Problems Faced by Early Christianity in Developing its Doctrine of God*

*(a)  God as Absolute and Related*

Catholic scholarship in Germany today has stressed the point that the seeds for trinitarian doctrine were sown as soon as God entered into a revelatory relationship with his world. Thus distinctions within the Godhead must be admitted once the Transcendent Mystery is affirmed to be related to creation.[6] Thus, for example, Raphael Schulte in his article 'The Self-Unfolding of the Triune God', makes the point: 'The revelation *of the Trinity*, which comes to speech in Christian faith and which can only be spoken about there, is first of all the *final* revelation *of God*, the absolute and genuine self-communication of God.'[7] And he continues,

In our general principles, we have already said, that the revelation of the Trinity is to be understood first of all as the final revelation *of God*, and that every genuine revelation of God (and therefore all genuine knowledge of God) is at the same time also revelation of the Trinity. This principle was not derived a priori, but from the theological

---

[6] Even a theologian such as Cyril Richardson who is sceptical about a specific threefoldness in God is prepared to admit the necessity for distinctions within the Godhead and believes that trinitarian thinking can basically be seen as an unsatisfactory attempt to deal with the paradox of God's absoluteness and relatedness. See his book *The Doctrine of the Trinity* (New York and Nashville: Abingdon Press, 1958).

[7] Raphael Schulte, 'Die Selbsterschließung des dreifaltigen Gottes', *Mysterium Salutis* II, p. 50.

insight into the factual, historically completed self-communication of God.[8]

It is not surprising then that the foundations for trinitarian thinking can already be found in the Old Testament as a number of recent studies have clearly indicated.[9] The Hebraic concept of God, while radically monotheistic, is by no means monistic. Just as Hebraic thinking conceived of man as one, yet believed his personality had an almost inexhaustible scope of extension,[10] so the Hebraic mentality admitted unity and diversity in regard to God. In order to see clearly how this is so, let us examine briefly three concepts of God which played an important role in Hebrew theology in elucidating God's relatedness to his creation. These are the divine name, the divine wisdom, and the divine *logos*.

Turning to God's name, we should bear in mind the following point made by John L. McKenzie in his *Dictionary of the Bible*. He writes,

It is a widespread cultural phenomenon that the name is considered to be more than an artificial tag which distinguishes one person from another. The name has a mysterious identity with its bearer; it can be considered as a substitute for the person, as acting or receiving in his place. The name is often meaningful; it not only distinguishes the person, but it is thought to tell something of the kind of person he is.[11]

All this is true *a fortiori* of God's name. To know God's name is to experience his reality. It is to know who he is. Thus God himself is present and active where his name is invoked.

In certain extra-canonical writings this idea is taken so far that the name is personified and becomes a substitute for God himself. In the *Apocalypse of Abraham* we have a long account of

[8] Ibid., pp. 77–8.
[9] See Aubrey R. Johnson, *The One and the Many in the Israelite Conception of God* (Cardiff: University of Wales Press, 1942); G. A. F. Knight, *A Biblical Approach to the Doctrine of the Trinity*, Scottish Journal of Theology Occasional Papers No. 1 (Edinburgh: Oliver and Boyd Ltd., 1953).
[10] Aubrey R. Johnson has shown how in Hebrew thinking a man's personality reaches beyond his body. His word of blessing, his servants and household, even his property were regarded as so embodying a man as literally to be regarded as extensions of his personality. They not only represent a man but in a certain sense can be said to *be* that man. See op. cit., pp. 5–17.
[11] John L. McKenzie, *Dictionary of the Bible* (London: Geoffrey Chapman, 1965), p. 603.

the angel Jaoel to whom God gave his ineffable name. From the text it is quite clear that this figure is God's Viceregent. But it is also clear that the figure is the mediator and bearer of Revelation since he is in possession of the ineffable name. By the second century AD this same angel was being designated as 'Little Yahweh' and thus we can see that Jaoel is really a substitute for the name itself.[12]

A similar instance can be found in the concept of God's wisdom. Here we can see a definite development as Hebraic thinking came into greater contact with Hellenism. In Job 28, for example, wisdom is said to be beyond man's capacity to search out. None the less God searched for her and found her. In Proverbs 8, God is said to have brought wisdom into being and used her in the creation of the world. But in the Book of Wisdom, wisdom is not merely a personification but a full *hypostasis*. Thus, for example, in Wisdom 7:25f., we read: 'She is a breath of the power of God, and a pure emanation from the glory of the almighty . . . For she is a reflection of eternal light, a spotless mirror of the working of God, an image of his goodness.' Wisdom is seen therefore not as a creation of God but as a divine *hypostasis* in a certain sense distinct from, though closely related to, the being of God.

Finally we turn to the concept of God's word. Here again we see that the word has a degree of objectivity and independence which is foreign to contemporary thought. As McKenzie notes, 'The Hebrews shared with most of the ancient Semitic world and many peoples of widely scattered cultures a belief in the distinct reality of the spoken word as a dynamic entity.'[13] G. A. F. Knight suggests an analogy with the current practice in cartoons and comic strips of circling the words that people utter and connecting them by a line to the mouth of the speaker. Knight remarks,

Their words have a very objective and solid look about them, framed as they are on the comic strip. You feel that the contents of the frame are now out of the speakers in actuality, that words that came out as thin sounds have condensed like steam into very tangible clouds, and

---

[12] See *The Jung Codex, A Newly Recovered Gnostic Papyrus. Three Studies by H. C. Puech, G. Quispel, and W. C. van Unnik*, trans. and ed. F. L. Cross (London: Mowbray, 1955), pp. 70–1.

[13] McKenzie, op. cit., p. 938.

that it is now too late to do anything about them. You cannot push the words back into the mouths of the speakers—they have solidified and become objectified.[14]

One of the best examples of this on the human level is Isaac's inability to recall his blessing when he has blessed the wrong son in Genesis 27:28–9. In regard to the objective power of the divine word we have a striking example in Isaiah 55:10–11.

For as the rain cometh down and the snow from heaven, and returneth not thither, but watereth the earth and maketh it bring forth and bud, that it may give seed to the sower and bread to the eater, so shall my word be that goeth forth out of my mouth: it shall not return to me void, but it shall accomplish that which I please, and it shall prosper in the things whereto I sent it.

In later Judaism the concept of God's *logos*, like that of his wisdom, became hypostasized. In fact the two were often identified. For example in Wisdom 9:1b–2a the author addresses God

who has made all things by thy word
and by wisdom hast formed man.

Thus Reginald Fuller can say,

Like *sophia*, the *logos* is distinct from, yet intimately related to, the being of God. He is the son of God,—so much so that Philo can go so far as to call the *logos* δεύτερος θεός ('second God'). Like *sophia* in Wisd. 7:26, the Philonic *logos* is the image (εἰπών) of God, and the agent of creation and revelation (cf. Wisd. 7:7–14, etc.).[15]

We can say then that God's name, God's wisdom, God's word have an almost independent existence and at the same time are practically indistinguishable from God himself. Thus Aubrey R. Johnson in his study *The One and the Many in the Israelite Conception of God* concludes, 'We must be prepared to recognize for the Godhead just such a fluidity of reference from the One to the Many and from the Many to the One as we have already noticed in the case of man.'[16] Concurring with this judgement, Arthur W. Wainright in his book *The Trinity in the*

[14] G. A. F. Knight, op. cit., pp. 14–15.
[15] Reginald H. Fuller, *The Foundations of New Testament Christology* (London: Lutterworth Press, 1965), p. 75.
[16] Johnson, op. cit., p. 20.

*New Testament* makes the following point: 'It is conceivable that a trinitarian doctrine should have grown on Jewish soil. While Hellenistic thought made a great contribution to the expression of the doctrine, the idea of plurality within unity was already implicit in Jewish theology.'[17]

If the resources for trinitarian thinking lay already in the Old Testament, the decisive impetus for the move in this direction is to be located specifically in the Christ-event. What distinguishes the Christ-event from those Old Testament concepts used to express God's relatedness to the world is that Jesus of Nazareth is a real person capable of entering into real dialogue with God. Thus the limits of Hebraic thinking are strained to the breaking point in the specific Christian belief in the incarnation. Wainright makes the point when he writes,

For the orthodox Jew, the trouble about Christ was not that he was regarded as an extension of the divine personality, but that he was believed to have been incarnate. If he had been a concept and nothing more, he would not have been a stumbling block to the Jews. It was the combination of beliefs about his exalted state with the fact that he lived a life of flesh and blood which offended the Jews. There was nothing else like it in Judaism. Although Jewish concepts were used in an attempt to explain Jesus' relation to the Father, these concepts were not sufficient for the task. Jewish thought did not admit of this kind of plurality within the Godhead. It had no room for a second person within the Godhead, who not only did the will of the Father but conversed with him, took counsel with him and pleaded with him . . . The idea of extension of divine personality is Hebraic. The idea of interaction within the extended personality is neither Hebraic nor Hellenistic but Christian.[18]

We have thus reached an important conclusion which has a significant bearing on our study as a whole. Christians were forced to rethink the doctrine of God because of their experience of Jesus Christ. The Christian doctrine of God, Christian thinking about the Trinity, has been and continues to be a function of christology.

### (b)  Christology and the Monotheism of Judaism

This leads us immediately to our second problem area: what is

[17] Arthur W. Wainright, *The Trinity in the New Testament* (London: S.P.C.K., 1962), p. 37.
[18] Ibid., pp. 39–40.

the relationship of Jesus of Nazareth to the God of the Old Testament, the God whom Jesus referred to as Father. How is it possible to ascribe to Jesus divine titles and functions without compromising the monotheism of the Judaic faith? At this point it is not our intention to indicate the solution to this problem but merely to point out that the trinitarian problem could not be avoided once the divinity of Christ was accepted. As G. L. Prestige puts it,

From the earliest moment of theological reflection it was assumed that Jesus Christ was true God as well as true man. . . . The problem which the Fathers had to solve was not whether he was God, but how, within the monotheistic system which the church inherited from the Jews, preserved in the bible, and pertinaciously defended against the heathen, it was still possible to maintain the unity of God while insisting on the deity of one who was distinct from God the Father.[19]

*(c) Jesus in Relation to Salvation-History*

The Christ-event not only forced Christians to explode the categories of Hebraic thought in regard to Christ's relation to the Father. It also impelled them to relate this event to God's revelatory action in creation and in the historical experience of Israel. As we have seen, they were aided in this task by the philosophical speculation about the *logos* as it was found in Hellenistic philososophy and in Jewish literature influenced by such philosophy. Thus Christian thinkers of the second century developed a theology of the *logos* which set the stage for the debates of the third and fourth centuries. In his *Christ in the Christian Tradition*, Aloys Grillmeier explains a five-fold role of the *logos* in the Apologists. In its cosmological aspect the *logos* functioned as creative word; in its noetic aspect as the basis of knowledge and truth; in its moral aspect as the basis and embodiment of the moral law; in its psychological aspect as the original form of· thought; in its saving historical aspect as the word and mediator of revelation. Grillmeier notes that the first and fifth aspects were suitable for interpreting the work of God *extra se* while the second and fourth were particularly helpful in clarifying the relation of the *logos* to the Father.[20]

---

[19] G. L. Prestige, *God in Patristic Thought* (London: S.P.C.K., 1952), p. 76.
[20] Aloys Grillmeier, *Christ in the Christian Tradition*, vol. i *From the Apostolic Age to Chalcedon (AD 451)*, trans. John Bowden (Oxford: Mowbrays, 1975). Revised ed. p. 109.

Thus the Apologists found in the *logos* a convenient device for relating the Christian experience both to the faith of Israel and to secular philosophy. The *logos* was at work in creation. All men have had a share in the *logos* and this accounts for the truth found in the great pagan philosophers. The *logos* was also active in the history of Israel inspiring the prophets. But now in Christ the work of the *logos* has come to its fulfilment by becoming incarnate in Jesus of Nazareth.

Helpful as this concept was in developing a Christian theology, it also contained within it threats to the Christian faith. On the one hand it was questionable whether this type of Platonism could easily be combined with the biblical doctrine of creation. According to Middle Platonism God's transcendence involved an infinite separation between himself and the world. Hence the union of God and the world had to be achieved by mediators. This was one of the functions of the *logos*. This problem immediately leads to another. Is the *logos* to be conceived on the side of God or on the side of creation? If the *logos* is placed on the side of God, the problem of the gap between God and creation remains unsolved. If the *logos* is placed on the side of creation, one is faced with the problem of subordinationism. Thus Karl Rahner states the trinitarian problem of the Fathers in this way:

The basic trinitarian question in the patristic age is whether the *logos* (and the *pneuma*) should be considered in the light of the 'hierarchical thinking' of Platonism and neo-Platonism and hence as a subordinate cosmic power other than the true God or whether he was really God 'consubstantial' with the Father, though not simply to be identified with him as in various types of modalism.[21]

### (d) Soteriology

Although the *logos* doctrine was fundamentally cosmological, we must not overlook the fact that early Christian reflections about the nature of God were equally motivated by soteriological concerns. As mentioned above, trinitarian speculation was a function of christology. Thus at the heart of all the debates about the nature of God was the question of the salvation experienced through Christ in the power of his Spirit. In the

[21] Karl Rahner, 'Trinity in Theology', *Sacramentum Mundi, An Encyclopedia of Theology*, vol. vi, ed. Karl Rahner *et al.* (London: Burns and Oates, 1970), p. 305.

debate with Arianism, Athanasius argued that if the *logos* was a creature, then Christ could not unite man with God and indeed himself stood in need of redemption. He went on to argue that the divinity of Christ implies the divinity of the Spirit, for the function of the Spirit is sanctification. The Spirit makes Christians participants in the divinization made possible by Christ. The Spirit cannot divinize us if he is not himself divine. Thus Maurice Wiles concludes that two great soteriological principles played an immensely important part in the doctrinal debates of the fourth and fifth centuries. 'On the one hand was the conviction that a saviour must be fully divine; on the other was the conviction that what is not assumed is not healed. Or, to put the matter in other words, the source of salvation must be God; the locus of salvation must be man.'[22] Grillmeier makes the same point in the first chapter of his *Christ in the Christian Tradition:*

The content of the kerygma, however, was always the person of Christ and his uniqueness. The theological struggles of the patristic period are nothing else than an expansion of this central question: this gives them their continuity. For from the gospel of Jesus Christ as Son of God, and of his subsequent history (as *pneuma, en pneumati*), grew the question of Christian monotheism (of the one God as Father, Son, and Holy Spirit). And this expanded theological horizon remained contained within yet another: the question of the peculiar nature of the salvation God has given us in Christ and in the Holy Spirit. Soteriology remained the actual driving force behind theological inquiry, even—as we shall see especially in the period from the third to the fifth century—behind reflection on the identity of Christ and the Holy Spirit.[23]

iii.   *The Doctrinal Decisions of the Councils of Nicaea and Constantinople*

Thus far we have looked at the problems which the church confronted as it reflected on the implications of its Christian experience. But the church not only asked questions. It also made judgements which are reflected in certain key doctrinal decisions of the patristic period. For our purposes it will be sufficient to consider the central affirmations of Nicaea and

22 Wiles, *The Making of Christian Doctrine*, p. 106.
23 Grillmeier, op. cit., p. 9.

Constantinople which provide the *sine qua non* for working out the Christian doctrine of God.

The doctrinal decisions of Nicaea were prompted by the Arian controversies which erupted in the early part of the fourth century. We may cite Dr Kelly who conveniently summarizes the major tenets of Arius's system in the following four propositions: 1. The Word must be a creature. 2. As a creature the Word must have had a beginning. This proposition is embodied in Arius's famous dictum 'There was when He was not'. 3. The Son can have no communion with and indeed no direct knowledge of the Father. 4. The Word is a demigod.[24]

More interesting, however, than what Arius actually taught are the motivations that lay behind his system. Although the outcome of the Arian controversy led directly to the formation of the doctrine of the Trinity, the concerns of Arius and the Council of Nicaea were strictly christological.

Fr. Grillmeier notes that the doctrine of the incarnation was the starting point of the whole Arian system.[25] Arius's problem is cosmological. He is trying to put together Greek cosmological speculation with the biblical doctrine of creation. Arius presupposes an unbridgeable gulf between the creation and the transcendent God. God the creator is impassible and so cannot come into direct contact with the world. Such presuppositions lead Arius to create a system in which the *logos* can act as mediator between God and the world. But when the question arises as to which side of the chasm the *logos* belongs, Arius believes he is forced to answer the created side. The whole problem is summarized succinctly by Prestige when he writes, 'Behind all expression of Arian thought lay the hard and glittering syllogism that God is impassible; Christ, being γεννητός, was passible; therefore Christ was not God.'[26]

In response to Arius, the Fathers gathered at Nicaea in 325 promulgated the following Creed:

We believe in one God, the Father almighty,
maker of all things, visible and invisible.

And in one Lord Jesus Christ, the Son of

[24] J. N. D. Kelly, *Early Christian Doctrines* (New York: Harper and Row, 1960), pp. 226–31.
[25] Grillmeier, op. cit., p. 246.
[26] Prestige, op. cit., p. 156.

God, begotten from the Father, only-begotten,
i.e. from the substance of the Father, God
from God, light from light, true God from
true God, begotten not made, of one substance
with the Father, through whom all things
came into being, things in heaven and things
on earth, who because of us men and because
of our salvation came down and became
incarnate, becoming man, suffered and rose
again on the third day, ascended to the
heavens, and will come to judge the living
and the dead;

And in the Holy Spirit.

But as for those who say, there was when he
was not, and before being born he was not,
and that he came into existence out of
nothing, or who assert that the Son of God
is from a different *hypostasis* or substance,
or is created, or is subject to alteration or
change—these the Catholic Church anathematizes.[27]

Piet Schoonenberg has suggested that the primary function
of dogma is polemical and that the main intention of a dogma
must be seen in terms of what it is directed against.[28] Certainly
this hermeneutical principle is valuable in interpreting the
doctrinal affirmations of Nicaea. In the light of this principle we
can agree with Dr Kelly when he writes,

The theology of the council . . . had a more limited objective than is
sometimes supposed. If negatively it unequivocally outlawed Arianism, postively it was content to affirm the Son's full divinity and
equality with the Father, out of whose being he was derived and
whose nature he consequently shared. It did not attempt to tackle the
closely related problem of the divine unity although the discussion of
it was inevitably brought nearer.[29]

What then did the Council of Nicaea accomplish? Grillmeier
mentions four points.[30] First, the Council taught that the Son
was begotten rather than created. Secondly, in contradiction to

---

[27] Kelly, op. cit., p. 232.
[28] Schoonenberg, art. cit., p. 133.
[29] Kelly, op. cit., p. 236.
[30] See Grillmeier, op. cit., pp. 267–72.

two theses of Arius, according to which the Father is above the Son and begot the Son by an act of the will, it affirmed that the Son is begotten 'from the substance of the Father'. Third, it maintained that the Son was true God of true God. This was affirmed without, as we have mentioned, reflecting on the question how the Father, Son, and Holy Spirit could be truly different and yet participate in the one undivided nature of the Godhead. Fourth, the technical term *homoousios* was introduced to describe the relation of the Son to the Father.

Concerning this term we should note a) that it was not a ready-made philosophical term which was simply imported into Christian dogmatics, and b) that the council fathers were most reluctant to employ it but did so out of constraint, with the conviction that alternative language was susceptible to an Arian interpretation.

It is therefore a gross exaggeration and misinterpretation to conclude that Nicaea was a sell-out to Hellenism. As John Courtney Murray notes,

The only place where one cannot find Hellenism is in the *homoousion*. It would be impossible to find a conception more remote from, at odds with, all the ontologies of the Graeco-Roman world than the conception embodied in this word, which says that the Son is all that the Father is except for the name of Father . . . It may be said that in the *homoousion* the Fathers of Nicaea christianized Hellenism in the single sense that they sanctioned the ontological mode of conception characteristic of the Hellenic mentality. But it may not be said, on peril of learned absurdity, that they hellenized Christianity.[31]

Lonergan draws the conclusion that in using the word *homoousios* Nicaea is enunciating a second-level proposition[32] to the effect that the Son is consubstantial with the Father if and only if what is true of the Father also is true of the Son, except only the Father is Father. In other words the language of Nicaea must be understood heuristically. Lonergan writes, 'It offers an open structure: it does not determine what attributes are to be

[31] John Courtney Murray, *The Problem of God* (New Haven: Yale University Press, 1964), p. 55.
[32] A first-level proposition is one that mediates reality directly. A second-level proposition is one that mediates reality through another proposition. Lonergan, 'The Dehellenization of Dogma', in *A Second Collection*, Papers by Bernard J. F. Lonergan, S. J. Edited by William F. J. Ryan, S. J. and Bernard J. Tyrrell, S. J. (London: Darton, Longman and Todd, 1974), pp. 19–20.

assigned to the Father and so must be assigned to the Son as well; it leaves the believer free to conceive the Father in scriptural, patristic, medieval or modern terms; of course, contemporary consciousness, which is historically minded, will be at home in all four.'[33] Nicaea therefore leaves a great deal open and great deal unsettled. But it does make a judgement and so provides a bare minimum which must be taken into account in any subsequent endeavour to formulate a Christian doctrine of God.

A glance at the Nicene Symbol reveals that little attention was given there to the role of the Holy Spirit. But in the wake of Nicaea, the divinity of the Holy Spirit was contested by the Tropici against whom Athanasius directed his *Letters to Serapion*. Athanasius argues for the full divinity of the Holy Spirit on the basis of the Spirit's close relationship to the Son. The Spirit belongs in essence to the Son as the Son does to the Father, so whatever belongs to the Son also belongs to the Spirit.[34] Athanasius also uses the soteriological argument which we cited earlier.[35]

The Cappadocians continued to wage battle for the divinity of the Holy Spirit later in the fourth century, Gregory of Nazianzus being the first to use the term *homoousios* for the Spirit as well as the Son.[36]

The efforts of Athanasius and the Cappadocians were vindicated at the Council of Constantinople in 381 which reaffirmed the faith of Nicaea, endorsed the consubstantiality of the Spirit, and affirmed that he is worthy of divine adoration.

Although there is no evidence that Constantinople produced a creed, the Nicene-Constantinopolitan Creed, ascribed to the Council of Constantinople since the Council of Chalcedon, has always been associated with it and may be regarded as a valid clue to interpreting the mind of the Council. The divinity of the Holy Spirit is affirmed through such titles as *kyrios* and *zoiopoios* and by the fact that the Holy Spirit is judged worthy of worship.

---

[33] Ibid., p. 23.
[34] See Athanasius, *Ep. ad Serapion*, I, 2; also I, 21.
[35] See, for example, Athanasius, *Ep. ad Serapion*, I, 24.
[36] *Oratio* 31, 10. 'What then? Is the Spirit God? Most certainly. Well, then, is he consubstantial? Yes, if he is God.' *A Select Library of Nicene and Post-Nicene Fathers of the Christian Church*, vol. vii, trans. Charles Gordon Browne and James Edward Swallow (Oxford: James Parker and Co., 1894), p. 321.

Over against the Macedonian Pneumatomachians who taught that the Spirit was a creature, the Creed stresses that the Spirit proceeds from the Father. To be sure, this Creed does not use the term *homoousios* or *theos* for the Holy Spirit. But these omissions should be seen as an effort at achieving moderate formulations which would facilitate compromise and avoid giving scandal to the weak.

Thus by the end of the fourth century, the church had solemnly affirmed the full divinity of the *logos* and of the Spirit, thus providing the foundations for a thorough elaboration of the Christian doctrine of God. As Lonergan has noted however, there is a difference between doctrines and systematics,[37] the former resting on the act of judgement, the latter on conceptual clarification. Nicaea and Constantinople provided fundamental doctrinal affirmations but how were these judgements to be conceptualized in such a way that a Christian could coherently affirm both the unity and indivisibility of the one God and his three-ness? Two major systematic efforts were made in this direction, in the East by the Cappadocian Fathers and in the West by Augustine. Let us turn immediately to an investigation of the major thrust of each school.

iv.   *Two Conceptual Systems: The Cappadocians and Augustine*

The pattern for subsequent Eastern thinking in regard to the doctrine of the Trinity was irrevocably established by the Cappadocian Fathers. They were the first to work out systematically the relationships within the divine essence and they did this by clarifying and distinguishing the meaning of *ousia* and *hypostasis*. In pre-Nicene thought *ousia* and *hypostasis* were used interchangeably and even Athanasius used the terms this way throughout his entire lifetime.[38] Dr Kelly points to three uses of the term *ousia* in the ancient world: 1. generic, a class to which a number of individuals belong (Aristotle's second substance); 2. a particular entity regarded as the subject of qualities; 3. matter or stuff (Stoic use).[39] One of the difficulties in using the term

---

[37] For the distinction see Bernard Lonergan, *Method in Theology* (London: Darton, Longman and Todd, 1972), p. 132. See also ibid., Chapters 12 and 13.
[38] Prestige, op. cit., p. 168.
[39] J. N. D. Kelly, *Early Christian Creeds* (3rd ed., London: Longman, 1972), pp. 243–44.

THE EARLY CHRISTIAN DOCTRINE OF GOD

*homoousios* to describe the relation of the Son to the Father was the danger of a materialist interpretation. This, however, was not the intention of Nicaea, as Eusebius of Caesarea explained to his flock and as Athanasius, Hilary, and Basil were at pains to point out.[40]

When the Cappadocians speak of the one divine *ousia*, they are using the term in the second of Dr Kelly's senses. Occasionnally they come dangerously close to the first sense, as for example when they compare the relation of God's *ousia* to the three divine *hypostases* as that of universal to particular.[41] Such a conception would obviously be open to the charge of tritheism. But if we remember that the fundamental conception of *ousia* for these writers is a concrete reality and not an abstract essence, and if we bear in mind their emphasis on the simplicity and indivisibility of the divine essence we will have to conclude that they are not tritheists.[42]

For the Cappadocians, then, God is one *ousia* in three *hypostases*, *hypostasis* being the term used to express the character of concrete objectivity.[43] To quote Dr Prestige,

When the doctrine of the Trinity finally came to be formulated as one *ousia* in three *hypostases*, it implied that God, regarded from the point of view of internal analysis, is one object; but that, regarded from the point of view of external presentation, he is three objects; his unity being safeguarded by the doctrine that these three objects of presentation are not merely precisely similar, as the semi-Arians were willing to admit, but, in a true sense, identically one.[44]

In other words God is one object *in* himself and three objects *to* himself.

A further question remains as to what distinguishes the three *hypostases*. Here the Cappadocians are not particularly illumin-

---

[40] Bernard J. F. Lonergan, *The Way to Nicaea, The Dialectical Development of Trinitarian Theology* (London: Darton, Longman and Todd, 1976), p. 90.

[41] See, for example, Basil, *Ep*. 214, 4. He writes, '*Ousia* has the same relation to *hypostasis* as the common has to the particular.' *A Select Library of Nicene and Post-Nicene Fathers of the Christian Church*, vol. viii, trans. the Rev. Blomfield Jackson (Oxford: James Parker and Co., 1895), p. 254. See also *Ep*. 236, 6. 'The distinction between *ousia* and *hypostasis* is the same as that between the general and the particular; as, for instance, between the animal and the particular man.' Ibid., p. 278.

[42] See Kelly, *Early Christian Doctrines*, pp. 267–69.

[43] See Prestige, op. cit., p. 174.

[44] Ibid., p. 169.

ating. For Basil, the distinguishing characteristics of the three *hypostases* are paternity, sonship, and sanctifying power.[45] The other Cappadocians define them more precisely as *agennēsia*, *gennēsis*, and *ekpempsis* or *ekporeusis*.[46] All three of the Cappadocians have this in common, that the ultimate *arche* or *aitia* in the Godhead is the Father. To be sure, the Cappadocian settlement represents the definitive defeat of all traces of subordinationism. But the East never abandoned its basic conviction that *ho theos* means primarily and in the first place the Father.

What then did the Cappadocians accomplish? In addition to doing away with subordinationism, they distinguished themselves in bringing conceptual clarity to the problem of God's unity and multiplicity. Equally important is their methodology. With their emphasis on the ultimacy of the Father and their stress on the threefold experience of God, the Cappadocians attempted to keep a foothold in the saving economy of God. Nevertheless the fact that they understood the distinctions within the Godhead in so formal a way coupled with their stress on the unified and indivisible activity of God *extra se* tended to sever the connection between the economic Trinity and the immanent Trinity.

For all their brilliance, we may still agree with Maurice Wiles when he says of the Cappadocians:

It cannot fairly be claimed that they found any philosophical solution to their problem. They simply expressed that problem with the use of philosophical terms. Perhaps that is all a philosophical statement ever does. But the point of doing so is to throw some new light upon the problem in hand. And this they failed to achieve. The most carefully articulated statement of the relation of *ousia* and *hypostasis* remains in the last analysis no less paradoxical than Gregory of

---

[45] In *Ep.* 214, 4 Basil writes, 'If you ask me to state shortly my own view, I shall state that *ousia* has the same relation to *hypostasis* as the common has to the particular. Everyone of us both shares in the existence by the common term of essence (*ousia*) and by his own properties is such an one and such an one. In the same manner, in the matter in question, the term *ousia* is common, like goodness, or Godhead, or any similar attribute; while *hypostasis* is contemplated in the special property of Fatherhood, Sonship, or the power to sanctify.' Op. cit., p. 254. See also *Ep.* 236, 6. 'If we have no distinct perception of the separate characteristics, namely Fatherhood, Sonship, and sanctification, but form our conception of God from the general idea of existence, we cannot possibly give a sound account of our faith.' Ibid., p. 278.

[46] See, for example, Gregory Nazianzus, *Oratio* 25,16; 26,19; 29,2.

Nazianzus' more direct declaration that the Trinity is 'separately one and unitedly separate'.[47]

Professor Wiles goes on to ask what has been gained by restating the problem in the terms of *ousia* and *hypostasis*. He writes,

It was right and necessary in the historical situation that the attempt should be made. But it may be equally right and necessary to conclude that the outcome of the attempt was to wrap up the nature of the problem in a way which is more likely to mislead than to illuminate. If in attempting to give philosophical expression to conflicting aspects of our experience, we are led to an apparently irreconcilable antinomy in our thinking, we do best to go back to the apparent conflict in experience in the hope that in due course some other form of philosophical expression may throw new light upon our problem.[48]

Before exploring at greater length the philosophical conundrums involved in this type of thinking and the theological impasses to which it can lead, let us complete this synopsis by examining the other major theological construction of the Christian doctrine of God, namely that developed in the West by Augustine. Here we encounter both a different methodology and a different conception of God.

The most important thing to be said about Augustine is that methodologically he begins with the divine essence as such. To quote Dr Kelly, 'While Augustine's exposition of trinitarian orthodoxy is scriptual throughout, his conception of God as absolute being, simple and indivisible, transcending the categories, forms its ever present background. So in constrast to the tradition which made the Father its starting point, he begins with the divine nature itself.'[49]

Within this framework, Augustine defines the three persons of the Trinity (his formula is *una substantia, tres personae*) as subsistent relations within the Godhead. The persons are identical considered as the divine substance. But they are distinguished from each other by their relations.[50] The Father is distinguished as Father because he begets the Son, and the Son is distinguished as Son because he is begotten.[51] The Spirit

[47] Wiles, op. cit., p. 139.
[48] Ibid., pp. 139–40.
[49] Kelly, *Early Christian Doctrines*, p. 272.
[50] See *De Trinitate* 5,12.
[51] See ibid., 5, 6.

similarly is distinguished from Father and Son inasmuch as he is bestowed by them, is their common gift, the communion between them.[52]

Augustine's theory of persons as subsistent relations together with his famous psychological analyses prepared the soil for the flowering of trinitarian theology in scholasticism, culminating in Aquinas's theory of processions in terms of intellect and will.

But a severe price has been paid for the subtleties of Western speculations. The Augustinian emphasis on the divine essence led eventually to the split in Aquinas between the tracts *De Deo Uno* and *De Deo Trino*. Trinitarian theology was superimposed on philosophical conceptions of God. Furthermore as the doctrine of the Trinity became more metaphysical, it also became more abstract and divorced from the trinitarian experience of God in the saving events of history.

Let us then conclude our overview of these two different systems of thought by quoting Jaroslav Pelikan who highlights the contrasts. He writes,

Opposed to each other were not only two systems of dogmatic authority, and two conceptions of tradition, and two methods of formulating theological distinctions, but, beyond and beneath all of these, two conceptions of the Godhead. In Western trinitarianism, the Holy Spirit was the guarantee of the unity of the Godhead . . . Eastern trinitarianism, by contrast, continued to begin with Father, Son and Holy Spirit, and it needed to formulate the relation between them in such a way as to assure their unity. This way was the identification of the Father—and only the Father—as the source (πηγή), the principle (ἀρχή), and the cause (αἰτία) within the Trinity. . . . But the Father was such a cause not according to his nature or essence (which was common to all three *hypostases*), but according to his *hypostasis* as Father. . . . The trinity could be compared to a balance scale, in which there was a single operation and center (the Father), upon which the two arms (Son and Holy Spirit) both depended.[53]

v.   *Evaluation of The Patristic Doctrine of God*

With the Cappadocians and Augustine we have come a long

[52] See ibid., 5,12.
[53] Jaroslav Pelikan, *The Christian Tradition, A History of the Development of Doctrine*, vol. ii, *The Spirit of Eastern Chrsitendom (600–1700)* (Chicago: University of Chicago Press, 1974), pp. 196–7.

way from the vivid and concrete imagery of the biblical expression of Christian faith, and so as a final question in this Chapter I would like to ask if and how much the Christian vision was corrupted by its contact with its Hellenistic environment. Obviously this is a vital question for contemporary efforts in reconstructing the Christian doctrine of God. Equally obvious is the danger of oversimplification. Harnack's theory of the wholesale sell-out of Christianity to Hellenism is clearly unacceptable today. As Wolfhart Pannenberg has noted, it is obviously

inappropriate to speak of such a complex matter as a 'Hellenization' in the sense of a coming under foreign control, a supplanting of the Christian idea of God by a 'deistic' one, as Harnack did in dependence upon Ritschl. Not only must the linkage with the philosophical concept of God which was effected by the Apologists be recognized as a legitimate task from the standpoint of the universal claim of the Judaeo-Christian God, but even with regard to the way in which this task was carried out in early Christian theology a more differentiated judgment is necessary.[54]

Writing in the same vein, Prestige comments:

Ideas were certainly adopted from pagan sources in the different efforts made to give a Christian explanation. But I do not think that any one such idea was ever imported without undergoing substantial modification to suit its new environment. The idea was cut to fit the Christian faith, not the faith trimmed to square with the imported conception. Conceptions of pagan philosophy were radically altered in their Christian context, and not seldom utterly discarded after trial.[55]

And so we may agree with Jaroslav Pelikan when he insists that although philosophy has intruded into Christian doctrine, it has equally been modified by Christian faith.[56]

Nonetheless the question remains as to how decisive the victory of Christian faith over Greek philosophy really was. To

---

[54] Wolfhart Pannenberg, 'The Appropriation of the Philosophical Concept of God as a Dogmatic Problem of Early Christian Theology', in *Basic Questions in Theology*, vol. ii, (London: SCM Press, 1971), pp. 177–8.

[55] Prestige, op. cit., pp. xiii–xiv.

[56] See Jaroslav Pelikan, *The Christian Tradition, A History of the Development of Doctrine*, vol. i, *The Emergence of the Catholic Tradition (100–600)* (London: University of Chicago Press, 1971), p. 55.

quote Pelikan again, 'Victory over classical thought there assuredly was, but a victory for which some Christians were willing to pay a rather high price.'[57]

As an approach to this problem, I suggest we investigate the presuppositions of classical thought which unconsciously affected the thinking of patristic authors both in the East and in the West. In other words we are searching for the pre-understanding of the patristic mind, a pre-understanding which cannot be identified with the definitions of the patristic period but which is implicit in them and underlies the attempts of the Church Fathers to systematize them theologically.[58] Here we must bear in mind the significant point made by Pannenberg in his important essay, 'The Appropriation of the Philosophical Concept of God as a Dogmatic Problem of Early Christian Theology'. Pannenberg writes, 'The formulation of the question that underlay the philosophical idea of God was so much taken for granted by the men of this Hellenistic period that they were not at all in a position to elucidate critically the presuppositions inherent in it.'[59]

Let us then examine in turn three presuppositions of the Hellenistic mind in approaching the problem of God: a) the relation of immanence and transcendence; b) God's immutability and a-temporality; c) the divine impassibility.

Pannenberg locates the basic tension between the biblical experience of God and Greek metaphysics in the method of causal inference. He writes,

The Greek gods need no special revelation in order to make their essence known, for they 'are a necessary part of the world'. That is their immanence. Philosophical theology's point of departure becomes intelligible from this standpoint. If it is the characteristic function of the divine to be the origin of normal events, then—under possible historical conditions which need not be discussed here—the reversal of this lies close at hand; the truly divine can be no other than the origin needed to bring about the familiar reality, and which every explanation of this reality presupposes. In this way it becomes

[57] Ibid., p. 45.
[58] Avery Dulles, op. cit., p. 176, lays down as a hermeneutical principle: 'An antiquated world-view, presupposed but not formally taught in an earlier doctrinal formulation, should not be imposed as binding doctrine.'
[59] Pannenberg, art. cit., p. 182.

possible to reason back from the normal state of affairs encountered in ordinary experience of the world to the true nature of the divine.[60]

The problem with this view is that it obscures the divine freedom and renders an historical action of God practically unintelligible. For if God is regarded exclusively as the origin of what is, in what sense can he be said to accomplish the genuinely new? In the Christian understanding of God, 'The constancy of God is realized as free act precisely in his contingent, historical action. In contrast to this, the concept of God who is by nature immutable necessarily obstructs the theological understanding of his historical action, and it has done so to an extent that can hardly be exaggerated.'[61] This is another way of saying that the locus of the divine presence for the Greeks is nature while for the Hebrew and Christian it is history. In his book *God and World in Early Christian Thought*, Richard A. Norris contrasts the two points of view admirably when he writes,

Whereas the Greeks transformed a primitive nature religion into a rational theology of nature, the Hebrews transmuted a similar nature religion into a theology of historical experience. . . . The Greek deity is the final point of stability in a world of apparently senseless change. The Hebrew Lord is the initiator of significant change which transforms the character of historical experiences. As such, he, like the events through which he is known, has a specific character. Hence, in the first instance he is named, not defined; and as the Lord of world history he is unique.[62]

In mentioning this presupposition of Greek religion, I am not claiming that the Church Fathers succumbed to this point of view. I am suggesting that as Christianity came into greater contact with Hellenism and tried to absorb Middle-Platonism, it sought to achieve a synthesis which was bound to break down precisely at this point. Let us now turn to two other presuppositions of Greek philosophical theology which rendered a synthesis of Greek thought and biblical faith highly problematic, namely the divine immutability and a-temporality and the divine impassibility.

[60] Ibid., p. 125.
[61] Ibid., p. 162.
[62] Richard A. Norris, *God and World in Early Christian Thought* (London: Adam and Charles Black, 1966), p. 32.

In dealing with the problem of God's immutability, Pelikan
writes,

In Judaism it was possible simultaneously to ascribe change and
purpose to God and to declare that God did not change, without
resolving the paradox; for the immutability of God was seen as the
trustworthiness of his covenanted relation to his people in the concrete history of his judgment and mercy, rather than as a primarily
ontological category. But in the development of the Christian doctrine of God, immutability assumed the status of an axiomatic
presupposition for the discussion of other doctrines. Hence the de-
Judaization of Christian thought contributed, for example, to the
form taken by the christological controversy, in which both sides
defined the absoluteness of God in accordance with the principle of
immutability even though they drew opposite christological conclusions from it.[63]

Pannenberg has likewise questioned the category of
immutability, judging that it is contrary to the biblical witness if
applied to God without qualification. He writes:

The concept of immutability rightly says that God is no originated
and transitory thing. Insofar as mutability is known to us only in
connection with the process of coming into being and passing away,
the author of the world cannot in fact be mutable if he is to be the basis
of the endurance of all things. But immutability says too little, since
God not only immovably establishes and maintains present reality in
its lawful course, but has within himself an infinite plenitude of ever
new possibilities in the realization of which he manifests the freedom
of his invisible essence. For this reason, while he is unoriginate and
indestructible, God is nevertheless not immobile, but rather, in this
inner plenitude, the living God. Therefore, it can also be said of him,
apparently in contradiction to 1 Sam. 15:29 and the other passages
mentioned above, that he allows himself to repent of some things (Jer.
18:8,10; Gen. 6:6). The durability of the world indeed does depend
upon the fact that God does not jump from one possibility to another
but abides by his creative decisions, 'not changing' them or simply
dropping them. But the fact that God does not change in his acts is an
expression not of an immobility constitutive of his essence but rather
of his free momentary, humanly unanticipatible decision, just as
much as his creative activity. It is identical with the faithfulness of
God.[64]

[63] Pelikan, *The Emergence of the Catholic Tradition*, p. 22.
[64] Pannenberg, art. cit., pp. 161–2.

Closely connected with the problem of God's immutability is his eternity. The flow of time is meaningless for that which remains ever the same. Pannenberg contends that the philosophical concept of eternity as separation from everything temporal intruded into the biblical idea of God's eternity as his powerful presence to every time.[65] Thus Christianity was faced with the task of assimilating the concept of God who is static, a-temporal and by definition uninvolved with his world. This has had the devastating consequence of rendering inexplicable the biblical affirmation of the contention of God with man and of necessitating that every innovation in the divine–human relationship has to be sought as much as possible on the side of man.

A final consequence results from God's immutability, namely the doctrine of the divine impassibility. As Pannenberg notes, this doctrine fatefully determined the christology of the early church right down to the theopaschite controversy in the sixth century.[66]

Many of the Church Fathers explicitly affirm the doctrine of the divine impassibility.[67] Yet they also see the necessity of theopaschitism, at least the passibility of the divine Word through the incarnation. Their motivation is primarily soteriological. It was necessary that God himself should subject himself to suffering and death in order thus to engage in combat with them and prove himself their Lord. Unless this were so, men would remain bound under their sway.

The difficulty is how to put these two affirmations together coherently. If the Word as such is impassible, how can it suffer? In his doctoral thesis *Theopaschite Expressions in Second-Century Christianity as Reflected in the Writings of Justin, Melito, Celsus and Irenaeus*, Michael Slusser suggests that, at least for these early writers, a solution was found in the divine will. The Word is by nature impassible but by an act of the will makes himself passible.[68]

[65] Ibid., p. 173.

[66] Ibid., p. 162.

[67] See, for example, Justin, *Dialogue with Trypho* 124, 4: *First Apology* 10, 1–2; 25, 2; Athenagoras, *Leg.* 8; Irenaeus *Adv.Haer.* II, 12, 1: Origen, *De.Prin.* 2, 4, 4; *Ioh. Comm.* 20, 36; *Num.hom.* 16, 3.

[68] Michael Slusser, '*Theopaschite Expressions in Second-Century Christianity as Reflected in the Writings of Justin, Melito, Celsus and Irenaeus*' (Oxford D. Phil. thesis, 1975), pp. 233 ff.

Yet this solution also involves a whole host of difficulties. For these writers still tenaciously held that the Father remains impassible. But if, as later trinitarian orthodoxy asserted, the action of the divine persons is one *ad extra*, how can the Father be free from suffering when the Son suffers?

These problems also affected the christological controversies. For it was the assumption of God's impassibility combined with the belief in the sufferings of Christ that led Arius to place the *logos* on the side of creatures. Again this same assumption prompted Cyril of Alexandria to speak in nearly docetic terms attributing Christ's suffering to the flesh. And it was the same principle that led Nestorius to separate the divine and the human in Christ lest the Word be made to suffer. Thus by the end of the fifth century, orthodox Christianity affirmed the paradoxical if not contradictory doctrine that the Word suffers but the Father does not along with the doctrine that the Word suffers in his human nature but not in his divine.

Furthermore the presupposition of divine impassibility led not only to impasses in christology and trinitarian theology but also had a deleterious effect on Christian spirituality, for divinization (*theōsis*), the ideal of Christian spirituality, was reduced to *apatheia*, the un-passioned life.[69] Such a doctrine carried to its logical conclusion would not only eviscerate Christian revelation by making the idea of incarnation unintelligible. It would also destroy the genuine *raison d'être* of Christian living which is not the transcendence of pain but active suffering with and for Christ's suffering members in the world.

What then are we to conclude from this analysis? We have seen that the systematic efforts of the patristic period were not merely the work of the Greek spirit on the soil of the gospel (Harnack). On the other hand the gospel, combined with certain Hellenistic presuppositions about the nature of God, led to impasses from which the church has yet to extricate itself. What then is to be done? In response let me quote again the remark of Maurice Wiles cited above: 'If in attempting to give philosophical expression to conflicting aspects of our experi-

---

[69] According to Jürgen Moltmann, the God of Christianity is far from Aristotle's idea of *theos apathes*. At the heart of Christianity is the suffering God and the vulnerable man. The ideal of Christian spirituality is not the apathetic man but the sympathetic man. See 'The Crucified God and the Apathetic Man', in *The Experiment Hope*, pp. 69–84.

ence, we are led to an apparently irreconcilable antinomy in our thinking, we do best to go back to the apparent conflict in experience in the hope that in due course some other form of philosophical expression may throw new light upon our problem.'[70]

This advice consists of two parts. First, there is a return to experience. This directive is certainly crucial for reconstructing trinitarian theology today. The doctrine of the Trinity is the Christian doctrine of God. This doctrine can be nothing other than an elaboration of Christian experience. As Rahner has tirelessly pointed out, the economic Trinity is the immanent Trinity.[71]

Secondly, there is the search for a new form of philosophical expression. As Professor Wiles remarks, 'A statement whose truth or falsity can be determined only in terms of a world-view that is dead and gone can hardly be a statement of direct relevance to subsequent ages; "Old formulas", to quote Loisy, "conceived in another intellectual atmosphere no longer say what needs to be said or no longer say it suitably." '[72]

We must emphasize that this search is absolutely indispensable. It is naïve to believe that the faith can be disengaged from ontology. As long as faith is a rational act of the human being, it must perforce be thought in some conceptual scheme, worldview, and ontology. Thus Langdon Gilkey can correctly assert,

No theological interpretation of fundamental symbols can have meaning for us unless it gives Christian shape to some *modern* ontology, expressive of our own being in the world. In providing understanding of the symbols expressive of our faith, theology for its own completion calls for the appropriation and use of contemporary philosophy if the symbols it expresses are to be reflectively alive, that is, meaningful and valid for us.[73]

This of course involves a risk, a risk similar to that taken by

[70] Maurice Wiles, op. cit., p. 140.

[71] Karl Rahner, *The Trinity*, trans. Joseph Donceel (New York: Herder and Herder, 1970), pp. 21–2. 'The *basic thesis* which establishes this connection between the treatises and presents the Trinity *as* a mystery of salvation (in its reality and not merely as a doctrine) might be formulated as follows: The "economic" Trinity is the "immanent" Trinity and the "immanent" Trinity is the "economic" Trinity.'

[72] Wiles, op. cit., p. 9.

[73] Langdon Gilkey, *Catholicism Confronts Modernity, a Protestant View* (New York: Seabury Press, 1975), p. 103.,

the early church. For in rethinking the gospel in a new conceptual framework, the theologian will transform the ontology in which it was once set and the ontology he has borrowed from contemporary philosophers. He will not merely be restating the old formulas in new language but will indeed be seeking a new synthesis.[74]

Yet it is precisely this that past dogmatic definitions invite. As Karl Rahner has written,

Work by the theologians and teachers of the church bearing on a reality and a truth revealed by God always ends in an exact formulation. That is natural and necessary. For only in this way is it possible to draw a line of demarcation, excluding heresy and misunderstanding of the divine truth, which can be observed in everyday religious practice. But if the formula is thus an end, the result and the victory which bring about simplicity, clarity, the possibility of teaching and doctrinal certainty, then in this victory everything depends on the end also being seen as a beginning.[75]

The definitions of Nicaea and Constantinople may therefore be seen as invitations to think the Christian doctrine of God anew. We have suggested that the two great patristic efforts along these lines were partially impeded by certain philosophical concepts which the Church Fathers had at their disposal and took for granted. Paradoxically, however, it may be that a deeper penetration into the mystery of the triune God will enable us to rethink our philosophical categories.[76] Pannenberg points the way when he writes,

It remains a task for the Christian doctrine of God to show that the otherness of God as well as his unity cannot really be conceived within the philosophical formulation of the question, but can be comprehended only as the unity of the Father with the Son and the Spirit, so that the revelation of the triune God is what brings the philosophical question to a genuine fulfilment for the first time.'[77]

[74] See ibid., p. 173.

[75] Karl Rahner, 'Chalkedon—Ende oder Anfang?' *Chalkedon* III, 3 as cited by Grillmeier, op. cit. p. 556.

[76] Whitehead once remarked that Christianity 'has always been a religion seeking a metaphysic, in contrast to Buddhism which is a metaphysic generating a religion'. *Religion in the Making* as collected in *Alfred North Whitehead, An Anthology* selected by F. S. C. Northrop and Mason W. Gross (New York: The Macmillan Co., 1961), p. 485.

[77] Pannenberg, art. cit., p. 182.

# III

# TRINITY AND PROCESS:
# THE CHRISTIAN DOCTRINE OF GOD
# IN PROCESS THEOLOGY

## i. *Introduction*

THE purpose of this chapter is to examine the doctrine of the
Trinity in the light of process theology. There are several
reasons why this investigation forms a critical part of our
general enterprise. First, there is the general conviction that
any valid interpretation of the Christian doctrine of God must
be trinitarian in scope. This is the case because as we have seen
the doctrine of God which emerged in light of Christian experience during the patristic period was precisely the doctrine of
Father, Son, and Holy Spirit. It is a sound principle then to
bridge the dichotomy which has become axiomatic since
Aquinas between the tracts *De Deo Uno* and *De Deo Trino*.[1]
Secondly, there is the hunch mentioned at the end of chapter
one that a trinitarian understanding of God may provide the
dynamic understanding of a God involved in history which has
been lacking in classical philosophical theism. If this is the case,
I believe it is critical for Christian theology today to examine
whether the specifically Christian experience of God can be
conceptualized not in the categories of Greek metaphysics but
in a metaphysics shaped by an evolutionary world-view.
Process metaphysics is one of the most compelling conceptual
tools available to us today, and therefore it is urgent to ask
whether a synthesis between the Christian doctrine of God and
process metaphysics is viable.

Beyond these intrinsic reasons for justifying our endeavour, a
number of extrinsic motivations also present themselves. The
first is that no such attempt has yet been made. Most of the
books and articles on process theology have either concentrated
exclusively on the philosophical side of the God-question and

---

[1] See Karl Rahner, *The Trinity*, pp. 16–17.

on the debate between classical philosophical theism and its
neoclassical revision, or they have struggled with the questions
of christology. To this extent process theology still labours
under the division mentioned above between the philosophical
tract on God and the theological tract on the Trinity. One of the
few attempts to examine the doctrine of the Trinity in the light
of process metaphysics is an essay entitled 'Trinity and
Process'.[2] In this essay, Anthony Kelly shows sympathy for the
project of a synthesis of trinitarian theology with process metaphysics but judges that the Whiteheadian version of such a
metaphysics is inadequate. Though Kelly's article is stimulating, its brevity certainly precludes anything like a final
verdict. This is all the more the case since Kelly does not have at
his disposal anything like a full process systematic theology but
must focus on some of the difficulties he finds inherent in
process philosophical theology.

This last point suggests a second extrinsic reason for the
present chapter. It has been noted by Jürgen Moltmann[3] that
process theology is inadequate as a Christian theology precisely
because it lacks the trinitarian perspective. Thus Moltmann
draws a sharp distinction between his own theology, which he
endeavours to develop in trinitarian terms, and process theology, which he says has a bipolar concept of God without a
doctrine of the Trinity. Moltmann then is sympathetic to the
key issues which have motivated process thinkers but finds their
shortcoming precisely in their bipolar view of God. We are led
then to ask whether the process view of God's bipolarity or
dipolarity necessarily results in binatarianism or whether it is
compatible with classical Trinitarianism.

Fortunately there is at least one thinker among the process
theologians who has come close to developing a thoroughly
elaborated systematic theology conceptualized in the categories
of process metaphysics. I am referring to Schubert M. Ogden.
Ogden's early work, *The Reality of God*,[4] initiated the dialogue

---

[2] Anthony J. Kelly, C.SS.R. 'Trinity and Process: Relevance of the Basic Christian
Confession of God', *Theological Studies* 31, 3 (Sept. 1970) 393–414. That this theme
merits further study is suggested by a recent seminar of the Catholic Theological
Society of America. See 'Seminar on Trinity and World Process', *Proceedings of the
Catholic Theological Society of America* 33 (1978) 203–28.

[3] Moltmann, *The Crucified God*, pp. 255–6.

[4] Ogden, *The Reality of God* (London: SCM Press, 1967).

between process philosophy and Christian faith. We find here Ogden's characteristic concern to develop a suitable philosophical analysis to state the meaning and the truth of the Christian faith. Yet he sets himself this philosophical task precisely as a theologian. Therefore it is not surprising to discover that from his first book *Christ Without Myth* to more recent articles, such as 'The Point of Christology' and 'On Revelation',[5] Ogden has had a keen interest in christology. I would agree then with Colin Gunton when he writes, 'Of the process theologians, S. M. Ogden is the most aware of the consequence of the introduction of process conceptuality into Christian theology.'[6] This judgement is all the more warranted if one takes into account not only the published writings but also the unpublished material. There, especially in the unpublished lectures presented to divinity students at Perkins School of Theology,[7] one can find a fairly comprehensive account of what comes close to a process system of Christian dogmatics. It is my intention in this chapter to take Ogden as a representative process thinker[8] and to pool the resources of both his published and unpublished writings to sketch how one process thinker at least looks to process metaphysics not only to provide a philosophical doctrine of God but to furnish a conceptual framework in which the specifically Christian doctrine of God, Father, Son, and Holy Spirit, can be meaningfully articulated.

## ii. *Methodology*

Ogden has made our task easier in that he not only does theology but also reflects explicitly on what it means to do theology and articulates clearly what are the criteria by which one can assess the success of one's theological work. In his

    [5] Schubert M. Ogden, *Christ Without Myth: A Study Based on the Theology of Rudolf Bultmann* (London: Collins, 1962); 'The Point of Christology', *Journal of Religion* 55 (1975) 375–95; 'On Revelation', in *Our Common History as Christians: Essays in Honor of Albert C. Outler*, edd. John Deschner, Leroy T. Howe, and Klaus Penzel (New York: Oxford University Press, 1975), pp. 261–92.

    [6] Colin Gunton, 'Process Theology's Concept of God: An Outline and Assessment', *Expository Times* 84 (1972–3), p. 295.

    [7] Perkins School of Theology is part of Southern Methodist University, Dallas, Texas, USA.

    [8] Though this chapter deals principally with Ogden's thought, indications will be given throughout of similarities with and differences from other process theologians as well as the philosophical influences of Whitehead and Hartshorne on Ogden's theology.

programmatic essay 'What is Theology?' Ogden defines Christian theology as 'the fully reflective understanding of the Christian witness of faith as decisive for human existence'.[9] As such, theology requires two poles as the condition of possibility for its existence, the pole of the Christian witness of faith and the pole of human existence. These two poles are in turn the source of the two criteria for the adequacy of theological statements. Ogden names these two criteria appropriateness and understandability. Let us examine each of these criteria briefly in turn.

Ogden writes, 'A theological statement may be said to be appropriate only insofar as the understanding expressed by its concepts is that also expressed by the primary symbols of the witness of faith.'[10] But how are we to know when this is the case? The classical Catholic answer was to appeal to the authority of scripture and tradition as interpreted by the *magisterium*. In opposition to this position, Protestant orthodoxy took as its only authority the principle *sola scriptura*. But Ogden recognizes that this criterion will no longer do, because today we recognize that scripture itself is tradition and indeed that there are various layers of tradition within the canonical scriptures. Thus he writes, 'The conclusion to which we are led is that, relative to Christ himself and to the apostolic witness that alone is directly authorized by him, there is no difference in principle, but only in fact, between the authority of scripture, on the one hand, and that of the church's tradition and *magisterium* on the other.'[11]

Are we then left with no norm by which to judge when our theological assertions are appropriate to the primary symbols of the witness of faith? Ogden argues that it is still possible to do justice to the motives of the reformation principle.[12] The re-

[9] Schubert Ogden, 'What is Theology?', *Journal of Religion* 52 (1972) 22.
[10] Ibid., p. 25.
[11] Schubert Ogden, 'The Authority of Scripture for Theology', *Interpretation* 30 (July, 1976) 252.
[12] See ibid., 250–4. Note that Ogden distinguishes doctrine and theology. There is a need for the Christian community to establish doctrinal standards. But theology is not subject to such standards, for its task is not to serve as the church's ideology but rather to critique those doctrinal standards both in terms of the apostolic witness and in terms of reason and experience. Thus no past dogmatic formulas are absolutely binding on the theologian as in the Catholic tradition. See Ogden's essay, 'Doctrinal Standards in the United Methodist Church', *Perkins School of Theology Journal* 28 (1974–5) 19–27. See also Schubert Ogden, *Faith and Freedom: Toward a Theology of Liberation* (Belfast–Dublin–

formers wanted an external authority and hence they looked to
the canon of scripture. But if we look to the criterion of canonicity in the early church, it was precisely apostolic authorship.
This was both an historical question and a theological one. The
early church asked if the documents of scripture bore witness to
Christ in the unique sense of being authorized by someone
directly authorized by Christ himself. Ogden goes on to argue
that if this is taken as the criterion for canonicity, then the
external authority can be neither the New Testament nor the
Old Testament but rather the apostolic witness that is prior to
the New Testament. Thus we must search through the layers of
tradition in the New Testament to find the core apostolic
witness. Relying on the work of the New Testament exegete
Willi Marxsen, Ogden identifies this core as the Jesus-kerygma.
In the Jesus-kerygma, Jesus is attested without christological
predicates and retains his status as proclaimer. [13] Ogden writes:

What is central in the Jesus-kerygma is the actual witness of Jesus
himself, his proclamation of the nearness of God's reign, his table
fellowship with the outcasts in anticipation of the eschatological meal,
his exorcisms of demons, his summons to faith with the promise or
threat that the coming Son of Man will judge according to his hearers'
present response to his own words and deeds. In other words, so far as
the Jesus-kerygma is concerned, Jesus is re-presented as the one who
through his words and deeds in the present places everyone whom he
encounters in the immediate presence of God whose gift and demand
is love. [14]

Ottawa–Christian Journals Limited, 1979), pp. 115–24. In the section with the title
'The Emancipation of Theology' (p. 121) Ogden writes, 'Because the real root of
theology's historic bondage is the underlying conception of its task as the
rationalization of positions already taken, the only way in which it can be emancipated
is by reconceiving its task, instead, as the critical reflection on such positions. Only
insofar as theology is consistently conceived as such reflection—on the positions taken
in the normative Christian witness as well as on those taken by men and women today
in their actual conflictive history—can it be said that theology really is free.'

[13] See Schubert Ogden, 'Sources of Religious Authority in Liberal Protestantism',
*Journal of the American Academy of Religion* 44, 3 (1976) 414–15, note 15. Marxsen
distinguishes three forms of kerygma in the New Testament: the Jesus-kerygma, the
Christ kerygma and the mixed Jesus–Christ kerygma. Only in the primitive Jesus-
kerygma is Jesus proclaimed as the proclaimer.
[14] Cited from the text of Ogden's unpublished lecture 'On Christ', p. 4. This lecture
forms part of a series given on the interpretation of the Christian message during
1975–6 at Perkins School of Theology. Note that unless otherwise indicated all references to unpublished lectures refer to this same series.

To summarize this point, we may say that the first criterion for judging theological assertions is their appropriateness. A theological statement is appropriate if its understanding expresses the understanding of the primary symbols of the Christian witness of faith. It does this if it expresses the understanding of the apostolic witness. Historical research indicates that the core of the apostolic witness is to be found in the Jesus-kerygma. The Jesus-kerygma then is normative for determining whether a theological statement is Christian.

There remains, however, the question of whether such a statement is either meaningful or true. To resolve this question, one must bring in the criterion of understandability. Ogden notes that a theological statement is understandable if 'it meets the relevant conditions of meaning and truth universally established with human existence.'[15]

In appealing to the criterion of understandability, Ogden places himself squarely in the tradition of liberal Protestantism. Classical Protestantism gave reason and experience only limited claims, whereas for liberal Protestantism scripture and revelation on the one hand and reason and experience on the other require mutual confirmation.

Ogden's reasons for this insistence are twofold.[16] First, he maintains that scripture itself demands an account of God as universally recognizable. The God of the scriptures is not one being among other beings, not even the supreme being. Rather the God of the scriptures is the 'Being of all beings', i.e. the all-inclusive reality that establishes the whole difference between something and bare nothing. Therefore to experience anything at all is to experience God as its necessary ground. Moreover, the scriptures affirm that man is radically free and therefore responsible for his sin. All men can be held responsible for their sin only if God has universally revealed himself to them. Only on this condition could they be held responsible for refusing to acknowledge him.

Secondly, Ogden argues that if theology is to claim to make intelligible assertions, it can do so only on condition of appeal-

[15] Ogden, 'What is Theology?', p. 25.
[16] For the first argument that follows, see Schubert Ogden, 'Present Prospects of Empirical Theology', in *The Future of Empirical Theology*, ed. Bernard E. Meland (Chicago: University of Chicago Press, 1969), pp. 73–4.

ing to those criteria of meaning and truth universally given in human experience. This implies that an adequate Christian theology requires a fully developed metaphysics. As Ogden writes, 'Thus not only is it evident that Christian faith alone is an insufficient ground for theology's assertions, but it is also clear that such assertions cannot even be established as meaningful except by establishing a theistic metaphysics which is true independently of specifically Christian faith.'[17]

The consequences of this position are quite significant. We have seen that no theological statement could be called Christian unless it is appropriate to the understanding expressed in the apostolic witness of faith. But this criterion alone is a necessary but insufficient guarantee that it is true. Ogden's methodology commits him to a thorough-going rejection of Barthianism. Theology cannot justify its assertions merely by appealing to special revelatory experiences or to the Word of God. Such a position amounts to fideism and implies that religious assertions are expressions of an unverifiable world-view. According to Ogden theology can avoid this cul-de-sac only by vindicating its assertions through a fully developed theistic metaphysics.

Finally, then, let us note that since metaphysical claims are ultimately rooted in human reason and experience, such claims being the conditions of possibility for any experience at all, it follows that theological statements must ultimately be judged in terms of experience and reason as well.

Is this then another form of rationalism? It is, in the sense that Ogden's method precludes an appeal to revelations or events that are heteronomous to human experience and reason. But it is not rationalism in the narrow sense, since for Ogden experience contains thought and not vice versa. The priority of experience to reason is irreversible.

Thus Ogden commits himself to an empiricism in which experience is broadly conceived.[18] Experience is reduced neither to sense data, as in Hume, nor to sense data plus the inner, non-sensuous perception of ourselves and of the world, as

[17] Schubert Ogden, 'The Task of Philosophical Theology', in *The Future of Philosophical Theology*, ed. Robert H. Evans (Philadelphia: The Westminster Press, 1971), p. 80.
[18] See Ogden, 'Present Prospects for Empirical Theology', pp. 80–8.

in the radical empiricism of William James. Ogden rather
conceives of experience in Whiteheadian terms as the awareness of ourselves and of our fellow creatures and of the infinite
Whole in which we are all included as somehow one. This
conception is a naturalism, in the sense that nature-history
forms one continuous order, and reality is one interrelated web
of spatio-temporal processes. But this form of naturalism is
unique in that it is not reductionist. Nature equals experience,
equals everything accessible to man as a human being including the Transcendent Whole to which he and every other
creature belong.

Having said this much, we have indicated all that needs to be
said about Ogden's method. We are ready to begin our investigation of Ogden's doctrine of God. But before doing so, we
might note at this point that Ogden's methodology has already
separated him from classical orthodox trinitarian theology
since he is committed from the outset to rejecting supernaturalism. For example, classical Catholic theology staunchly
defended the ability of reason to know the existence of God but
just as staunchly maintained that such strict mysteries as the
Trinity, incarnation, and grace could only be known by a
special revelation from God that is totally gratuitous. Even a
modern interpreter such as Karl Rahner, though he is committed to the universality of grace even to the point of maintaining that there neither is nor ever has been a man who exists
as a pure nature without any knowledge of the gracious God of
Jesus Christ, is none the less committed to the position that all
this is strictly gratuitous and hence supernatural.[19]

But Ogden is prepared to deny such supernaturalism from
the outset both on methodological and on religious grounds.
Ogden's whole theological enterprise is an attempt to vindicate
the truth of the Christian claims about God solely on the basis of
reason and experience. Any other approach, he believes,
justifies the charge that Christianity distracts our attention
from this world to another world and that therefore its claims,
far from offering the hope of the fulfilment of our deepest human

[19] See, for example, Karl Rahner, 'Concerning the Relationship Between Nature
and Grace', *Theological Investigations*, vol. i (London: Darton, Longman and Todd,
1961), pp. 297–317; also 'The Concept of Mystery in Catholic Theology', *Theological
Investigations*, vol. iv (1966) pp. 36–73.

desires, in fact offer a heteronomous understanding of the nature of human fulfilment.[20] Ogden's whole theological system is a defence of the proposition that man and God literally belong together so that neither God nor man can realize himself apart from the other. For Ogden any compromise of this position means that man and God ultimately appear over against one another. Any form of supernaturalism therefore must be rejected from the outset as leading to heteronomy.

We can conclude this section then by noting that for Ogden there are no *mysteria stricte dicta* in the Christian faith. The Christian doctrine of God, even the so-called supernatural mysteries of Trinity, incarnation, and grace, must be doctrines that can be vindicated on the basis of that reason and experience which every man has simply as a man. The Christian affirmation of Father, Son, and Holy Spirit, if it is to be true, must be affirmed at least implicitly in human experience as such.

### iii. *The Object of Faith: God the Son*

In our second chapter we noted that the Christian doctrine of God, Christian thinking about the Trinity, has been and continues to be a function of christology.[21] It was the Christian experience of God in Jesus Christ that impelled the Christian community to rethink the monotheism of the Old Testament. The thesis that the doctrine of God is a function of christology is

[20] See, for example, Schubert Ogden, 'The Christian and Unbelievers', *Motive* 25, 8 (May 1965) 22, where he writes, 'The conventional formulations of Christian belief usually have been marked by an abstract, or one-sided other-worldliness. Instead of conceiving of God as the infinite depth or ultimate significance of our present historical life, they have portrayed him as something merely alongside our life, without any real organic relation to it. The result is that men have been distracted from their proper tasks and opportunities in this world by the imagined consolations and demands of another. Then, too, there has been the fateful divorce of sacred from secular, of religious from non-religious, which has contributed just as surely to man's betrayal. Given this divorce, Christians have either abandoned the world to shift for itself—as when they have claimed, say, that "Religion has nothing to do with politics"; or else they have treated the world as but a means to "religious" ends ... Far too frequently they (Christians) have exempted their claims from the common tests of experience and reason, insisting that they be accepted blindly on sheer authority. Hence even Christian faith itself has come to seem something alien to man, something he could bring himself to affirm only by sacrificing his own integrity.'

[21] See chapter 2, section ii (a).

one with which, I believe, Ogden would concur. For as he noted in his article, 'The Point of Christology', the question to which 'Jesus is the Christ' is the christological answer is not the question 'Who is Jesus?' but rather the question 'Who is God?' It is the question of God which is man's radical existential question which ultimately asks about the worth and meaning of our existence, and to that question the Christian community proposes the answer 'Jesus is the Christ', which is to say that 'what is re-presented to us in him is the answer to our question about God as the question of our own existence.'[22]

The theological task which then presents itself is how to understand this christological assertion. The path Ogden follows here was opened to him by his early study of Bultmann. Like Bultmann, Ogden wants to assert that the point of christ-ology is a strictly existential point. So much does Ogden want to commit himself to this position that he even affirms that christ-ological assertions are existential assertions without remainder. They literally have no other function than the existential one.

Ogden's early study of Bultmann led him to the conviction that while Bultmann's initial instincts were correct, he failed to carry out his christological project with the rigour it demanded. Bultmann had set out to show that Christian faith is to be interpreted exhaustively and without remainder as man's original possibility of authentic historical existence which is to be clarified and conceptualized by an appropriate philo-sophical analysis. But then Bultmann went on to affirm that authentic existence is actually realized only because of the particular historical event of Jesus of Nazareth, which is the originative event of the church and of its distinctive word and sacraments.

Ogden finds this position inconsistent and maintains that Bultmann has failed to carry out his demythologizing prog-ramme sufficiently.[23] For what Bultmann precisely leaves as mythology is the Christ-event as the unique act of God consti-tutive of man's possibility of authentic existence. For Bultmann, 'Jesus not only decisively *reveals* God's love . . . but

---

[22] Schubert Ogden, 'The Point of Christology', p. 378.
[23] See Schubert Ogden, *Christ Without Myth*; also 'Bultmann's Project of Demytho-logizing and the Problem of Theology and Philosophy', *Journal of Religion* 37 (1957) 156–73.

actually *constitutes* it as an event, so that apart from him (or the witness of the church that proclaims him), man cannot actually realize his authentic life.'[24] Ogden finds that this position contradicts his stated contention that all men have the same possibility of authentic existence in principle, for if authentic existence is a human possibility for every man, how can it be said to be possible in fact only in Jesus Christ and how can all men, even those who have never heard of Jesus Christ, be held accountable for failing to realize it? Thus Ogden maintains that Bultmann's understanding of the Christ-event undermines the very self-understanding that it is supposed to ground.

How then would Ogden propose to revise Bultmann so as to carry out Bultmann's original intention more faithfully? In general we can say that Ogden endeavours to press Bultmann's existential demythologizing to its logical limits. Thus in the christological assertion 'Jesus is the Christ', 'Jesus' does not refer to the historical person Jesus of Nazareth. Rather 'Jesus' is that which is re-presented in the apostolic witness. As Ogden puts it,

What is meant by the subject term 'Jesus' in the constitutive christological assertion is not 'the so-called historical Jesus' but rather, 'the historic biblical [sc. apostolic] Christ'. The referent of that term is not some past figure or event behind the apostolic witness but the present figure and event constitutive of and, in another sense, constituted by that very witness.[25]

Now the objection can immediately be raised that the New Testament makes many statements about the historical Jesus, and Ogden agrees that this is the case. But Ogden believes that we must distinguish what the New Testament assumes and what it asserts. The New Testament makes many assumptions about Jesus, not the least of which is the fact that he existed. But none of these assumptions are essential to its claims. Thus even if it could be demonstrated on historical grounds that Jesus never existed, this would have no bearing on the truth claim of the New Testament kerygma.[26]

From this it follows that the Jesus who is asserted to be the

[24] Ogden, *The Reality of God*, p. 173.
[25] Ogden's unpublished lecture 'On Christ', p. 5.
[26] See Ogden, 'The Point of Christology', pp. 381 ff.

Christ is not a blank to be filled in by historical research behind the apostolic witness. Rather, he is the Jesus who is the origin and principle, the noncompressible core, of that very witness as actual historical event—the human word which that witness asserts implicitly or explicitly to be God's own word to us and to every human being.

Now so far all that we have said is merely formal. But if we turn to an examination of that human word which the Christian claims is the divine word addressed to him, what do we find it to be? Ogden answers in this way, 'All that Jesus is represented as saying or doing in the apostolic witness is but a single witness to the truth, or to what the Christian witness of faith attests as the truth, that all things have their ultimate beginning and end solely in God's pure unbounded love and that it is in giving ourselves wholly unto the keeping of that love, by surrendering all other securities, that we realize authentic life.'[27] In short, the kerygma proclaims the radical gift and demand of God's love not as an eternal truth but as an event confronting me here and now.[28]

On this interpretation, the Christian kerygma does not proclaim some new content about God nor a new possibility of authentic existence in fact. As Ogden once boldly put it, 'There is not the slightest evidence that God has acted in Christ in any way different from the way in which he primordially acts in every other event.'[29] This interpretation is faithful to Bultmann's original insight that every man has the genuine possibility of authentic existence. Ogden takes this quite seriously and argues that this is so because the constitutive event of human existence as such is God's unbounded love.

---

[27] Ogden's unpublished lecture 'On Christ', pp. 8–9.

[28] In Ogden's essay 'On Revelation', p. 286, he considers Kierkegaard's famous alternatives between 'the Socratic point of view', according to which Christian revelation is merely the recollection of the eternal truths, and Kierkegaard's own point of view, according to which the Christian revelation gives man the possibility he in no way already possesses even implicitly. As Kierkegaard sees the alternatives, either no event is constitutive of man's authentic possibility or some event is. Ogden argues that there is a third possibility, namely that '*every* event is constitutive of man's possibility, because, while it is in no way his eternal possession, it is given to him at least implicitly in every event that is constitutive of his existence'.

[29] Ogden, 'Bultmann's Project of Demythologizing and the Problem of Theology and Philosophy', 169.

This constitutive event is the revelation of God's love to every man.

Given the fact of this constitutive revelation to every man, the Christian kerygma cannot add anything new. Thus Ogden writes, '*What* Christian revelation reveals to man is nothing new, since such truths as it makes explicit must already be known to him implicitly in every moment of his existence. But *that* this revelation occurs does reveal something new to him in that, as itself event, it is the occurrence in his history of the transcendent event of God's love.'[30]

From this analysis it should be clear that the event of Jesus Christ is not strictly necessary for man's salvation. But by no means does this imply that Christian revelation is superfluous. Though the Christ-event is not constitutive of God's love and though Christian revelation is not constitutive of man's authentic possibility, they nevertheless have a critical role to play. Ogden specifies this role as re-presentation. According to Ogden's anthropology and phenomenology of faith, every man at least implicitly has a confidence in the meaningfulness or worthwhileness of life. In other words, each of us somehow believes that his life is worth living and that his having lived does not add up to zero. For Ogden this basic confidence is ineradicable. Even the man who commits suicide or writes about the absurd somehow sees these actions as meaningful. Yet this basic confidence is continually called into question, for example, in the awareness of one's finitude and guilt. Therefore man desperately needs symbols that re-present his original confidence and re-assure him of life's basic meaningfulness. This is the function of religious symbols. They re-present the boundless love of God to man burdened with the anxiety of having to face his own sin and death.[31]

For the Christian the christological symbol is the decisive religious symbol. The Christian kerygma re-presents the original event of God's gift and demand as an event confronting me. In that it re-presents the original possibility of every human life, it is universally true; in that it re-presents this possibility to me, it is decisive. Thus Jesus Christ is not absolutely necessary

[30] Ogden, 'On Revelation', 287.
[31] See *The Reality of God*, pp. 21–43.

to authentic human existence but he is relatively necessary in so far as man as an historical being requires an objectification of his original confidence in life through concepts and symbols. As Ogden puts it in his essay 'On Revelation',

Although such revelation cannot be necessary to the *constitution* of human existence, it can very well be necessary to the *objectification* of existence, in the sense of its full and adequate understanding at the level of explicit thought and speech. . . . Whereas original revelation, we may say, is *immediately* and *proximately* necessary to man's authenticity, decisive revelation is only *mediately* and *remotely* necessary to it, being necessary in the first instance not to the constitution of his possibility, but to its full and adequate explication.[32]

Or as Ogden put it in another place, the function of Christian revelation is not to *limit* man's consciousness of the sacred but to define it.[33]

Now how far does this christology accord with the traditional christological claims? We have already seen that Ogden's stated intention is to understand the primary symbols of the Christian witness of faith. To do this he is willing, if necessary, to call into question any of the church's traditional doctrines.[34] Let us then at this point ask whether and to what extent this christology conforms to the traditional christologies as enunciated at Nicaea and Chalcedon.

On this point we may be surprised to find in Ogden a striking conservative tendency. For example, one of his preoccupations with Bultmann's theology is the tendency there toward subjectivism. He cites two of Bultmann's celebrated statements. Bultmann writes, 'The cross of Christ is not the salvation event because it is the cross of Christ. It is the cross of Christ because it is the salvation event.'[35] Again Bultmann asks, 'Do [the titles ascribed to Jesus] speak of his φύσις or do they speak of Christ *pro me?* To what extent is a christological assertion about him at

---

[32] Ogden, 'On Revelation', p. 284.

[33] Schubert Ogden, 'Christliche Theologie und die neue Religiosität', in *Chancen der Religion*, ed. Rainer Volp (Gütersloh: Gütersloher Verlagshaus Gerd Mohn, 1975), p. 172.

[34] See Ogden's 'Doctrinal Standards in the United Methodist Church', 22–3.

[35] Rudolf Bultmann, *Kerygma and Myth*, ed. H. W. Bartsch and trans. R. H. Fuller (New York: Harper and Row, 1961), p. 41 as cited by Ogden, 'The Point of Christology', p. 389.

one and the same time an assertion about me? Does he help me because he is the Son of God, or is he the Son of God because he helps me?'[36] To this Ogden replies definitively, 'The only reason Christ can help me, provided he really does so, is that he is, in truth, the Son of God, who alone has the power to give me that kind of help. Similarly, if the cross really is the salvation-event in that it has the power to save me from death and from the burden of guilt, there can be no sufficient reason for this other than it really is the cross of Christ.'[37]

To avoid this subjectivism, Ogden wants to stress the divine origin of the kerygma. The human word of the kerygma is the divine word addressed to me. This is what Ogden understands to be the theological significance of the mythological story of Jesus's resurrection.[38] If 'Jesus' is the origin and principle of Christian witness and faith, 'resurrection' is God's judgement that this witness and faith are true. The resurrection of Jesus is that divine event to which my act of faith is a human response. Thus the event of faith is both divine event and historical event, divine summons and human response.

Within the context of this existential hermeneutic Ogden interprets the doctrinal decisions of Nicaea and Chalcedon. He is willing to affirm with Nicaea that Jesus is true God and with Chalcedon that Jesus is one person in two natures—human and divine. But he interprets these affirmations strictly existentially. He writes,

Thus, what I properly mean when I assert that Jesus is 'divine' is that

[36] Rudolf Bultmann, *Essays, Philosophical and Theological*, translated James C. G. Greig (London: SCM Press, 1955), p. 280 as cited by Ogden, 'The Point of Christology', p. 389.

[37] Ogden, 'The Point of Christology', p. 389.

[38] Resurrection does not mean that '"the act of God" which the faith of Easter signifies is yet another historical happening in space and time, subsequent to the events of Jesus' life and death. The New Testament's representations of it as though it were such a happening are undeniably mythological and demand to be critically interpreted—and that, primarily for the sake of expressing more appropriately its own distinctive reality as an act of *God*. The crucial point, however, is that the witness of faith, which did originate in history at some time after Jesus crucifixion, is by no means something completely independent or primary. On the contrary, it is by its very nature the response to another and altogether different "witness" on which it absolutely depends, namely, the "*self*-attestation" of the risen Lord, or, as the New Testament also expresses it, *God's own* testimony to the decisive significance of Jesus and his cross (cf. Rom. 1:4).' *The Reality of God*, pp. 217–18.

the possibility here and now re-presented to me in the Christian witness of faith is God's own gift and demand to my existence. On the other hand, what I properly mean when I assert that Jesus is 'human' is that I am here and now actually confronted with this possibility, that is actually re-presented to me as a historical event and hence is not merely an idea or a general truth.[39]

He concludes, 'The value of the dogmas of Nicaea and Chalcedon, so far as they have any permanent value, is entirely dependent on their being a more or less adequate witness to this same existential truth'.[40]

Is there then any difference between Ogden and the tradition? There is at least one central difference and it is critical. The classical tradition including most of its modern interpreters affirms as a central claim of Christian faith that Jesus, being God's Incarnate Word, not only re-presents the gift and demand of God's love but also actualized them in his own life. Ogden vigorously denies this claim. He maintains that there is not a single passage in the New Testament that speaks of Jesus's own personal faith and love as a man in such a way as to point to their perfection as the reason for his being the Christ. He further contends that this is as it should be, since there is no way that any objective historical proof could be given to substantiate the claim, since any man's existential faith perforce remains hidden. Thus, 'as far as the New Testament witnesses are concerned, Jesus is the Christ not because he *actualized* the possibility of faith, and unlike us, actualized it perfectly, but

---

[39] Ogden, 'The Point of Christology', p. 385. Ogden notes that his understanding of the person of Jesus Christ as the divine word re-presented as human word enables him to accept certain classical doctrines such as the *enhypostasia* of Christ's human nature, who is fully personal only as the incarnate Word of God. He writes, 'This doctrine I can accept as a more or less adequate way of expressing the point that it is the one divine meaning re-presented through human words and deeds that defines the unity of the Christ-event. Just as, in general, it is the meaning of an expression of meaning that is its principle of unity as such—the expression itself being but instrumental to the meaning and not a meaningful expression at all apart from it—so the principle of unity of the divine-human expression of meaning that we call Jesus the Christ is the divine meaning expressed by human words and deeds—such expression being strictly instrumental to that divine meaning and not a meaningful expression at all apart from it.' Ogden, unpublished lecture 'On Christ', p. 14. Of course, when Ogden says he can accept the doctrine of the *enhypostasia* of Christ's human nature, he means that he can accept it as existentially interpreted.

[40] Ogden, unpublished lecture 'On Christ', p. 18.

because he *re-presents* the possibility of faith, and for us, he re-presents it decisively'.[41]

Ogden has often said that his theology is a modern version of Melanchthon's famous adage, 'To know Christ is to know his benefits.' To know Christ is to know a re-presented possibility of authentic existence, existence lived in trust in the pure unbounded love of God. The object of Christian faith is not Jesus. Faith's object can never be less than God himself. The object of faith is therefore the God whom the event of Jesus Christ re-presents. But the ground of this faith can also be nothing less than God. It is only God who makes faith possible. To believe in the possibility re-presented in Jesus Christ as my possibility requires the self-attestation of God himself.[42] This self-attestation, this ground of faith, is what Christians have traditionally called the Holy Spirit. Let us then turn to Ogden's theology of the Spirit which completes the trinitarian circle in any Christian account of the doctrine of God.

iv.   *The Ground of Faith: God the Holy Spirit*

Ogden takes as his starting point for the theology of the Spirit the fact that Christian faith in Christ always begins in and with

[41] Ogden, 'The Point of Christology', p. 391. It is this point which separates Ogden from the other process approaches to christology. Among the important process views on christology which have recently appeared are W. Norman Pittenger, *The Word Incarnate, A Study of the Doctrine of the Person of Christ* (Digswell Place: James Nisbet and Co., 1959); *Christology Reconsidered* (London: SCM Press, 1970); David R. Griffin, *A Process Christology* (Philadelphia: The Westminster Press, 1973); John B. Cobb, Jr., *Christ in a Pluralistic Age* (Philadelphia: The Westminster Press, 1975). All of these theologians understand the relation of God to Jesus in process categories rather than in those of substance and have a common allegiance to the Antiochene christological tradition and take as their model the total openness of the man Jesus to the fullness of God's presence. John Cobb, for example, speaks of the 'I' of Jesus being co-constituted by the incarnate Logos. But they all reject the way in which Ogden distinguishes the historical Jesus and the Christ of faith and his substitution of the 'Jesus' of the primitive 'Jesus-kerygma' for the 'Jesus of history'. For Ogden's critique, see 'Christology Reconsidered: John Cobb's *Christ in a Pluralistic Age*', *Process Studies* 6,2 (Summer 1976) 116–22; also 'The Point of Christology', p. 390, note 23. Ogden has trenchantly summarized his critique in these words, 'On my view, all such rationalizations are exegetically without warrant, historically indemonstrable in fact as well as in principle, and systematically beside the point.' Letter of Schubert Ogden to Robert Baker, 19 June 1973, quoted in the excerpt of Baker's doctoral dissertation *Symbol in the Thought of Schubert M. Ogden* published by the Gregorian University Press, Rome, 1977, pp. 72–3.

[42] As Ogden once noted in class, his argument is a modern version of that first propounded by Athanasius: we are saved, we are saved by Jesus, only God can save, Jesus is God.

the church. The believer first encounters Christ in the Christian community. As John Knox once pointed out, from the historical point of view, we can say that the sole residuum of the event of Jesus's own witness of faith is the church. The only empirical, observable difference between the world before the coming of Jesus and the world after his crucifixion is the existence of the witnessing community.[43]

But this historically verifiable fact also has its theological counterpart. As Knox also observed,

The early church not only shared a common memory. It also partici- pated in a common Spirit. . . . The two belong inseparably together. If the event had not been remembered, the Spirit could not have come; but without the Spirit, the event could not have been remembered just as it was remembered, for the reason that it could not have happened just as it did happen. For the event was, in its final issue, the coming of the Spirit. Only those who had received the Spirit could really remember the event, for it was only to them that the event had really occurred.[44]

This means then that the church as a witness to faith is the gift of the Spirit.

What then are the theological implications of this event? In short we must say that if the immediate ground of the believer's faith in Jesus Christ is the church, the ultimate ground of such faith is God the Holy Spirit. Thus if, as we have previously developed, the object of Christian faith is the God decisively re-presented by Jesus Christ, so the ground of such faith is the same God. The Holy Spirit is the active presence and power of God himself as the only ultimate ground of authentic faith and love.

But we can go on to say that what God is for us is precisely what he is in himself. We have seen that Jesus Christ re- presents God as pure unbounded love. This is the object of his witness. But we have also seen that the only ground that makes our believing that witness possible is the same God. Thus Ogden specifies that the meaning of God the Holy Spirit in himself is God as active subject. He writes, 'The Holy Spirit

---

[43] John Knox, *The Early Church and the Coming Great Church* (London: The Epworth Press, 1957), p. 45 as cited by Schubert Ogden, unpublished lecture 'On the Holy Spirit', p. 5.

[44] Knox, op. cit., pp. 55 f. as cited in Ogden, 'On the Holy Spirit', p. 6.

whom Christians understand to be the active power and presence of God himself as the ultimate ground of their experience
and faith *is* precisely God himself with respect to his subjectivity
as eminent love, such love alone being the sole sufficient ground
of the answering faith and love which are the essence of
Christian experience.'[45]

As the eminent subject of love, the Holy Spirit makes authentic existence possible. There are various ways of elaborating
what authentic existence is. Sometimes Ogden speaks of it as
faith working through love. Yet perhaps the simplest word to
describe it is freedom. In his book *Faith and Freedom*, in which he
attempts to sketch a theology of liberation, Ogden speaks of
faith as existence in freedom and for freedom.

First of all, faith brings freedom *from* all things. Ogden
indicates what he means by this when he writes,

To exist is to be freed from any compulsion to find the ultimate
ground of one's life in something else alongside God. Being bound
utterly and completely to God, the believer is utterly and completely
freed from everything else. Indeed, the believer exists in the knowledge that, no matter what happens, good or bad, it is finally indifferent or of no consequence insofar as we always exist under God's loving
care and, together with all our fellow creatures, are finally safe—in
the sense that our lives, like theirs, are embraced within God's
boundless and everlasting love, where they have an abiding meaning
in spite of our own death and sin and the transience of all things.[46]

Secondly, faith is existence in the freedom *for* all things—
literally for everything else, for ourselves and the whole world as
worthy of our love and our devoted service.[47] In this we are
invited to share in God's creative work, taking the other into our
lives and letting it be to the full scope of its potentiality. This
freedom for the other is what the bible describes as 'faith
working through love' (Gal. 5:6), the test of love being precisely
freedom, both in the sense that the test of whether one loves
another is whether one intends to speak and act in such a way as
somehow to optimize the scope of the other's freedom, and in
the sense that the test of whether one is loved by another is

[45] Ibid., p. 10.
[46] Schubert Ogden, *Faith and Freedom*, pp. 55–6.
[47] See ibid., p. 56.

whether the scope of one's own freedom is in some respect thus optimized by what the other says and does.[48]

In summary then, the effect of the Holy Spirit in our lives is experienced in this way:

> As I appropriate the meaning of God for me, which is to say respond in authentic faith and returning love to God's love, to his own active presence and power in *my* life, to that extent my life is emancipated, liberated life—a life freed not only from the *guilt* of sin but also from its *power*, from the anxious, faithless self-concern which is the innermost core of concupiscence or desire—as well as a life which is free for all things, myself and my fellow creatures, to be loyal to them, to love and to serve them, and to help bring them to their proper fulfillments—to the glory of God.[49]

In concluding this section, I would like to observe that Ogden's method in both his christology and his pneumatology has been thoroughly experiential. He has tenaciously adhered to his principle that all theological statements are existential statements. The logic of his argument has proceeded from man's need for reassurance that his basic confidence in life is warranted. But this confidence is warranted only if God is the source and end of our lives as pure unbounded love. The Christian believer finds this reassurance in the community which witnesses to Jesus Christ as the decisive re-presentation of God's pure unbounded love for every man. Thus both the object and the ground of the believer's faith is the same God revealed as love. In presenting this argument, Ogden has in effect been proceeding to give an account of the economic Trinity. But underpinning this argument has been the conviction that what God is for us, he is in himself. Or as Rahner has put it, the economic Trinity is the immanent Trinity.[50] Let us then turn to the question of the immanent Trinity and examine how Ogden uses the tools of process philosophy to conceptualize the reality of God's being in himself.

## v.   *God's being in Himself*

In this section our purpose is to examine the being of God in

---

[48] See ibid., pp. 63–4.
[49] Ogden, unpublished lecture 'On the Holy Spirit', p. 11.
[50] Karl Rahner, *The Trinity*, p. 22.

himself in distinction to God's being for us. Of course there must be a correspondence between the two, given the fact that God has genuinely revealed himself. For Ogden the distinction between the economic and the immanent Trinity is not that between the meaning of God for us and the meaning of God in himself. Rather the economic Trinity is the reality of God for human experience. The immanent Trinity is the reality of God for any experience including the divine experience.[51]

Before proceeding to investigate how Ogden proposes to use process categories to shed light on this reality, we must pause and fill in some necessary philosophical background on the doctrine of God in Whitehead and Hartshorne.

Whitehead proposed a metaphysical doctrine according to which God was to be treated not as an exception to the metaphysical categories but as their chief exemplification.[52]. Now in Whitehead's system, the fundamental building blocks of reality are called actual entities, each of which has two poles which Whitehead calls the physical pole and the mental pole. The mental pole is the actual entity's desire for and realization of ideal forms (called by Whitehead eternal objects). The physical pole is the actual entity's direct rapport with the environment from which it springs. Since Whitehead conceives of reality as essentially temporal, the environment of any given entity is its past.[53] An actual entity is formed as other actual entities perish and contribute to the new entity.

[51] In his unpublished lecture 'On God', pp. 12–13, Ogden writes, 'The distinction between the *immanent* and the *economic* Trinity is not the same as the distinction between the *being of God in himself and the meaning of God for us*. Even the doctrine of the economic Trinity is a doctrine about the being of God in himself as the ultimate ground and object of Christian and, implicitly, of human experience of God, although if the doctrine of the economic trinity—to say nothing of the doctrine of the immanent Trinity—is properly developed, it will be developed in function of, not in abstraction from the meaning of God for us. Economic = the Trinity that God is for *human* experience—implicitly for *all* human experience, explicitly for specifically *Christian* experience; while immanent = the Trinity that God is for all experience, or experience as such, even *divine* experience—assuming only that human, or explicitly Christian, experience is an experience precisely of God.'

[52] 'God is not to be treated as an exception to all metaphysical principles, invoked to save their collapse. He is their chief exemplification.' Alfred North Whitehead, *Process and Reality*, p. 521.

[53] 'According to the classical "uniquely serial" view of time, two contemporary actual entities define the same actual world. According to the modern view no two actual entities define the same actual world. Actual entities are called "contemporary" when neither belongs to the "given" actual world defined by the other.' Ibid., p. 102.

Whitehead speaks of God as the non-temporal actual entity.[54] And as any actual entity, God must have two poles, the mental pole and the physical pole.[55] Whitehead calls God's mental pole his primordial nature. The primordial nature of God is the realm of possibilities including the structure of relevance, the qualities and potential meanings which characterize the world. This realm of possibilities exists in abstraction from all particular matters of fact.

Whitehead calls the physical pole of God his consequent nature. This is God's concreteness as he is related to the world and as the world's events are objectified in him. God receives from the world the effects of the world's action.

These two natures of God lead Whitehead to speak of God as dipolar. A succinct summary of the meaning of God's dipolarity is given in *Process and Reality* when Whitehead writes,

One side of God's nature is constituted by his conceptual experience. This experience is the primordial fact in the world, limited by no actuality which it presupposes. It is therefore infinite, devoid of all negative prehensions. This side of his nature is free, complete, primordial, eternal, actually deficient, and unconscious. The other side originates with physical experience derived from the temporal world, and then acquires integration with the primordial side. It is determined, incomplete, consequent, 'everlasting', fully actual and conscious.[56]

The difficulties of such language are immediately apparent, for Whitehead's way of speaking suggests a dualism between the two natures. It appears as if he is speaking of two gods rather than one. John Cobb and David Griffin have given lucid expression to these difficulties in their book *Process Theology: An Introductory Exposition*, where they write

Unfortunately, in some passages Whitehead does not describe the two 'natures' of God as if they were truly integrated. Sometimes the primordial nature is described as if it were a static ordering of the eternal possibilities and the 'initial aim' for each worldly actuality is said to be derived from this primordial nature. This would mean that the creative input of God into the world in each moment would be based upon a completely inflexible vision; it would not be based upon

[54] See ibid., p. 73.
[55] For Whitehead's discussion of the two natures of God, see ibid., pp. 521–4.
[56] Ibid., p. 524.

a sympathetic response to the previous state of affairs. However, in other passages Whitehead makes clear that the ideals toward which the world is called by God in one moment are based upon God's loving response to the facts of the previous moments. . . . The world does not really have to do with two 'natures' of God that stand externally related to each other, the one influencing the world and the other being influenced by it. Rather, the primordial nature is abstract, while the consequent nature is God as fully actual.[57]

Such difficulties as these led Whitehead's disciple Charles Hartshorne to seek a more adequate expression that would be faithful to Whitehead's intention while avoiding the ambiguities of his language. The fundamental insight of Hartshorne's philosophy is the relation between the abstract and the concrete. He argues that the concrete is greater than and includes all abstractions. Ralph E. James in his commentary on Hartshorne's work interprets this fundamental insight in the following way: 'The inclusive concrete contains the abstract; is ontologically prior to the abstract; precedes the abstract temporally.' Furthermore the changing concrete is superior to abstractions which do not change.[58]

In applying this insight to philosophical theology, Hartshorne follows Anselm in arguing that God must be the unsurpassably perfect being, for only the unsurpassably perfect is worthy of worship. The difficulty with classical philosophical theism is that it has mistaken abstractions about God for the concrete God. But in the case of God as well, the concrete must contain the abstract. God is the inclusive concrete, i.e. reality itself equals God containing within himself his cosmic body the universe.

How are we to conceive this inclusive concrete, the unsurpassably perfect one? There are two logical possibilities, either unsurpassable by another or unsurpassable in every respect even by oneself. Hartshorne argues that the former alternative is a logically inconsistent idea. Certain ideas admit of a maximum, for example, moral perfection. But other ideas do not, for example, mathematical infinity or aesthetic harmony.

---

[57] John B. Cobb, Jr. and David Ray Griffin, *Process Theology: An Introductory Exposition* (Belfast: Christian Journals Limited, 1977), p. 62.

[58] Ralph E. James, *The Concrete God, A New Beginning for Theology—The Thought of Charles Hartshorne* (Indianapolis: Bobbs-Merrill, 1967), p. 58.

God's perfection falls into the latter class. God is unsurpassed by all others in principle but not unsurpassed by himself. He is the self-surpassing surpasser of all others.[59] Hartshorne accepts Anselm's discovery that the unsurpassably perfect one necessarily exists.[60] His only disagreement with Anselm is the interpretation of the meaning of perfection. Hartshorne's neoclassical interpretation mentioned above leads him to make a distinction between the divine existence and the divine actuality.[61] The divine existence is necessary. It is necessarily the case that the most perfectly conceivable being exists. But how the divine being exists, in what particular state, is not necessary but contingent. This contingent dimension of God is the divine actuality. Hartshorne writes,

Existing necessarily, God nevertheless, like any individual you please, exists by virtue of concrete states ('experiences') which themselves, in their concreteness, are contingent. Thus, on his concrete side, God is of the same logical type as other individuals. Where then is his necessity? In this: the class of his possible states could not be empty; whereas with other individuals there might not have been *any* such states. . . . God has no option between existing and not existing, but—and there is no inconsistency in this—he has options as to *how* he exists, in what particular states.[62]

With these presuppositions in mind we can easily understand Hartshorne's reformulation of Whitehead's dipolar God. The single concept from which God's dipolarity emerges is that of 'the self-changing whole which includes all other beings as its (more or less) self-changing parts.'[63] As the self-transcending being God includes two poles, the absolute pole which is abstract, necessary, eternal and unchanging, and the relative pole which is contingent, changing and temporal.

[59] See, for example, Charles Hartshorne, *Creative Synthesis and Philosophic Method* (London: SCM Press, 1970), p. 243; also *Aquinas to Whitehead, Seven Centuries of Metaphysics of Religion* (Milwaukee: Marquette University Publications, 1976), p. 33.

[60] For Hartshorne's interpretation of Anselm, see *Anselm's Discovery, A Re-examination of the Ontological Proof for God's Existence* (LaSalle, Ill.: Open Court, 1965); *The Logic of Perfection and Other Essays in Neoclassical Metaphysics* (La Salle, Ill.: Open Court, 1962).

[61] Schubert Ogden employs this distinction in developing his argument for a new theism in *The Reality of God*, pp. 47–8.

[62] Hartshorne, *Creative Synthesis and Philosophic Method*, p. 144.

[63] Charles Hartshorne, *Man's Vision of God and the Logic of Theism* (New York: Harper and Brothers, 1941), p. 349.

We need not further clarify Hartshorne's meaning in speaking of God as actually temporal, finite, and contingent, but perhaps a little more clarity is required to understand the meaning of God's absolute pole. The absolute pole is an abstraction from the contingent, changing, and temporal God. It is that which is always true (necessary), because it is that aspect of God which must be concretized in any of God's contingent actual states. In *Creative Synthesis and Philosophic Method*, Hartshorne writes, 'God is the only individual identifiable by abstractions alone. This does not imply that God is a merely abstract entity, but only that what makes him God and no other individual is abstract.'[64] Hartshorne further specifies the absolute pole as the realm of pure possibility.[65] For process thought, to be actual is to be definite, hence limited and finite. Thus the divine actuality must be affirmed to be finite in any of its contingent states. But it is equally the case that in his divine existence God must be affirmed as infinite, the infinite being precisely that which is unlimited, the realm of the possible as such.

We have thus come to see that the absolute pole must be characterized as abstract, necessary, and infinite. From this it follows that a number of other attributes must be predicated of the divine existence. Hartshorne writes, God's character

can be described in utterly abstract terms which yet are unique to him as the one divine individual. Only one individual can ever be omniscient, primordial-and-everlasting, all-loving, supreme cause of all effects, supreme effect of all causes. Only one individual can ever be divine. Here is an extremely abstract character which yet is the definite characteristic of a self—or person. This character, though individual to God, is so abstract or nonspecific that it can be correlated with any possible character you please in its correlate, the world. Whatever the world may be, God can know that world in his uniquely adequate way, whereas some possible worlds would exclude human knowers altogether. The utter abstractness of the individual essence of God is what makes him, as concrete individual, completely independent of relational alternatives for his mere existence. Because the defining characteristic of his self-identity is utterly neutral to such

---

[64] Hartshorne, *Creative Synthesis and Philosophic Method*, p. 246.

[65] Hartshorne, *The Logic of Perfection*, p. 38. 'The absolute infinity of the divine potentiality might also be called its *coincidence with possibility as such*. (Perhaps "co-extensiveness" with possibility would be more accurate.)'

alternatives, the concrete embodiment can be wholly expressive of and variable with relations. The character can be expressed in any relational pattern, hence God can contain any relational pattern and still be himself.[66]

This then is Hartshorne's dipolar conception of the eminent individual. We should notice that in describing God as eminent individual, Hartshorne also calls God a person. In doing so, he is once again making a significant revision of the Whiteheadian scheme. Whitehead had spoken of God as an actual entity, and interpreters such as Lewis S. Ford and William Christian continue to understand his doctrine of God in this way.[67] But Hartshorne and his theological disciples John Cobb and Schubert Ogden have felt it more consistent with his fundamental insights to interpret God as a living person.

The key here is obviously Whitehead's understanding of personal identity. We have seen that process philosophy is based on the conviction that the building blocks of reality are not substances but events. Within this scheme, however, Whitehead has to be able to interpret the macrospcopic objects of our ordinary experience. He refers to these as enduring objects. Conceived metaphysically, an enduring object is 'a society whose social order has taken the special form of "personal order."'[68] A personally ordered society is ordered serially—i.e. it is a purely temporal society, a mere thread of continuous inheritance containing no two actual entities that are contemporaries.[69] The human person is an instance of a personally ordered society. The key to personal identity is inheritance. Whitehead writes, 'An enduring personality in the temporal world is a route of occasions in which the successors with some peculiar completeness sum up their predecessors.'[70] Following this basic Whiteheadian doctrine, Hartshorne defines the self as 'a "society" of past and future experiences bound together by a mode of sympathy which in a specifically

[66] Charles Hartshorne, *The Divine Relativity, A Social Conception of God* (New Haven: Yale University Press, 1964) pp. 80–1.
[67] See William A. Christian, *An Interpretation of Whitehead's Metaphysics* (New Haven: Yale University Press, 1967), pp. 393, 407–9; also Lewis S. Ford, 'The Non-Temporality of Whitehead's God', *International Philosophical Quarterly* 13 (1973) 347–76.
[68] Whithead, *Process and Reality*, p. 50.
[69] See ibid., p. 51.
[70] Ibid., p. 531.

different but generically similar way, unites us also to the experiences belonging to the temporal societies constituting other personalities.'[71]

It is the conviction of Hartshorne's school of interpretation that although Whitehead speaks of God as an actual entity, it is more proper to speak of God as a living person in the sense developed above. Hartshorne notes,

On my view God is the supreme form of 'personally-ordered' society. His defining characteristic, the divine perfection, his gene structure, as it were, is precisely his perfection, his necessary surpassing of all, including self. Each of his states will be the uniquely adequate summing up of the cosmic actuality correlated with it and of all past states of the divine society. And it will be the only society whose defining characteristic could not fail to be actualized in ever new (and greater) states.[72]

Thus as Cobb has put it, God 'at any moment would be an actual entity, but viewed retrospectively and prospectively he would be an infinite succession of divine occasions of experience.'[73] In conclusion then let us say that if the human person is an individual self in being a personally-ordered society, God is the eminent individual and the supreme person experiencing in his own life the temporal succession of all events in his cosmic body, the universe.

Turning now to specifically theological concerns, we must ask how Ogden employs this process conceptuality to explicate the doctrine of the immanent Trinity, or God's being in himself. We can begin with the general conviction that God is not merely an individual but the eminent individual, i.e. the one whose own reality constitutes reality as such. Thus while God transcends the world, he is nevertheless affirmed to be immanent in the world as its primal ground just as he is affirmed to be the ultimate end of the world since the world is immanent in him.

Now since God is not an individual but the eminent individual, neoclassical metaphysics affirms that God is at once

[71] Charles Hartshorne, *Reality as Social Process, Studies in Metaphysics and Religion* (Glencoe, Ill. and Boston: The Free Press and Beacon Press, 1953), p. 64.
[72] Hartshorne, *Anselm's Discovery*, p. 291.
[73] John B. Cobb, Jr., *A Christian Natural Theology* (London: Lutterworth Press, 1966), p. 188.

both the eminent object and the subject of love, that is, the one individual whose essence is both to love and be loved by *all* individuals, himself as well as all others. In asserting this, Ogden is merely echoing Hartshorne's doctrine of God. Thus, for example, in dealing with the problem of God's relatedness to the world in his book *The Divine Relativity*, Hartshorne observes,

Only God can be so universally important that no subject can ever wholly fail or ever have failed to be aware of him (in however dim or unreflective a fashion). Thus the unique status of object-for-all-subjects is to be correlated with the more commonly recognized one of subject-for-all-objects. The difference between them is that the latter means 'having relations to all objects' and thus implies universal relativity; the former means that all subjects have relation to the one object, without the latter having relation (other than extrinsic or nominal) to them.[74]

Now traditional trinitarian theology affirms that God is one *ousia* or *substantia* in three *hypostases* or persons. The neoclassical theory affirms this as well in that God is the eminent individual.

But this one eminent individual, the concrete God, must also be said to have an essence. The divine essence can be said to be the individuality of the eminent individual as both loving himself and all others and being loved by himself and all others. The divine essence is an abstraction from the concrete God. Ogden notes that the analogue in human experience for the distinction between the eminent individual and his individuality is the distinction between what we call the 'person' as the concrete unity of his own sequence of experiences and his 'personality' as the complex of abstract traits or characteristics which identify him as this person rather than any other.[75]

In order to show how this position is related to Hartshorne's dipolar doctrine of God, let me cite the following comment of Ogden on Hartshorne's position:

God's essence is neither A (Absolute) or R (Relative), but AR. God's essence is absolute relativity. A and R are both abstract aspects of God's essence with A being constant and R being variable. God's eternal purpose is to be God. Included in this purpose is a constant absoluteness of love and awareness and a necessary relatedness to

[74] Hartshorne, *The Divine Relativity*, pp. 70–1.
[75] Schubert Ogden, 'On the Trinity', *Theology* 83 (March. 1980) p. 98.

some, but not any, particular value. The key to this difficult concept is· to recognize that A and R are both abstract aspects of God's essence which is related to nothing but to which everything is related. God's concreteness is not in AR, but is that God whose character is AR.[76]

The next critical point is to notice that God's essence (which we have seen is an abstraction) necessarily consists in two subsidiary abstractions which makes it possible and necessary to distinguish between three divine persons, though in the ancient, rather than the modern, sense of the word 'person'.[77]

In the first place, there is the divine essence as such, which is properly designated 'Father' since it is in fact 'the fountain of the whole Trinity'. God as Father is God as both loving all individuals and being loved by them, himself as well as all others, or the divine subjectivity and the divine objectivity in their original unity. But, as we have seen, it is also necessary to distinguish within God both his objectivity and his subjectivity. The divine objectivity as the integral objectivity of all love, both of God and of all others, may be said to be the divine Logos. The divine subjectivity as the one holy God loving both himself and all others may appropriately be called the Holy Spirit.

In concluding the exposition of this section, let me make two ·comments. First, the Dutch Catholic theologian Piet Schoonenberg has pointed out that contemporary trinitarian theology tends to avail itself of two models: the modalistic model and the communitarian one.[78] By the modalistic model, Schoonenberg does not mean the Sabellian heresy, but rather those theologies which explicate God's being in himself in terms of 'modes of being'. He has in mind such theolgians as Karl Barth and Karl Rahner. The personalistic school represented by such thinkers as Leonard Hodgson conceives of God as a community of persons with real intersubjective relations. If these are the two primary options confronting theologians today, certainly Ogden's approach falls within the modalistic school. He

[76] Schubert Ogden, 'The Christian Doctrine of God: Summary of Seminar Proceedings', p. 20 as cited by Robert J. Baker, 'Symbol in the Thought of Schubert M. Ogden', Pontifical Gregorian University, unpublished STD thesis, pp. 177–8, note 66.
[77] Ogden, 'On the Trinity', p. 99.
[78] Piet Schoonenberg developed this point in a public lecture given in Oxford on 5 May 1977. The title of Father Schoonenberg's lecture was 'Modalistic and Personalistic Views of the Trinity'.

stresses the unity of the eminent individual and does not envisage any type of divine archetypal community.

Secondly, there is a strong recognition today that the church has two divergent approaches to the doctrine of the Trinity. Eastern theology has emphasized the priority of the Father and has always sought to anchor its trinitarian theology in salvation history. The Augustinian tradition has begun with the divine nature and has stressed the equality of the three persons within the one nature. Clearly Ogden's position is more Eastern in character. Ogden's doctrine of the divine subjectivity and objectivity resembles the ancient iconography of the Son and the Spirit as the two arms of God.

Yet there is one point on which Ogden's approach is more Western, namely the *filioque*.[79] We recall that the Western doctrine asserts that the Spirit proceeds from the Father and the Son whereas the Eastern view asserts that the Spirit proceeds from the Father alone. In Ogden's view, does the divine subjectivity proceed from the divine essence alone or from the divine essence and the divine objectivity? In process metaphysics, a subject depends on its object but an object is independent of the subject. Thus, for example, in knowing an object, the knower is dependent on that object for the content of his knowledge whereas the object is independent of him. In other words, the subject is internally related to the object and this implies dependence. But if the Holy Spirit is the divine subjectivity and if the Logos is the divine objectivity, and if the subject depends on the object, and if in this case the divine objectivity (Logos) depends on the divine essence (Father) since the Father is the original unity from which the divine subjectivity and the divine objectivity are derivative, then we must say that the Holy Spirit proceeds both from the Father and from the Son.

Having said this much, I have outlined all I believe needs to be said in presenting the substance of Ogden's position on the doctrine of the immanent Trinity. Nevertheless there are a few critical questions to consider. According to this theory it is not only convenient but necessary for the Christian to conceptualize the doctrine of God in trinitarian terms, first because the

---

[79] Ogden developed this point in an interview with the author on 23 Sept. 1977. See also 'On the Trinity', p. 99.

logic of Christian experience requires it. As we have seen, the believer first encounters Christ in the church and through Christ encounters the Father. Secondly, a metaphysical account of God's being requires that distinctions be made between God as eminent individual and his individuality or essence and within his essence between his subjectivity and objectivity.

Yet a number of serious objections have been raised today against this type of analysis. Let me comment on two typical objections briefly at this point. In 1958 Cyril Richardson wrote a book entitled *The Doctrine of the Trinity* in which he raised a number of objections against the classical formulations of orthodox trinitarian doctrine.[80] The fundamental thesis of Richardson's book is that distinctions must be made within the Godhead, in particular between God as absolute and God as related. Hence to this extent Richardson affirms a dipolarity. Richardson, however, argues that this fundamental distinction does not lead to a trinitiarian doctrine and this for the following reasons. First, the New Testament symbols of Father, Son, and Holy Spirit are vague and fluid and cannot be forced into a trinitarian pattern. Secondly, a fundamental ambiguity arose when the relation between the man Jesus and his Father was translated into the heavenly sphere of God's own life. The human Jesus is indeed God's Son, but a confusion arises when one tries to develop the idea of Father and Son in the Godhead. Richardson sees no reason to justify the distinction between unbegotten and begotten. The unbegotten is no more primordial than the begotten. Furthermore Richardson argues that this ambiguity is a result of the desire to set up mediators between God and his creation so that God can be brought close to the suffering of the world without ceasing to be God. But here again Richardson argues that we are faced with a basic paradox, namely that God both suffers with man and remains pure joy. Richardson sees no way of getting behind these fundamental paradoxes. Historically he sees no way of justifying the distinction between the Logos and the Spirit and concludes that logically the New Testament should have identi-

---

[80] Cyril C. Richardson, *The Doctrine of the Trinity* (New York and Nashville: Abingdon Press, 1958).

fied them. Therefore trinitarian thought is at best arbitrary and
one cannot justify a three-ness in God.

In his book Richardson also enters into an interesting discussion with Karl Barth's trinitarian thought. Barth, in his
*Church Dogmatics*, argues for three modes of God's being,
because he believes it is essential to distinguish the objective
dimension of revelation from the subjective apprehension of it.
The Logos is for Barth the objective dimension of revelation
whereas the Spirit is the subjective pole, our response to God
which is God's own response in us. To this Richardson replies,

The question, however, is whether this leads us necessarily to say that
the Spirit is an entity over against the Son, that God exists in a third
mode of being as the self-imparter. Granted that the distinction is of
crucial importance as *we* look at the matter—differentiating God's
inward working from his objective presentation of himself in the
revealing event—does this mean that the distinction is to be carried
back to the Godhead? In order that it may find a proper metaphysical
ground, must the distinction be so grounded in the Godhead?[81]

Before dealing with Richardson's objections, let us turn to
the similar critique by Maurice Wiles in his article 'Some
Reflections on the Origins of the Doctrine of the Trinity.'[82] As
with Richardson, Wiles sees the symbolism of the New Testament as essentially fluid. None the less the threefold symbolism of the New Testament determined the early confessions of
the church and was standard in liturgical rites such as baptism.
The difficulty for Wiles is that the church was forced to fit its
experience of God into the trinitarian pattern dictated by scripture. In other words, the experience of God didn't generate the
doctrine but the doctrine was made to conform to the symbols.
Thus before Nicaea there was a threefold pattern of confession
but no clear delineation was made between the activity of the
different persons. After Nicaea the issue was the ontological
status of the persons, not the distinctness.of their activities,
since the works of the persons were affirmed to be *indivisa ad
extra*. Wiles concludes that if the works of the three persons are
*indivisa ad extra*, then an explicit threeness could only be known if

    [81] Ibid., p. 109.
    [82] Maurice F. Wiles, 'Some Reflections on the Origins of the Doctrine of the Trinity',
*The Journal of Theological Studies* N.S. vol. viii (1957) 92–106.

God so reveals it by a direct propositional revelation or if revelation itself involves an essential three-foldness. Wiles rejects the former alternative as involving a highly suspect idea of revelation and is doubtful of the latter. Ogden's position is in effect a defence of this alternative and thus the question is: can Ogden maintain his position in the face of these criticisms against it?

Ogden agrees with two points made in these criticisms.[83] First, the scriptural symbols of Father, Son, and Holy Spirit are essentially ambiguous and do not form a precise trinity. Secondly, there are distinctions that must be made with regard to the Godhead, notably the distinction between God as absolute and God as related which cannot be construed as distinctions between the divine persons.

None the less Ogden's theory is able to withstand the criticisms made by Wiles and Richardson. For example, in Ogden's theory, there is no attempt to derive God in his relatedness to creatures from God as absolute. For in the neoclassical view, God himself, the eminent individual, is both absolute and related. A and R as describing the essence of God must be descriptive of the derivative aspects of God's essence as well. Thus the Father does not refer to God as absolute, while the Son and Spirit refer to God's ways of being related to the world. In this doctrine, the one God, Father, Son, and Holy Spirit, is both absolute and related. As Ogden writes, 'God's relatedness is just as original and underived as his absoluteness, and the three divine persons are equally relative and equally absolute—God the Father being as relative as God the Son or God the Holy Spirit, and they in turn being as absolute as God the Father.'[84]

Secondly, Ogden addresses himself to Richardson's strictures against Barth. The crux of this objection is Richardson's claim that the distinction between God as object and God as subject is arbitrary, since 'this difference is no greater than other differences we are forced to make in discerning God's manifold operations'.[85] To this Ogden replies

There is hardly a greater difference than that between internal and external relatedness, and that is the difference between subject and

---

[83] Ogden, 'On the Trinity', p. 100.
[84] Ibid., p. 101.
[85] Richardson, op. cit., p. 130.

object, which certainly applies to God, who in all his 'operations' is the eminent individual who both loves and is loved by himself and all others. Of course, what we know in revelation, in the first instance, is the God whose love for us is itself the ground as well as the object of our faith in him—God himself being thereby disclosed as not only he in whom we believe but also why and what we believe in doing so. But beyond the necessary threeness evidently involved in this 'economic Trinity' of revelation, there is the necessary threeness involved in the 'immanent Trinity' of God's own essential being. For if it is nothing other or less than God's very self that is revealed to us as the ground and the object of our faith in him—and just this is the claim of Christian revelation—then God exists as God only by existing as the eminent subject and object of love in their primordial unity and difference, and hence as Father, Son, and Holy Spirit. Thus it is doubly true that revelation involves a necessary threeness; both because of its own intrinsic structure and because of the necessary conditions of its possibility as precisely God's self-disclosure.[86]

Ogden notes in conclusion that one of the merits of his neoclassical interpretation is that it overcomes the modern forgetfulness of the ancient doctrine of the *vestigia trinitatis* in man and the world. Indeed, his doctrine even permits one to say that the doctrine of the Trinity is in a way a truth of secular reason and philosophy as well as of Christian revelation and theology.[87] Thus to return to questions of methodology, Ogden has shown that the Christian doctrine of God is both appropriate and understandable. What Christian revelation attests is that which a fully developed theistic metaphysics confirms, namely

that there is one integral life from and for which all other lives are lived; and that the essence of this life is the primordial unity and difference both of integral objectivity, or the one life as self-loved and loved by all others, and of integral subjectivity, or the same life as loving all others as well as itself.[88]

### vi.  *Trinity and Temporality: The Divine Becoming*

The focus of our work as a whole is God and time. We have been searching for a model of God's relation to history that obviates

---

[86] Ogden, 'On the Trinity', pp. 101–2.
[87] Ibid., p. 102.
[88] Ibid.

the religious difficulties which appear to be inherent in the model of classical philosophical theism. Having spoken in this chapter about the God who is revealed to us in Jesus Christ and in his Spirit, let us now turn specifically to the question of the relation of the Christian God to history. Perhaps we can best understand the process view of God's relation to time by contrasting it with two others. Let us then take three views of God's relation to history, summing up each in a thesis.

1. God's being does not become (classical philosophical theism).
2. God's being is in becoming (Jüngel).
3. God's being becomes (process theology).

The first thesis sums up the position of classical philosophical theism. According to this position, all change is excluded from God's being, for change in the classical Aristotelian sense is the transition from potency to act. Since God is the full plentitude of being, his creation exists only by participation in him and as such can add nothing ontologically to his being. There is in him no change or shadow of alteration. He is the same yesterday, today, and forever.

A second position is expressed in Eberhard Jüngel's book on Barth's trinitarian theology, *The Doctrine of the Trinity, God's Being Is In Becoming*.[89] Jüngel sees in Barth's theology of the Trinity an attempt to think through the relatedness of God's being. Barth is certainly not committed to the tenets of classical philosophical theism. Working strictly from the perspective of revelation, he is prepared to surrender even the classical philosophical doctrine of God's impassibility. At the same time, Barth wants to cling to the absolute sovereignty of God with the same tenacity as do the classical philosophical theists. Thus Jüngel works out what might be seen as a mediating position between classical philosophical theism and process theology. God's being does not become. To maintain this position, Jüngel affirms, would make God dependent on the world and thus compromise his sovereignty. Nevertheless because in the event of revelation God does truly disclose himself, we can say that God's being itself is a self-movement toward the world. Only if God is such a self-movement is revelation possible. Thus God's

[89] Eberhard Jüngel, *The Doctrine of the Trinity, God's Being is in Becoming*, trans. Horton Harris (Edinburgh and London: Scottish Academy Press, 1976).

being as self-movement requires a history. Revelation means the correspondence between the being of God and the history of the divine life. As Jüngel says, 'God *makes space* within himself for *time*.'[90] In this way Jüngel believes he can satisfy the demands of the religious consciousness without surrendering the religious insights of the classical tradition. As he writes:

So long as the becoming in which God's being is, is understood as the becoming *proper* to God's being, the statement 'God's being is in becoming' remains from the first guarded from the misunderstanding that God *would* first *become* that which he is, through his relationship to an other than himself. God therefore does not first become in the faith which he grants. But certainly God chooses to become in faith what he *already is*. And in so far God, in the self-relatedness of his being in becoming, is already ours in advance.[91]

In this context the radicality of the process position should be clear. In the process view, reality is basically made up of events not substances. Creativity is the category of the ultimate. In Whitehead's famous remark, 'The many become one and are increased by one.'[92]

If reality is ultimately an endless series of events of becoming, what then is being? Being is the abstract identity factor in becoming. According to Hartshorne, becoming includes being in at least three ways: 1. Process includes past events as immortally remembered or objectified. 2. Becoming includes structures generic to process as such (Whitehead's eternal objects). 3. Becoming includes emergent structures as less abstract constituents of process subsequent to the emergence.[93] Now, as we have seen, in the Hartshorne-Ogden interpretation of Whitehead, God is the eminent individual, the personally ordered series of all actual entities. According to this model, how should one understand the relationship between God's becoming and God's being?

Hartshorne explains that God is the categorially supreme instance of becoming in which there is a factor of categorially supreme being. As Hartshorne wrote in *Philosophers Speak of God*,

[90] Ibid., p. 96.
[91] Ibid., pp. 100–1, note 152.
[92] Whitehead, *Process and Reality*, p. 32.
[93] Charles Hartshorne, 'Tillich's Doctrine of God', in *The Theology of Paul Tillich*, edd. Charles W. Kegley and Robert W. Bretall (New York: Macmillan Co., 1952),. p. 169.

God is neither being as contrasted to becoming nor becoming as contrasted to being; but categorially supreme becoming in which there is a factor of categorially supreme being, as contrasted to inferior becoming, in which there is inferior being. Both poles have two levels, analogically but not simply comparable. The divine becoming is no more divine than the divine being; but both are incomparable (except analogically) to other being or becoming.[94]

But note that the doctrine of the divine becoming has an immediate corollary. If in every instance of becoming the many become one and are increased by one, then God as supreme becoming must be the eminent individual who integrates the many into his one life. This means, as process doctrine explicitly recognizes, that God and the world are correlative terms. One cannot exist without the other. How then do process thinkers reconcile this doctrine with the Christian understanding of creation and eschatology? In other words, how does God relate to the beginning and end of time?

In regard to the doctrine of creation, process theology wants to say at least two things. First, there is no beginning to temporal process. The world never had a beginning in time. There never was a time when God was without *some* world.

On the other hand, against all forms of metaphysical dualism, process theology denies that there is any being or ground save God alone which is the necessary ground of whatever is or is even possible.[95] Thus for any given actual world of

---

[94] Charles Hartshorne and William L. Reese, *Philosophers Speak of God* (Chicago: University of Chicago Press, 1953), p. 24.

[95] In spite of this affirmation, we should note that in *Process and Reality* (p. 31) Whitehead speaks of creativity rather than God as the category of the ultimate. Thus the creativity of the universe is not to be ascribed to God's volition. In Whitehead's view, to do so would be to make God the source of all evil as well as all good. In *Process and Reality*, pp. 343–4, Whitehead writes, 'God can be termed the creator of each temporal actual entity. But the phrase is apt to be misleading by its suggestion that the ultimate creativity of the universe is to be ascribed to God's volition. The true metaphysical position is that God is the aboriginal instance of this creativity, and is therefore the aboriginal condition which qualifies its action. It is the function of actuality to characterize the creativity, and God is the eternal primordial character. But of course, there is no meaning to "creativity" apart from its "creatures", and no meaning to "God" apart from the creativity and the "temporal creatures", and no meaning to the temporal creatures apart from "creativity" and "God"'.

It is this point which most sharply divides process theology from the classical Christian interpretation of creation. See Robert C. Neville, 'The Impossibility of Whitehead's God in Christian Theology', *Proceedings of the American Catholic Philosophical Association* 44 (1970) pp. 130–40; 'Whitehead on the One and the Many', *Southern Journal*

creatures, that world was itself created 'out of nothing' in the
sense that there once was when it was not. Any given world then
is a co-creation. God creates himself out of the physical feelings
of the universe and each actual entity creates itself out of the
data of its world with the help of God's initial aims which are the
source of novelty.[96]

According to Ogden then, the real meaning of the doctrine of
*creatio ex nihilo* is

that everything other than God does have a beginning and that he
alone is the primal source of whatever comes to be. In this sense,
everything other than God comes 'out of nothing', though the
'nothing' here is the *relative* nothing of the real potentiality of God and
of the already existing creation as well as the *absolute* nothing that
determines every contingent existent or event. This implies, of course,
that the *complete* source or origin of any world that comes to exist is not
only the primal creative activity of God but also the derived creativity
of the already created world. Nevertheless, since any world that is
co-creative with God of a subsequent world was itself thus created,
God alone is the *primal* source of any world that comes to be.[97]

Turning now to the end of history and the question of
Christian eschatology, a number of points must be made. First
of all, from the philosophical perspective, process theologians
are committed to the doctrine that there will never be a consummation of temporal process. Like their views on creation,
this doctrine too is rooted in the conviction that creativity is the
category of the ultimate. As Daniel Day Williams once
observed, the process world-view consists in a loosely organized
universe in which there is an endless plurality of events and
therefore there is no final event which consummates or determines the unity of the whole. In this world, though every event
grasps possibility as an element in its becoming, there is no
ultimate future.[98] Thus Schubert Ogden writes,

The promise of faith can be adequately explicated only as entailing
the belief that *all* the stages in the natural-historical process find their

[96] See Schubert Ogden, *The Reality of God*, pp. 62–3; pp. 213–14.
[97] Schubert Ogden, unpublished lecture 'On Creation and Man', p. 3.
[98] Daniel Day Williams, 'Response to Pannenberg', in *Hope and the Future of Man*, ed.
Ewert H. Cousins (Philadelphia: Fortress Press, 1972), pp. 85–6.

ultimate end, even as they have their primal ground, in the encompassing reality of God's love. But this belief in no way requires . . . that there sometime will be, nay even must be, a last stage of the cosmic process. To suppose that the promise of faith in itself requires us to make any such claim is as wrong as to hold that faith in God as the creator implies that the world process sometime had a first stage.[99]

How then would Ogden deal with the New Testament language about resurrection from the dead, the second coming of Christ and the surrender of Christ's kingdom to the Father? Ogden argues that all such statements must frankly be acknowledged as mythological, and interpreted existentially.[100] In regard to the New Testament eschatological symbols, Ogden finds two distinctive types. The first type is based on Jewish apocalyptic, and expresses the cosmic dimensions of man's hope. The early church merely christianized the characteristic hope of late Jewish apocalyptic on the basis of its experience of Jesus. The second type is the christianization of gnosticism. Here Christianity incorporated the Hellenistic interpretation of man's destiny and gave expression to the individual's hope of the survival of death. Ogden writes, 'While the apocalyptic hope is projected along the horizontal line of historical development and anticipates the resurrection of the body, the gnostic hope is really a vertical projection, which envisages solely the immortality of the human soul.'[101]

Ogden proposes to demythologize both types of symbols. And he notes that the specifically Christian hope must interpret the symbols, not vice versa.[102] But what is this specifically Christian hope? It is nothing less than God himself. The object of man's hope as well as its ground can be nothing less than God's pure unbounded love. Ogden writes,

Even as this love is at once the ground and object of man's faith, of his trusting consent to reality as such, so it is also the ground of his own capacity to love and the one inclusive object toward which all his love

[99] Ogden, *The Reality of God*, p. 213.
[100] Schubert Ogden, 'The Meaning of Christian Hope', in *Religious Experience and Process Theology: The Pastoral Implications of a Major Modern Movement*, edd. Harry James Cargas and Bernard Lee (New York: Paulist Press, 1976), pp. 202–3.
[101] Ibid., p. 201.
[102] Ibid., p. 203.

is directed. Being freed to love by God's limitless love for him and for
the whole creation, he loves both himself and all others in his
returning love for God. But, in the same way, the love of God is also
the ground and object of Christian hope.[103]

Let us now see how this hope is the answer to man's
existential predicament in the face of his own death and the
transience of all things. From a philosophical perspective death
is not just an event that will one day overtake us. As Heidegger
has so forcibly made clear, death is a reality in whose midst each
of us lives.[104]

Death is for each man his ultimate possibility. This is even
more so in the process perspective according to which there is
no substantial self but rather the self is a route of occasions.
Thus we are literally perishing all the time.

This perpetual perishing of all actual occasions is the core of
the theological problem of time and the source of man's deepest
anxiety. For as Ogden has said,

Even if we suppose that death in the first sense is somehow to be
escaped and our lives as subjects endlessly prolonged beyond that
uncertain hour, still the deeper problem posed by the 'perpetual
perishing' of all creaturely things remains to plague us. What profit
would it be for us to go on and on living—even to eternity—if the net
result of all our having lived were simply nothing; if our successive
presents in no way added up to a cumulative accomplishment such as
no creature is able to provide either for himself or his fellows?[105]

The message of Christian hope is that man's life does not add
up to zero because it is embraced by God's love and is taken
everlastingly into his life. Ogden writes

Our final destiny, as Christian faith understands it, is not merely to be
loved by our human successors, but also, and infinitely more important, to be loved by the pure unbounded love of God, for whom each of
us makes a difference exactly commensurate to what he is and of
everlasting significance. Because God's love, radically unlike ours, is
pure and unbounded, and because he, therefore, both can and does
participate fully in the being of all creatures, the present moment for
him never slips into the past as it does for us. Instead, every moment
retains its vividness and intensity forever within his completely

---

[103] Ibid., p. 204.

[104] See Martin Heidegger, *Being and Time*, trans. John Macquarrie and Edward
Robinson (Oxford: Basil Blackwell, 1967), pp. 279–311.

[105] Ogden, *The Reality of God*, pp. 224–5.

perfect love and judgment. He knows all things for just what they are, and he continues to know and cherish them throughout the endless ages of the future in all the richness of their actual being. In other words, because God not only *affects*, but is also *affected by*, whatever exists, all things are in every present quite literally resurrected or restored in his own everlasting life, from which they can nevermore be cast out.[106]

For process theology, this ultimate hope is both a philosophical doctrine and a theological one. Philosophically, it springs directly from Whitehead's dipolar conception of God and his doctrine of objective immortality. In *Process and Reality* Whitehead writes, 'The consequent nature of God is the fluent world become "everlasting" by its objective immortality in God.'[107] There Whitehead envisages four phases in God's ongoing relation with the world.[108] The first phase is the phase of conceptual origination in God's primordial nature. The second phase is that of physical origination, with its multiplicity of actualities. In the third phase there is perfected actuality. The many become one everlastingly. Immediacy is reconciled with objective immortality. In the fourth phase, perfected actuality passes back into the temporal world, and qualifies this world so that each temporal actuality includes it as an immediate fact of relevant experience.

This, however, is only the philsophical side. The theological dimension is the doctrine of God's pure unbounded love. Process thinkers believe that their doctrine can make the conviction that 'God is love' intelligible. For these thinkers love implies receptivity. As we have already noted, God not only affects all things but is affected by them. Thus he is not only eminent cause but also eminent effect.[109] Love lets the other make a difference, takes the other into account. This is precisely what the dipolar account of God allows. Our lives are not ultimately meaningless because they do literally make a difference to the one integral life that is eternal.

Nevertheless even though Ogden is convinced that Christian faith enables us to say that our lives are ultimately meaningful,

[106] Ibid., p. 226.
[107] Whitehead, *Process and Reality*, p. 257.
[108] See ibid., p. 532.
[109] See Ogden, *The Reality of God*, p. 223.

he is equally convinced that Christian faith gives us no guarantee that we shall survive death as personal subjects enjoying beyond this life the same kind of subjective immortality which God alone enjoys.[110] He views such a demand on our part as *hubris*. Just as the church denied the doctrine of personal pre-existence, so it should logically deny that of post-existence. To be a creature is to be finite and hence to be subject to death. Christian faith does not promise that we shall personally survive death but that our lives are meaningful in spite of transience and death. As Ogden puts it,

The continuity that the Christian witness undoubtedly affirms between present and future is the continuity established by *God's* subjectivity, not by ours, by his redemption and judgment of the world, and, in the human case, by his universal offer of salvation to all men and women—not by our continued subjective existence beyond the limit of our death.[111]

The conclusion to be drawn from this discussion is that eschatological assertions do not tell us anything about another life or another world beyond this one. They tell us rather about the ultimate significance of our world for God. Therefore the tense of eschatological assertions is really the present not the future. Ogden writes,

Being really and truly *last* things, that is, *ultimate* things, things constituting the most essential reality of *all* places on the time-line, they are always and only matters of the present—though, of course, of *every* present. Just as the reality of God the creator is not something belonging to the past of nature and history, but is their ever-present primordial ground, so the reality of God as judge and redeemer is not a particular event of the future, but the ever-present final consequence of each passing moment in the stream of time.[112]

According to Ogden, such an interpretation has the added merit of addressing the indictment of other-worldliness made against Christianity by Marxists. He writes,

On this interpretation, such mythology in no way expresses hope in some other life beyond this life but, precisely as symbolic of Christian hope in God's love, expresses hope in the ultimate significance of this

---

[110] See ibid., pp. 229–30; also 'The Meaning of Christian Hope', pp. 206–10.
[111] Schubert Ogden, unpublished lecture 'On the Last Things', p. 13.
[112] Ogden, *The Reality of God*, p. 210.

life itself. Therefore, so far from compromising our concern with this world and our responsibility for humanizing it, Christian hope is disclosed to be the best of reasons for having such concern and responsibility. Just because it is hope in God's love, it is also hope in the world's significance, and this means that it is the kind of hope that issues in concerned and responsible action for the world's fulfillment.[113]

In this whole discussion of God and time, we see Ogden's effort to mediate between two extreme positions. As we saw in chapter one, a principal reason why so many modern men reject God is that faith in God seems to contradict a humanistic affirmation of life. As Ogden once put it,

The Christian God often appears to be nothing more than a *deus ex machina*, who, as Sartre and Camus have eloquently argued, is the most insidious threat of all to man's fully assuming his rightful freedom and responsibility for his own existence. And matters in this respect are, if anything, even worse with the more sophisticated conception of God in the classical theistic tradition. By virtue of the philosophical assumptions determinative for this tradition, God can only be so understood that his relation to man and his history is the wholly external one of absolute, unchanging being. Small wonder, then, that Nietzsche could think that a God so conceived is already dead and that the announcement of the fact but frees man to involve himself in the relativity and change in which life alone is to be found.[114]

Thus Ogden's whole theological project is an attempt to do justice to an integral humanism without landing on the other horn of the dilemma, namely secularism. Secularism tries to affirm the value of this world and life's meaningfulness without any reference to the transcendent. The whole burden of Ogden's doctrine of God has been to demonstrate that neither the Christian gospel itself nor man's own commitment to secularity are justified unless the ultimate reality with which any of us must perforce come to terms is the eminent individual, necessary in his existence but contingent in his actuality, absolute and yet relative, supreme cause and supreme effect, the ultimate ground and final end of everything that is.

---

[113] Ogden, 'The Meaning of Christian Hope', p. 211.
[114] Schubert Ogden, 'Beyond Supernaturalism', *Religion in Life* 33 (1963–4) 16–17.

### vii.   *The Christian God and the Problem of Suffering*

At the end of the last section we tried to show how Ogden's doctrine of God sought to meet the problems of modern atheism raised in chapter one. Ogden has endeavoured to give us an account of God which takes secularity seriously and which demonstrates the place of God in secular experience. He argues the case that man's confidence in the meaning of this life is itself undermined without the transcendent God to ground it.

Still this is only one aspect of the problem of modern atheism which emerged from our study in chapter one. As we observed there, a significant number of contemporary atheists base their case on the insoluble mystery of human suffering, especially the suffering of the innocent. Such atheists as Camus and Rubenstein are 'protest atheists'. They prefer to act as if God does not exist in order to undertake a movement of rebellion against a world in which the innocent suffer and die. Let us now consider whether process theology has anything to say to these people.

In discussing the problem of suffering, Ogden quotes the famous passage from Bonhoeffer's *Letters and Papers from Prison* where he writes, 'The God who makes us live in this world without using him as a working hypothesis is the God before whom we are ever standing. Before God and with him we live without God. God allows himself to be edged out of the world and onto the cross. God is weak and powerless in the world, and that is exactly the way, the only way, in which he can be with us and help us. ... Only a suffering God can help.'[115] Commenting on this passage, Ogden writes, 'All his statements about God, expressed as they are in concrete language that is obviously metaphorical, cry out for conceptual clarification that he nowhere provides.'[116]

Thus the first response of process theology to the problem of human suffering is to affirm a dipolar conception of God in which it is intelligible to affirm that God actually suffers with us. There is no need for us to examine this doctrine more closely, for we have already seen that God is affected by the world, that he

---

[115] Dietrich Bonhoeffer, *Letters and Papers from Prison*, ed. Eberhard Bethge, trans. R. H. Fuller (London: SCM Press, 1953), p. 164, as cited by Ogden, *The Reality of God*, p. 53.

[116] Ogden, *The Reality of God*, p. 54.

is supreme effect as well as supreme cause and that in this way
God is affirmed to be love. For process theology love literally
involves suffering, for suffering minimally involves being
affected. As Daniel Day Williams once put it,

I affirm that God does suffer as he participates in the ongoing life of
the society of being. His sharing in the world's suffering is the
supreme instance of knowing, accepting, and transforming in love the
suffering which arises in the world. I am affirming the doctrine of the
divine sensitivity. Without it I can make no sense of the being of God.
Sensitive participation in this world means suffering, or else our
human experience is completely irrelevant to anything we can say
about God.[117]

There still remains, however, the cause of our suffering and
evil. Is God somehow responsible for all the suffering that goes
on in our world? To this question process thinkers respond that
suffering and evil are not cogent objections against the reality of
God's love, for they do not have their origin in God but in a
universe of free subjects. Hartshorne writes,

Those who think God cannot mean well toward us because he 'sends'
us suffering can prove their point only by showing that there is a way
to run the universe, compatible with the existence of other real powers
than just the supreme power which would be more fully in accord
with the totality of interests, or by showing that God sends us the
suffering while himself remaining simply outside it, in the enjoyment
of sheer bliss.[118]

The key then is the community of being as a community of
free subjects. In process metaphysics, every actual entity from
God to the least atomic particle is characterized by freedom.[119]

[117] Daniel Day Williams, 'Suffering and Being in Empirical Theology', in *The Future of Empirical Theology*, pp. 191–2.

[118] Hartshorne, *Man's Vision of God*, p. 31.

[119] Ogden writes, '*Nothing whatever, not even God, can wholly determine the being of something else.* Taken in a completely generalized, analogical sense, "freedom" means self-creation and therefore, determination by self in contrast to determination by others. Assuming, then, as process metaphysics maintains, that freedom in this sense is a strictly universal metaphysical principle, one must infer that anything that is even conceivably actual is and must be, in its own way or to its own degree, self-created. This need not mean and, as we shall see, must not mean that self-creation ever occurs in the complete absence of creation by others, any more than creation by others ever occurs in the complete absence of creation by self. But since it clearly belongs to the very idea of freedom as self-creation to exclude being completely determined by others, what anything is, is always, in part, the result of its own free decision, as distinct from the decisions of others that it must somehow take into account.' Ogden, *Faith and Freedom*, p. 76.

As we have seen, creativity is the category of the ultimate. Every actual entity decides what it will become. In this freedom of self-determination lies its power. This means that power is essentially a social concept. Thus although God must be affirmed to be the eminent instance of power in that he synthesizes in his own life the freedom of all creatures, his omnipotence cannot mean a monopoly of power in such wise that creatures have no power. To quote Hartshorne once again, 'Omnipotence . . . is power to the highest degree possible and over all that exists, it is "all" the power that *could* be exercised by any *one* individual over "all" that is; but it remains to be shown how much power *could* be exercised in this fashion. The minimal solution of the problem of evil is to affirm the necessity of a division of powers, hence of responsibilities, as binding even upon a maximal power.'[120]

This then is essentially Ogden's solution. The problem of evil is a pseudo-problem which dissolves as soon as one takes seriously the freedom of creaturely events and the real interaction of God and his world. He writes,

To be an individual at all, even a created individual, is one and the same with having some freedom, however slight, to decide what up to then remains undecided. Consequently, it is not only false but meaningless to suppose that God is somehow responsible for whatever happens in the sense that he himself has freely decided it. So far as what happens does not follow simply from general metaphysical conditions that no one decides, since they are precisely the conditions of free choice rather than its *consequences*, it is the outcome always both of God's free choices *and* of the free choices of his creatures. Such evil as exists, then, is either the 'metaphysical evil' of creaturely existence as such—the price that *must* be paid if there is to be any concrete value at all—or else the 'factual evil' that results from the free, but always also finite, choices of the creatures themselves—and thus the price that in fact is paid for the actual exercise of their freedom.[121]

Thus far our response to the problem of suffering has proceeded in two stages. We have shown that God neither causes our sufferings nor remains oblivious of them. This can be understood on the basis of process metaphysics. But we might also ask if this solution is adequate to the burning religious

[120] Hartshorne, *Man's Vision of God*, p. 30.
[121] See Ogden's unpublished notes on 'Tillich's Theological Anthropology', IV, p. 6.

question which suffering raises. As critics of process theology ask: is the God of process strong enough to save? To this question process theologians reply that their God is not strong enough to save if one demands a guarantee of final victory or triumph either in one's individual life or in the cosmos as a whole. Process theology admits that there is a tragic dimension to life and that even God himself embraces this tragic dimension in his own life. God does not overcome every evil. To maintain this would be to deny that evil is real and that it has real effects which God's *fiat* cannot simply eradicate. None the less process theology affirms that there are resources in God to deal with every evil, that is, God draws what good he can out of suffering and evil by responding to them with new initiatives for realizing the greatest possible harmony between himself and his creation.[122]

In conclusion then let me cite a quotation of Norman Pittenger which epitomizes the process perspective on God and suffering. 'More and more, some of us are convinced that a basic difficulty in Christian theology has been, and is, an inability to rest the case upon love. Somehow or other, it is felt, love must be backed up by force or there is no assurance of its triumphant quality.'[123] Yet Christian faith is convinced that 'The Cosmic Lover will not triumph by being changed from love into coercion; but then anybody who thought that this was his way of victory must have failed utterly to understand what the gospel of God's love in action in Jesus Christ, to the point of death on Calvary yet through that death to the assurance of resurrection, really declares to us about the divine nature and the divine mode of activity in the creation.'[124]

viii.   *Process Theology and the Theology of the Church Fathers*

We began our chapter on patristic theology by noting that contemporary approaches to the doctrine of God must take a stand on tradition. Let us at this point note briefly how the doctrine of God worked out by Schubert Ogden compares to that developed in the patristic period.

[122] See, for example, Daniel Day Williams, 'Tragedy and the Christian Eschatology', *Encounter* 24 (1963) 61–76, especially 74–6.

[123] Norman Pittenger, 'Trinity and Process: Some Comments in Reply', *Theological Studies* 32, 2 (June 1971) 296.

[124] Ibid.

Again we might take as our point of departure Maurice
Wiles's observation that true continuity with the Church
Fathers lies not in the repetition of their doctrinal conclusions
but in the continuation of their doctrinal aims. In chapter two,
we listed a number of problems which directed the questioning
of the Fathers: God's absoluteness and relatedness, the relation
of God's revelation of himself in Jesus Christ to his revelation in
creation and in the history of Israel, christology and the monotheism of Judaism, soteriology.

I think we can say that Ogden's theological project has been
directed to all of these questions. First, his entire effort has been
to work out a theology in which God's absoluteness and relatedness are equally primordial, and his critique of the classical
philosophical tradition is precisely that it failed to do adequate
justice to the pole of God's relatedness. Secondly, Ogden has
sought to construct a theology in which Christ has a role of
central importance for human existence without being the constitutive mediator of God's grace. Jesus re-presents God's grace
truly and decisively, but not exclusively. This is a theological
system which takes seriously both the particularity of the
Christian kerygma and the universality of God's offer of grace.
Thirdly, Ogden considers the relation of Jesus to the Father to
be of critical importance in that the question of christology is
not 'Who is Jesus?' but 'Who is God?' For Ogden the Christian
kerygma can only be a salvation event if it is God's Word as
human word. Thus Ogden has been at pains to correct
Bultmann's one-sided subjectivism with an insistence on the
objective foundation of the kerygma in God as ground and
author.[125] Finally, we can say that Ogden's theology is from
first to last a treatise on soteriology. His insistence that all
theological statements are *strictly* existential statements and his
call for radical demythologizing, even to the point of
demythologizing the Christ-event as an act of God, are both
part of a contemporary reinterpretation of the meaning of
salvation. For Ogden salvation is the realization of authentic

---

[125] One of the critical questions, however, that we shall return to is the distinction
which Ogden makes between the Jesus of history and the Christ of faith, and his
insistence that the referent of the term 'Jesus' in the constitutive christological assertion
'Jesus is the Christ' is 'not some past figure or event behind the apostolic witness but the
present figure and event constitutive of and, in another sense, constituted by that very
witness'. Ogden, 'On Christ' (unpublished), p. 5.

existence, and his theological hermeneutic is an attempt to
show how the Christian faith renders such authentic human
existence possible.

Granting that Ogden's theological aims are consistent with
those of the Church Fathers, we must nevertheless ask whether
his conclusions are equally consistent with them. In addressing
this question, a number of distinctions must be made. First of
all, though Ogden does not believe himself bound by the
judgements of the great ecumenical councils, he none the less
explicitly accepts them, at least if properly interpreted.
Negatively this means that he rejects the conceptualizations in
which they were articulated and what I termed in chapter two
the philosophical presuppositions of the patristic mind.
Positively this entails an existential hermeneutic and a process
metaphysics. Whether Ogden can employ such tools and
remain faithful to the tradition remains much more problematic. Certainly it is appropriate and even necessary to restate
the faith of the church in an idiom intelligible by contemporary
standards of meaning and truth. But it may be the case that just
as certain philosophical conceptions and presuppositions made
a synthesis of Greek thought and Christian faith untenable, so
certain presuppositions and conceptions of the 'secular' man
whom Ogden is addressing may likewise render it impossible to
translate the Christian faith into that idiom and remain faithful
to the original experience. To that more difficult question we
shall turn at the end of this chapter and again in chapter five.

ix.  *Trinity and Dipolarity*

We began this chapter by asking whether the Christian doctrine of God, Father, Son, and Holy Spirit, could be conceptualized in process categories or whether, as Moltmann believes,
process philosophy with its dipolar God will always be
inadequate as a resource for Christian theology, precisely
because dipolarity does not do justice to the trinitarian experience which for Moltmann has its foundation in the cross.

In response to that problem I hope that I have shown that
Moltmann's objection is unfounded. Process theology, at least
as practiced by Schubert Ogden, intends to say more than that
God is dipolar, absolute, and relative. Ogden has argued that,
while such a philosophical doctrine can overcome the diffi-

culties inherent in classical philosophical theism, it cannot do justice to specifically Christian experience.[126] The logic of this experience proceeds from our encounter with God in the church through the witness of the kerygma of Jesus Christ. This logic demands as its ultimate foundation one God, known through Jesus Christ, in his Spirit. When this logic is thought out, it demands both the doctrine of the Trinity and that of God's dipolarity. It demands a God absolute and relative in all three persons.

Nevertheless the issues between Moltmann and Ogden are substantial. For if, as we have argued, the doctrine of God is a function of christology, as both Moltmann and Ogden would agree, then the critical issues are christological. In particular they involve one's understanding of Jesus Christ as the revelation of the Father. And this issue is, in my judgement, the critical one in Ogden's theology, for at the core of this issue lies the question of Jesus's decisiveness and at the heart of this question lies the problem of eschatology and so of time. Thus once again there is the hermeneutical circle involving Jesus and God, God and time.

### x.  *Critical Reflections*

In concluding this chapter let me indicate the critical issues that lie before us. The first is, in my judgement, the reference of the term 'Jesus' in the constitutive christological assertion. For Ogden 'Jesus' does not refer to the past historical figure Jesus of Nazareth. No doubt the kerygma assumes certain things about him, not least of which is that he existed, but the kerygma does not assert anything about him. For Ogden, the kerygma proclaims the apostolic Christ as the re-presentation of faith, not the historical Jesus as the actualization of faith.

Yet it is my judgement that the kerygma allows no such dichotomy. Rather, the faith of the apostolic church asserts a strict identity between the Jesus of history and the Christ of faith. Let me cite the recent testimony of several scholars in the fields of biblical, historical, and systematic theology.

Turning first to the New Testament, we note the following judgement of the former Lady Margaret Professor in the University of Cambridge, C. F. D. Moule. He writes,

[126] Ogden emphasized this point in an interview with the author, 23 Sept. 1977.

At no point in the New Testament . . . is there any suggestion that Christian experience meant no more than that it was the teaching and example of a figure in the past which now enabled Christians to approach God with a new understanding and confidence, or that it was merely because of what Jesus had done and been in the past that they found the Spirit of God lifting them up to new capacities and powers. On the contrary, they believed that it was because the same Jesus was alive and was himself in some way in touch with them there and then that the new relationship and the new freedom were made possible. They believed in the continued aliveness and presence, in some spiritual dimension, of the person who had been known in the past in the dimensions of hearing, sight and touch. The transcendent, divine person of present experience was continuous and identical with the historical figure of the past.[127]

Writing along the same lines, the German patristic scholar Aloys Grillmeier observes,

So today . . . a synthesis is being sought between the extremes (pure Jesus of history—pure Christ of faith); the Jesus of history is taken as a presupposition of the Christ of faith. There is a recognition that the primitive community itself already achieved this conjunction. It identified the humiliated Jesus of Nazareth with the exalted *Kyrios*. With this twofold recognition it was in a position to withstand the error of docetism on the one hand and the denial of the transcendence of the *Kyrios* on the other. Indeed, it was just this tension, this war waged on two fronts by the New Testament authors, that demanded clarity of expression in talking about Jesus and hence depth in theological interpretation. They knew that the earthly, crucified Jesus was to be seen only in the light of Easter day. But it was also realized 'that the event of Easter cannot be adequately comprehended if it is looked at apart from the earthly Jesus'. It follows from this that for the understanding of the primitive church 'the life of Jesus was constitutive for faith, because the earthly and the exalted Lord are identical'.[128]

Turning finally to contemporary dogmatics, let us record the judgement of the Tübingen Catholic theologian Walter Kasper in his book *Jesus the Christ*. Speaking of the necessity of the historical Jesus for faith, he comments,

[127] C. F. D. Moule, *The Origin of Christology* (Cambridge: University Press, 1977), pp. 98–9.
[128] Aloys Grillmeier, *Christ in the Christian Tradition* vol. i: *From the Apostolic Age to Chalcedon (AD 451)*, pp. 4–5.

It is a question of the rejection of myth. The eschatological process is 'not a new idea and not a culminating-point in a process of development', but happens once and for all. This historical contingency reflects the freedom of the divine action. It also grounds the new *kairos*, the great turning-point, the new historical possibility of our decision. On the other hand: it is a question of the rejection of docetism and of the conviction that the revelation occurs 'in the flesh'. Therefore everything focusses on the identity of the exalted Lord with the earthly Jesus. It is a question of the reality of the incarnation and of the specific meaning of the true humanity of Jesus. Ultimately, it is a question of the rejection of enthusiasm and of a purely contemporary understanding of salvation. The reference is to 'the *extra nos* of salvation as the presumption of faith'. A faith which refers only to the kerygma becomes the end of faith in the church as the bearer of the kerygma. In the quest for the historical Jesus, on the other hand, what has to be elicited is 'the non-assignability of salvation, the *prae* of Christ before his own, the *extra nos* of proclamation, the necessity of the exodus of the faithful from themselves'. It is a question of the primacy of Christ before and over the church.[129]

In citing these authors, I am arguing for the position that christological statements are not strictly existential statements or existential statements without remainder. The Christian kerygma not only assumes certain things about the historical Jesus but also makes assertions about him. To this extent I judge Ogden's existential hermeneutic to be inadequate.

But now I would like to press this question even further and ask what it is that drives Ogden to take this position. No doubt many of his motives are strictly theological. Following Bultmann, he argues that the New Testament itself demands a radical demythologizing.[130] But I belive that other motives are also at work. Among them is Ogden's commitment to process metaphysics. This metaphysics is hard pressed to express some of the convictions of Christian faith because of its understanding of the relationship between God and the world.

Let me explain my position in three stages. First of all, process metaphysics has great difficulty in dealing with a unique act of God. Some years ago, Daniel Day Williams wrote an essay entitled 'How Does God Act?': An Essay in

[129] Kasper, *Jesus the Christ*, pp. 33–4.
[130] See, for example, Ogden, *Christ Without Myth*, pp. 49–50.

Whitehead's Metaphysics'.[131] In that essay, he argued that according to Whitehead God acts in his primordial nature by being what he is, that is, by presenting to the creatures the unity, the richness, and the limits of possibility as ordered by his vision. In his consequent nature God acts by being felt by his creatures. From this analysis two things are clear. Firstly, it is hardly accurate to refer to either of these functions of God as actions in the strict sense. The action of the primordial nature is an action of final causality better described as a lure rather than as an action. The action of the consequent nature is more accurately a passivity. Secondly, even if we understand these as actions, we note that they are uniform. There is hardly scope for a unique activity of God in history.

The point is taken up in Ogden's essay 'What Sense Does it Make to Say, "God Acts in History?"' There he argues that the primary sense of God's action 'is the act whereby, in each new present, he constitutes himself as God by participating fully and completely in the world of his creatures, thereby laying the ground for the next stage of the creative process'.[132] Beyond this we may also give a derivative sense of God's action *in* history. Just as in human life, certain words and gestures are considered particularly expressive of the person, so there are some distinctively human words and deeds in which God's characteristic action as creator and redeemer is appropriately re-presented or revealed. But this requires as a minimal condition that these words or events be received and understood by someone as having decisive revelatory power.[133] The difficulty with this position, as David Griffin has pointed out, is that the criterion for divine action is not something God does but something that we do.[134]

The foregoing analysis indicates that, whatever other theological motives influence a process theologian, his commitment

[131] Daniel Day Williams, 'How Does God Act? An Essay in Whitehead's Metaphysics', in *The Hartshorne Festschrift, Process and Divinity, Philosophical Essays Presented to Charles Hartshorne*, edd. William L. Reese and Eugene Freeman (La Salle, Ill.: Open Court, 1964), pp. 161–80.
[132] Ogden, *The Reality of God*, p. 177.
[133] See ibid., 184–5.
[134] See David Ray Griffin, 'Schubert Ogden's Christology and the Possibilities of Process Theology', in *Process Philosophy and Christian Thought*, edd. Delwin Brown, Ralph E. James and Gene Reeves (Indianapolis and New York: Bobbs-Merrill, 1971), pp. 352–4.

to process metaphysics is an incentive to demythologize the Christ-event as the unique act of God since the process world-view rules out such particular divine acts *a priori*. As Eugene H. Peters writes in his book *The Creative Advance*,

The process theologian will not speak of miraculous, divine intervention in the world. He will try to conceive creation, incarnation, resurrection, and so forth, not as bewildering acts of God, which have no affinity with the structures and processes of the experienced world; rather, he will conceive these as expressions in mythical or symbolic form of facts which, however religiously profound, are yet within the warp and woof of the world's single order.[135]

The second point is really an elaboration of the first. If God never does anything at one time that he does not do at another, then he does not really do anything new. Now, of course, in process metaphysics God is always the source of novelty in that all creative advance in the universe is dependent on God's offer of initial aims to each actual occasion. But as Peters has reminded us, this is understood in such a way that the new which God initiates is always in continuity with the old. The New Testament, however, proclaims an action in Jesus Christ which is so explosive that it shatters the categories of the old. The language of resurrection suggests the language of creation. The God who raises the dead is the God who creates out of nothing. But this perspective is alien to that of the process world-view.

Coming now to the last point, let me state my case in another way by noting that the ultimate reason for this stance of the process theologians is their conviction that God's relation to the world must be conceived metaphysically. As Langdon Gilkey writes,

Process theology better than most understands how God can relate individually and so novelly to each particular occasion. But nonetheless in understanding these unique or particular actions *meta-physically*, it understands them always under an identical category necessarily applicable alike to all events and thus special to none. God's redeeming activity is thus understood categorically as a part of his general creative activity as such, and is necessarily related to all

---

[135] Eugene H. Peters, *The Creative Advance* (St. Louis: Bethany Press, 1966), p. 107.

events everywhere. In this situation, it is hard for one decisive act, let alone an ontologically unique act, to enter the system intelligibly.[136]

Thus Gods's freedom *vis-à-vis* the world is understood within the limits of the metaphysical principles of the process system, God being not an exception to them but their chief exemplification. God, therefore, acts but he does so according to metaphysical necessity, the necessity that he prehend everything perfectly (necessary redemption) and the necessity that everything prehend his influence (necessary creation).[137]

The issue confronting us then is whether the only alternatives for the Christian theologian today are classical philosophical theism, leading to an apparent religious cul-de-sac, or process metaphysics, leading to severe restrictions on the kinds of divine initiatives that Christians have traditionally wanted to affirm. To put it another way, must we, as one contemporary theologian has put it, accept our lot bequeathed to us by the Enlightenment and make the most of it,[138] or can we affirm God's involvement in time and history without surrendering his transcendence? As a first step in exploring this question, I propose to turn to the German eschatological school, which more than any other today has sought to synthesize the divine transcendence with involvement in temporal process. For these theologians, God is transcendent precisely by being the initiator of a new heaven and a new earth. Focusing our attention on Jürgen Moltmann, who launched the movement with his book *Theology of Hope*,[139] let us examine how he works out these insights in developing his account of the Christian doctrine of God.

[136] Langdon Gilkey, 'Process Theology', *Vox Theologica* 43 (1973) 25.

[137] See Robert C. Neville, 'Neoclassical Metaphysics and Christianity: A Critical Study of Ogden's *Reality of God*', *International Philosophical Quarterly* 9 (1969) 620. Ogden would not see this type of necessity as incompatible with God's freedom. God has positive freedom to do this or that but not the negative freedom to do nothing at all (e.g. the freedom not to create or redeem). See his unpublished notes 'On the Concept of God's Freedom', 29 May 1971.

[138] Leslie Houlden, 'The Creed of Experience', in *The Myth of God Incarnate*, ed. John Hick (London: SCM Press, 1977), p. 125.

[139] Jürgen Moltmann, *Theology of Hope, On the Ground and the Implications of a Christian Eschatology* (London: SCM Press, 1967).

# IV

# THE TRINITARIAN HISTORY OF GOD: GOD AND HISTORY ACCORDING TO JÜRGEN MOLTMANN

i. *Introduction: Context and Goal of Moltmann's Theology*

IN attempting to interpret the thought of a theologian it is critical to discern the central problematic that motivates his reflections. Although the thought of Jürgen Moltmann has undergone shifts of perspective and various dialogue partners since the appearance of *Theology of Hope*,[1] the central focus has remained constant. This is the problem of human liberation. One can recognize the consistency of this concern in Moltmann's own explanations of his theological enterprise. Reflecting on the reactions to his provocative first book on hope, he wrote 'The Christian faith wants not only to interpret the world differently and to bring existence to a different understanding of itself, but also wants to change the world and existence by establishing freedom and obedience.'[2] More than ten years later, in his answer to the critics of *The Crucified God*, he sounded the same theme: 'The goal of those three books, which were of a type and method that should not be pursued further, is a new ordering of the theological system toward a messianic dogmatics, in which, under the guiding view-point of the

---

[1] In the development of Moltmann's dialectic of cross and resurrection, his early book *Theology of Hope* emphasized the perspective of the resurrection, whereas *The Crucified God* concentrated on the cross. In the third work of the trilogy, *The Church in the Power of the Spirit, A Contribution to Messianic Ecclesiology* (London: SCM Press, 1977), Moltmann elucidated his understanding of the Holy Spirit, who is the link keeping the dialectic in tension. The conversation partner in the early period was Ernst Bloch (philosophy of the resurrection); in the later books the principle dialogue partners have been Camus, Horkheimer, and Adorno (philosophy of the cross).

[2] Jürgen Moltmann, 'Antwort auf die Kritik der Theologie der Hoffnung', in *Diskussion über die 'Theologie der Hoffnung' von Jürgen Moltmann*, herausgegeben und eingeleitet von Wolf-Dieter Marsch (München: Chr. Kaiser Verlag, 1967), p. 230.

Trinity and of the Kingdom of God, the path from history to freedom is opened up.'[3] Moltmann's goal for theology then is a messianic dogmatics. The critical concepts for developing such a dogmatics will be the doctrine of the Trinity and the kingdom of God. Before speaking of these two central concepts in more detail, we should ask: what impels Moltmann to develop such a messianic theology?.

The answer to this question leads us straightaway to the context of Moltmann's theological enterprise, namely the suffering of the world. Just as Israel's religious experience was shaped by its liberation from bondage in Egypt, so Christian faith is rooted in the promise of liberation which is grounded in the event of the cross and resurrection. Israel's messianic faith was kept alive by the unredeemed character of the world. In the same way the Christian prays for the parousia, which will bring the final liberation from the power of suffering and death.

In the meantime, Christian faith is constantly assaulted by the cries of the suffering and the abandoned. If God is understood in a messianic sense, then God is known in his Lordship over his creation. God is only fully God when his kingdom has come, when his Lordship is manifest, and suffering and death are no more.[4] But God in this sense precisely does not exist. The question then which troubles Moltmann is whether belief is an honest option in the face of an apparently godless world. Moltmann writes, 'The question about God arises most profoundly from the pain of injustice in the world and from abandonment in suffering.'[5] He asks, 'In the face of the innocent suffering of children, in the face of Auschwitz and Hiroshima, in the face of this world where all happiness passes

[3] Jürgen Moltmann, 'Antwort auf die Kritik an *Der Gekreuzigte Gott*' in *Diskussion über Jürgen Moltmanns Buch 'Der Gekreuzigte Gott'*, herausgegeben und eingeleitet von Michael Welker (München: Chr. Kaiser, 1979), p. 168.

[4] Thus, for example, in his collection of essays *The Future of Creation* (London: SCM Press, 1979), Moltmann writes (p. 27): A theological eschatology, if it is to remain eschatology at all, cannot develop the future and the sphere of God's existence on the basis of the temporal concept of his eternity, or the impression of his sovereignty gained from the Christ event. It must rather see to it that—just as the kingdom of God is not the mere "accident" of his divinity or something added to it, but is that divinity's quintessence—so the future too is the mode of his being that is dominant in history.'

[5] Jürgen Moltmann, 'Der gekreuzigte Gott, neuzeitliche Gottesfrage und trinitarische Gottesgeschicte', *Concilium* 8 (1972) p 408.

away and where human beings die without recognizable meaning, how should I believe in the goodness and fatherly rule of a God in heaven?'[6] In the experience of suffering then, Moltmann finds the rock of atheism. He draws the conclusion that any authentic theology today must come to terms with the theodicy question.

I said above that the critical concepts for developing such an authentic theology are for Moltmann the doctrine of the Trinity and the kingdom of God. Moltmann turns to the trinitarian conception of God, first of all, because he is convinced that a monotheistic God leads directly to the atheistic cul-de-sac from which the Christian believer wishes to extricate himself. Why is this the case? Monotheism so stresses the unity of God that there is no room for any distinctions within God. God is absolutely simple. This implies that God cannot undergo any change. Metaphysically this implies that God cannot make room for anyone besides himself, nor can he be affected by any reality outside of himself. Although it might be possible to affirm a doctrine of creation in which other beings are dependent on God, it is impossible to affirm a mutual reciprocity between God and creatures. In any human understanding of love, love makes room for the other, takes the other into account. Without this ability to be affected by the other person, love has no meaning. If then we accepted the monotheistic idea of God that I have briefly sketched, it is difficult to see how we could affirm that 'God is love'.[7] Moltmann further believes that monotheism has as its correlate monarchy, that is, the being of the one God is linked to the absolute sovereignty of his rule. According to Moltmann, this monotheistic God is 'a lonely world-ruler and world-possessor'.[8]

---

[6] Jürgen Moltmann, *Umkehr zur Zukunft* (München and Hamburg: Siebenstern Taschenbuch, 1970), p. 19.

[7] See Jürgen Moltmann, *The Crucified God* p. 222. 'A God who cannot suffer is poorer than any man. For a God who is incapable of suffering is a being who cannot be involved. Suffering and injustice do not affect him. And because he is so completely insensitive, he cannot be affected or shaken by anything. He cannot weep, for he has no tears. But the one who cannot suffer cannot love either. So he is a loveless being. Aristotle's God cannot love, he can only be loved by all non-divine beings by virtue of his perfection and beauty, and in this way draw them to him. The "unmoved Mover" is a "loveless Beloved". If he is the ground of the love (eros) of all things for him (*causa prima*), and at the same time his own cause (*causa sui*) he is the beloved who is in love with himself; a Narcissus in a metaphysical degree: *Deus incurvatus in se*.'

[8] Moltmann emphasized this idea in his lectures on the doctrine of the Trinity,

Moltmann argues that such a concept of God gives rise to
protest atheism. First of all, because if God is absolute ruler and
possessor of all power 'there is no room for freedom, not even the
freedom of the children of God'. Secondly, such a conception of
God raises the question why guiltless children suffer and die.
Moltmann writes, 'If God is omnipotent, the misery of the earth
proves he is not good; or he is good, but then obviously not
omnipotent. The question of freedom and the outcry of suffering are the bases for every serious atheism which resists
banality.'[9]

The only way out of this impasse is to develop a specifically
Christian idea of God. The Christian idea of God confronts both
the monotheists and the atheists, since it follows from the
experience of the suffering of God in the cross of Christ. It is
Moltmann's conviction that an adequately developed theology
of the cross leads to a trinitarian theology. To show how this is
so will be the burden of this chapter.

Although we must come back to this point in greater detail
later, it is important to note here at the outset that history plays
a crucial role in this development. We have seen that the
context of Moltmann's thought is the suffering of the world.
Man finds himself over against a world which appears to him
godless and unredeemed. But an adequate anthropology
cannot content itself merely with these two terms, man and the
world, for precisely what mediates the relationship of man and
world, subject and cosmos, is history.[10] If then there is any
answer to the cry of man in the face of the unredeemed
character of the world, it must be found in history. And this is
precisely the key to the Christian understanding of God. The
Christian account of God has its origins in an historical event,
more precisely in the event of the cross. In this slice of history

Tübingen, Winter Semester, 1978. See, for example, 'Der Dreieinige Gott', p. 17
(unpublished lecture notes).

[9] Moltmann, *The Experiment Hope*, p. 50.

[10] See, for example, Jürgen Moltmann, *Religion, Revolution and the Future* (New York:
Charles Scribner's Sons, 1968), p. 206. 'Man and the world are mediated today in the
realm of history, and that means in social, political and technological history. Without
humanization of the world, man will not find his inner identity, and without a solution
to the identity crisis of modern man there is no imaginable solution to the social and
political crises of the world. The theodicy question and the identity question are two
sides of the same coin.'

God encounters man in his suffering and death, even in his God-forsakenness. Moltmann contends that when this history is adequately interpreted—and that means theologically interpreted—it is seen to be nothing less than the history of God himself. And in this historical event God shows himself to be the trinitarian God, i.e. this history is itself the event involving Father, Son, and Holy Spirit.

In summary, we can see that the way to a messianic dogmatics must be the way of history, and more precisely the way of the cross. This history is nothing less than the trinitarian history of God.[11] Moltmann's entire theological enterprise is an effort to work out the theological implications of this vision. In this chapter I intend to follow his effort, always keeping an eye on the central experience from which it arises, namely the suffering of the world and the goal toward which it moves, namely the liberation of man.[12]

## ii.   *Questions of Methodology*

Before turning to the experience of the cross which is the focal point for establishing Moltmann's trinitarian theology, we should briefly clarify a few methodological questions which indicate why Moltmann finds the cross the only adequate ground for faith in God today.

I have already mentioned that history is the mediating factor between man and the world. History turns out also to be the mediating factor between man and God. Moltmann rejects an existentialist interpretation of man according to which access to God can be found in the experience of human subjectivity. From the beginning of his career Moltmann has contended that

---

[11] In the Foreword to the tenth edition of *Theologie der Hoffnung* (München: Kaiser, 1977) Moltmann writes (p. 7): 'The *Theology of Hope* has led me to intensive work in developing a trinitarian conception of God, which has the suffering and the passion of the crucified God at its centre. With the new edition of this book I would like to point beyond this book in the direction of these movements.'

[12] See, for example, Jürgen Moltmann, *Im Gespräch mit Ernst Bloch, Eine Theologische Wegbegleitung* (München: Kaiser, 1976), p. 70. 'Faith or atheism is not the theoretical question whether or not there is a God, but the political question of the liberation to freedom.' Peter Momose in his study of Moltmann's theology of the cross also understands Moltmann's soteriology as a theology of liberation. He writes, 'According to Moltmann, contemporary man's expectation of salvation can be summarized in a word: the search for the liberation of man and for the righteousness of the world.' Peter F. Momose, *Kreuzestheologie, Eine Auseinandersetzung mit Jürgen Moltmann* (Freiburg: Herder, 1978), p. 114.

all such interpretations, which have found an important place in twentieth-century theology through the work of Bultmann, founder in the storm of suffering which human beings have inflicted on one another in this century. An anthropology which does not take into account Hiroshima and Auschwitz and an anthropology which does not provide the means whereby one can effectively protest against such barbarisms is decidely one-sided. There is no direct route from subjectivity to the transcendental ground of the self which is able to bypass the tragedies of human brutality.

For the same reason Moltmann rejects the classical cosmological proofs for God's existence. He contends that the difficulty in all such arguments lies not in the character of their reasoning but in their starting point. The world that we experience simply is not a cosmos but in large measure a chaos. In *The Crucified God*, Moltmann writes:

> The cosmological arguments for the existence of God presuppose a God who is indirectly evident and manifest through his works. Therefore they draw conclusions from *ea quae facta sunt* to the invisible being of God. This process of argument is not questionable in itself, but stringent; however, its presupposition, that everything that is corresponds to God and is connected with his being through an *analogia entis*, probably is.[13]

Moltmann argues that in fact atheists have taken theists too seriously. The atheist reasons correctly that if the world as we know it is a mediation of God's presence, then God must be a monster. Moltmann writes,

> Metaphysical atheism, too, takes the world as a mirror of the deity. But in the broken mirror of an unjust and absurd world of triumphant evil and suffering without reason and without end it does not see the countenance of a God, but only the grimace of absurdity and nothingness. Atheism, too, draws a conclusion from the existence of the finite world as it is to its cause and its destiny. But there it finds no good and righteous God, but a capricious demon, a blind destiny, a damning law or an annihilating nothingness.[14]

What conclusions does Moltmann draw from this situation? First of all, we must not say that Moltmann is hostile to philoso-

---

[13] Moltmann, *The Crucified God*, p. 210.
[14] Ibid., pp. 219–20.

phy. He rejects the Barthian tradition which sees philosophical theology only as human arrogance in the face of God's own proof of his existence and love. Hostility to philosophy can only lead theology into the ghetto.[15] Moltmann even goes so far as to accept what Vatican I taught about the capacity of man to attain the knowledge of God on the basis of the creation. Moltmann stresses, however, that the capacity to achieve such knowledge and the reality of attaining it are quite distinct. The real question, he asks, is where God can *de facto* be known. The only absolutely certain place where God can be recognized is in the cross.[16]

Moltmann advocates therefore not an analogical epistemology but a dialectical one. By this he means that we do not move from below to above, from partial likeness to the source of the likeness. Rather proceeding from the experience of the cross, we must suppose that God can be known and revealed in his contrary. If the cross is the epistemological criterion of truth, then we must say, 'So God is not known through his works in reality, but through his suffering in the passiveness of faith, which allows God to work on it: killing in order to make alive, judging in order to set free. So his knowledge is achieved not by the guiding thread of analogies from earth to heaven, but on the contrary, through contradiction, sorrow and suffering.'[17]

However, many difficulties lie hidden in this seemingly plausible account of God's revelation in his contrary. On the one hand, for example, Moltmann is fond of quoting 2 Tim 2:13, 'God remains faithful, for he cannot deny himself.'[18] On the

---

[15] In *The Future of Creation* (p. 35) Moltmann writes, 'Christianity has to talk and think under the conditions of mission. It has no language and no theological way of thinking of its own. Consequently it has to talk in the sphere of contemporary philosophy, even though it is not under the pressure of that sphere's own particular structure. If this is not the case Christianity arrives at a kind of linguistic isolation which cuts it off from solidarity with its companions in time and in suffering.'

[16] In response to the critique of the Catholic theologian Peter Momose, Moltmannn writes, 'The thesis that "God, the origin and goal of all things, *can* be recognized with certainty with the help of the natural light of human reason from created realities" (Vatican I) does not say very much, if it is not also said with certainty, where, how and through what God *is* also *de facto* recognized. Here also, it seems to me, following the *ratio cognescendi*, one should proceed from the reality of the knowledge of God by faith in the crucified Christ, in order then to investigate the natural possibilities of the natural knowledge of God and their transcendental conditions.' Momose, op. cit., p. 179.

[17] Moltmann, *The Crucified God*, p. 212.

[18] See, for example, Moltmann, 'Antwort' in *Diskussion über Jürgen Moltmanns Buch 'Der Gekreuzigte Gott'*, p. 171.

other hand, he can quote Schelling with approval, ' "Every being can be revealed only in its opposite. Love only in hatred, unity only in conflict." Applied to Christian theology, this means that God is only revealed as "God" in his opposite: godlessness and abandonment by God.'[19] Do we have here an inconsistent epistemology? Walter Kasper speaks in this respect of a 'lack of precision'.[20] Richard Bauckham comments.

If it should mean that God is the opposite of that which reveals him, it is difficult to understand how revelation can ever take place at all. To take only one of the examples of Schelling which are cited by Moltmann: how can love be revealed only in hate? The example is appropriate, because Moltmann believes, that God is 'himself love in his entire Being'. The expression that love is revealed only in hate' cannot mean that hate is a revelation of the love of God. It must mean that love is revealed only *in the context* of hate.[21]

In spite of the imprecision of this dialectical principle of understanding, the general thrust of what Moltmann wants to say is clear, namely that the criterion for knowledge of God is the cross of Christ. Moltmann writes, 'In concrete terms, God is revealed in the cross of Christ who was abandoned by God.'[22] This theology then attempts to be a biblically-grounded theology in so far as it brings no independent philosophical presuppositions or ontological preconceptions to interpret the biblical revelation. It attempts to let the biblical revelation create its own ontology.[23]

[19] Moltmann, *The Crucified God*, p. 27.
[20] Walter Kasper, 'Revolution im Gottesverständnis? Zur Situation des ökumenischen Dialogs nach Jürgen Moltmanns *Der Gekreuzigte Gott*', in *Diskussion über Jürgen Moltmanns Buch 'Der Gekreuzigte Gott'*, p. 144.
[21] Richard Bauckham, 'Moltmanns Eschatologie des Kreuzes', ibid., p. 47.
[22] Moltmann, *The Crucified God*, p. 27.
[23] See, for example, Moltmann, *Theology of Hope*, p. 95. 'If we would trace out the Old Testament's peculiarly ambiguous, unemphatic and yet widely broadcast observations on "revelation" and turn them to good account for dogmatics, then it is not advisable to set out from the assumption that every man's existence, threatened as it is by chaos and transience, leads him to ask after "revelation", nor yet to start with the question how the hidden God, the Origin and the Absolute, becomes manifest to men estranged from him. Rather, it is essential to let the Old Testament itself not only provide the answers, but also pose the problem of revelation, before we draw systematic conclusions. If this is to be attempted in the following pages, it is of course impossible to enter into questions of detailed exegesis. But it will have to be a case of clarifying and defining the concepts employed in exegesis. In doing so we shall often come upon religious-historical ideas, and shall also have to employ such ideas. That, however, is not intended to imply any general religious-historical presuppositions.'

On the other hand, Moltmann wants to make it clear that his rejection of natural theology does not mean an ultimate and insuperable hostility between philosophy and theology. For this reason he does not see the Catholic emphasis on analogy and the Protestant emphasis on the cross as ultimately opposed. He argues rather that a dialectical epistemology works in the service of an analogical one. In replying to Kasper's critique, he writes, 'According to my understanding of the matter, the *theology of the cross* should not replace the *theology of analogy* but should rather make it possible without leading to illusionary points of view.'[24] This implies as a final consequence, that natural theology will be possible ultimately only in the eschaton, when God will be all in all, and when the world will correspond to God's purposes for his creation.

iii.   *The Cross as the Foundation of the Christian Doctrine of God*

We have already noted that the cross is the decisive epistemological criterion for our knowledge of God. Moltmann is so insistent on this point that he claims the cross is either the end of all theology or the beginning of specifically Christian theology. He writes, 'Either Jesus who was abandoned by God is the end of all theology or he is the beginning of a specifically Christian and therefore critical and liberating, theology and life.'[25] Let us look a little more closely at the two poles of this disjunction. First, the cross could mean the death of God or atheism. Jesus preached a message of the coming kingdom of God. He preached a God whom he called Father, a God with whom one could live in the most intimate union. Moreover, he linked this gospel to his own person. The kingdom of God was breaking into history in his preaching, miracles, and symbolic actions such as eating with tax-collectors and sinners. Yet it is this Jesus who dies in utter abandonment by the Father. Jesus dies with the desperate cry, 'My God, my God, why have you abandoned me?'[26] If there is no more to the end of Jesus than

---

[24] Jürgen Moltmann, 'Dialektik, die umschlägt in Identität—was ist das?, Zu Befürchtungen Walter Kaspers', in *Diskussion über Jürgen Moltmanns Buch 'Der Gekreuzigte Gott'*, p. 152.

[25] Moltmann, *The Crucified God*, p. 4. See also ibid., p. 153.

[26] Although this cry of Jesus is taken from Psalm 22, Moltmann insists that we must interpret the psalm in terms of the God-forsakenness of Jesus upon the cross and not vice versa. See *The Crucified God*, p. 150.

this abandonment on the cross, then atheism is the only authentic response to the suffering of the world. Since the cause of Jesus is so linked to his person, he must either transcend the death on the cross, or his cause must perish with his death. The other term of this disjunction says that the cross is the beginning of a specifically Christian theology. Moltmann understands specifically Christian theology to be trinitarian theology as opposed to the classical philosophical theism which we have described above. According to classical philosophical theism God cannot suffer. According to Christian faith, Jesus, true God and true man, suffered and died on the cross. Moltmann believes one is forced either to abandon the classical philosophical theistic account of God or to abandon the event of the cross, as decisive for our knowledge of God. Moltmann explains,

If God is an indivisible, eternal subject, then he can only be either dead or not dead, and because his immortality belongs to his unity and eternity, he cannot be dead. The Christian assertion about the crucified Son of God presupposes a self-differentiation in God: the incarnate Son of God has died for us; but God, the eternal Father of Jesus Christ, has not. The unity in this self-differentiation of God, which encompasses death as well, lies in the Holy Spirit, in whom occurs the surrender of the Son to death and through death his resurrection to glory. The one divine life cannot be completed only by one subject or one person. Only the doctrine of the tri-unity of God is in the position to perceive the enormous contradiction of the cross and to integrate it into the infinite life of God.[27]

The event of the cross cannot then be understood either in an atheistic sense or in a theistic sense, but only in a specifically Christian sense, that is, as a trinitarian event. The central concept which Moltmann employs to interpret the event of the cross is the biblical idea *paradidonai*, in German *Dahingabe*, in English 'deliver up'.[28] In the event of the cross Moltmann sees a double *paradidonai*. First of all, the Father delivers up the Son. Moltmann explains the full import of this action by citing the

[27] Moltmann, 'Antwort', in *Diskussion über Jürgen Moltmanns Buch 'Der Gekreuzigte Gott'*, p. 175.
[28] Critical biblical texts for supporting Moltmann's position are Rom. 8:32; Gal. 2:20. 'He who did not spare his own Son but gave him up for us all, will he not also give us all things with him?' 'The life I now live in the flesh I live by faith in the Son of God, who loved me and gave himself for me.'

study of W. Popkes on the meaning of *paradidonai* in the New Testament. Popkes explains,

That God delivers up his Son is one of the most unheard-of statements in the New Testament. We must understand 'deliver up' in its full sense and not water it down to mean 'send' or 'give'. What happened here is what Abraham did not need to do to Isaac (cf. Rom. 8:32): Christ was quite deliberately abandoned by the Father to the fate of death: God subjected him to the power of corruption, whether this be called man or death. To express the idea in its most acute form, one might say in the words of the dogma of the early church: the first person of the Trinity casts out and annihilates the second. . . . A theology of the cross cannot be expressed more radically than it is here.[29]

Such an interpretation of the Father's action would be one-sided without the corresponding *paradidonai* of the Son. Moltmann writes,

In Gal. 2:20 the 'delivering up' formula also occurs with Christ as its subject: '. . . the Son of God, who loved me and gave himself for me'. According to this it is not just the Father who delivers Jesus up to die godforsaken on the cross, but the Son who gives himself up. This corresponds to the synoptic account of the passion story according to which Jesus consciously and willingly walked the way of the cross and was not overtaken by death as by an evil, unfortunate fate. It is theologically important to note that the formula in Paul occurs with both Father and Son as subject, since it expresses a deep conformity between the will of the Father and the will of the Son in the event of the cross, as the Gethsemane narrative also records. This deep community of will between Jesus and his God and Father is now expressed precisely at the point of their deepest separation, in the godforsaken and accursed death of Jesus on the cross. If both historical godforsakenness and eschatological surrender can be seen in Christ's death on the cross, then this event contains community between Jesus and his Father in separation, and separation in community.[30]

We can further say that this communion in separation is precisely what we mean by the Holy Spirit. Moltmann writes 'What proceeds from this event between Father and Son is the

[29] W. Popkes, *Christus Traditus: Eine Untersuchung zum Begriff der Dahingabe im Neuen Testament*, 1967, p. 286 f., as cited in *The Crucified God*, p. 241.
[30] Moltmann, *The Crucified God*, pp. 243–4.

Spirit which justifies the godless, fills the forsaken with love and
even brings the dead alive, since even the fact that they are dead
cannot exclude them from this event of the cross; the death in
God also includes them.'³¹ Thus far we have spoken of a double 'delivering up'. The
Father delivers up the Son and the Son delivers up himself in
obedience to the Father's will. The roles of the Father and the
Son, however, cannot be understood simply in an active sense.
The action of the Son, for example, is clearly also a passion. His
active obedience consists in his acceptance of his abandonment.
But it is equally true that the Father's role involves a passion,
namely the suffering of the death of his only Son. In affirming
the suffering of the Father, Moltmann is breaking new ground
in theology, taking a position not previously acknowledged
either in the patristic period or even in modern theology. Thus,
for example, even Karl Barth, who had no hesitation in breaking
with classical theism in order to adhere consistently to the event
of the cross, did not take the additional step of affirming that
God the Father actually 'suffered' the death of his only Son.
Moltmann criticizes Barth in this respect, maintaining that his
thought is still too theistic and not sufficiently trinitarian.³²
Moltmann argues that we must press the question: what
meaning has the death of the Son for the Father? Unless we are
willing to say that it has no meaning, then we must say the
Father suffers the death of his Son. The logical consequence of

³¹ Ibid., p. 244.
³² See Moltmann, *The Future of Creation*, pp. 63–4. Speaking of Barth's theology of the
cross, he writes, 'God's being is found in the history of the humiliation of the Son of God
and in the exaltation of the Son of Man. Consequently we find in Barth many "theopaschite" statements about God's suffering and involvement in the cross of Christ.'
Yet these too stand in the framework of the doctrine of election and reconciliation, i.e. in
a soteriological context. Barth has really "etched the harshness of the cross into the
concept of God" thereby deepening Luther's theology of the cross, not merely criti-
cizing it. In my view Barth's limitations lie, strangely enough, in the fact that at these
points he does not argue expressly enough in *trinitarian* terms. Because he always
stresses—and rightly so—that *God* was in Christ, *God* lowered himself, *God himself*
wanted to be the loser on the cross so that man might be the gainer, he uses the simple
concept of God in considering miserable and reconciled man, not yet a concept
developed in trinitarian terms. That is why Barth, rather like Rahner, has to distinguish the God who in his primal decision proceeds from himself, from the God who is
previously in himself "untouched by evil and death". This certainly makes it possible
for us to conceive the very being of God as being present in the death of Jesus; but the
converse is difficult; how can we conceive of Jesus' death on the cross as belonging
within the being of God?'

this position is panentheism, that is, the doctrine that God is not only in suffering but suffering is in God. Moltmann writes,

A trinitarian theology of the cross perceives God in the negative element and therefore the negative element in God, and in this dialectical way is panentheistic. For in the hidden mode of humiliation to the point of the cross, all being and all that annihilates has already been taken up in God and God begins to become 'all in all'. To recognize God in the cross of Christ, conversely, means to recognize the cross, inextricable suffering, death and hopeless rejection in God.[33]

In this section we have tried to show that one can interpret the event of the cross adequately only when one interprets it in trinitarian terms. Because of the crucifixion of Jesus of Nazareth, the world finds itself in a totally new God-situation. The theological expression of this new God-situation is the doctrine of the Trinity. The doctrine of the Trinity is therefore not an arcane mystery or a piece of idle speculation. Far from being a Platonic idea that hangs suspended above the world of space and time, it is anchored in the hard-rock historical event of Golgotha. The hermeneutical principle, therefore, which guides Moltmann's thinking is the following: 'The content of the doctrine of the Trinity is the real cross of Christ himself. The form of the crucified Christ is the Trinity.'[34]

### iv.  The Role of the Holy Spirit

In his first two major books, Moltmann stressed the dialectic of cross and resurrection. This dialectic can be expressed in the correlative expressions: the resurrection of the crucified Christ and the cross of the risen Jesus. Especially in *Theology of Hope* Moltmann dwelt upon the promise contained in the event of the resurrection. The meaning of resurrection is the promise of the future of Christ, his parousia, which is the absolute future of the

[33] Moltmann, *The Crucified God*, p. 277. See also Moltmann, 'Antwort', in *Diskussion über Jürgen Moltmanns Buch 'Der Gekreuzigte Gott'*, pp. 187–8 Moltmann writes, 'As to the activity of God, one asks: what do the surrender of Christ, his suffering and his dying mean for us? But if there lies in this activity a reciprocal relation, then one must also inquire the other way round: what does the cross of Christ mean for God? Only if one had assumed that God is incapable of any receptivity, because he is the mere causality for everything else, does this question seem meaningless or speculative. It is no different with the assertions: God suffers—suffering is in God.'
[34] Moltmann, *The Crucified God*, p. 246.

world. This promise in fact sets history in motion. The resurrection of Jesus of Nazareth is not an historical event (in the sense understood by the empirical science of history) but rather a real history-making event. Thus, for example, in the introduction to *Theology of Hope*, Moltmann writes,

The present of the coming parousia of God and of Christ in the promises of the gospel of the crucified does not translate us out of time, nor does it bring time to a standstill, but it opens the way for time and sets history in motion, for it does not tone down the pain caused us by the non-existent, but means the adoption and acceptance of the non-existent in memory and hope.[35]

In his later writings Moltmann specifies this history created by the promise as the presence of the Holy Spirit. Thus, for example, in the third book of his trilogy, his study of the church, Moltmann writes,

Pneumatology is developed historically and eschatologically, in the sense that the history of the church, the communion of saints and the forgiveness of sins are to be interpreted as the history of the future; while the eschatology of the resurrection of the body and life everlasting are to be seen as the future of history. That is why we understand this mediation of eschatology and history as the presence of the Holy Spirit.[36]

This development in Moltmann's thought is a welcome one, for it gives greater balance to the one-sided emphasis in *Theology of Hope* on the God whose mode of being is future.[37] Critics of this early work objected that Moltmann had evacuated history of God's presence.[38] But in his later works Moltmann clearly indicates that one of the central functions of the Holy Spirit is to

---

[35] Moltmann, *Theology of Hope*, p. 31.

[36] Moltmann, *The Church in the Power of the Spirit*, p. 198.

[37] Thus, for example, in *Theology of Hope*, Moltmann writes, 'The God spoken of here is no intra-worldy or extra-worldy God, but the "God of hope" (Rom. 15:13), a God with "future" as his essential nature (as E. Bloch puts it), as made known in Exodus and in Israelite prophecy, the God whom we therefore cannot really have in us or over us but always only before us, who encounters us in his promises for the future, and whom we therefore cannot "have" either, but can only await in active hope.' p. 16. See also ibid., p. 141.

[38] Among others see the critique by Langdon Gilkey, 'The Universal and Immediate Presence of God', and John Macquarrie, 'Eschatology and Time', in Jürgen Moltmann' and Frederick Herzog, *The Future of Hope: Theology as Eschatology* (New York: Herder and Herder, 1970), pp. 81–109; 110–25.

create anticipations of the fullness of God's presence in the kingdom. Moltmann writes,

It is possible to see this real presence of God, pointing beyond itself, as the history of the Shekinah wandering through the dust, as the history of the spirit which comes upon all flesh. We understand it here in the process of the trinitarian history of God. Thus the real presences of God acquire the character of a '*praesentia explosiva*'. Brotherhood with Christ means the suffering and active participation in the history of this God. Its criterion is the history of the crucified and risen Christ. Its power is the sighing and liberating spirit of God. Its consummation lies in the kingdom of the triune God which sets all things free and fills them with meaning.[39]

What then are these anticipations? Certainly they are to be found in the preaching of the gospel, in the fellowship of the Christian community, in the celebrations of baptism and eucharist. But we cannot limit the presence of the Holy Spirit to such experiences. That would be too narrow and parochial an understanding of the working of the Holy Spirit in the world.

The presence of the Holy Spirit can also be found wherever men and women receive the power to enter into the struggle for the liberation of God's creation, for justice among men, and for the freedom of mankind. The Holy Spirit is precisely the presence of this power of liberation. These anticipations of the kingdom of God are experienced in a special way in the power of resistance against the forces which bind mankind in various forms of slavery. The present experience of the world is the experience of the lack of freedom. The Holy Spirit on the other hand as the power of the future, as the power of the risen Christ, empowers persons to resist the given reality of the present and create anticipations of the freedom to come in all the multi-faceted dimensions of life. These anticipations must be created not only in the specifically religious dimension of life but in all other dimensions as well, in the realm of economics, politics, psychology, culture, even in the realm of man's relation to nature.

Thus the two key words for understanding the working of the Holy Spirit are anticipation and resistance. These two categories represent the two sides of the dialectic of cross and resurrection. The Holy Spirit is the anticipation of the future of

---

[39] Moltmann, *The Crucified God*, p. 338.

the risen Jesus. But this Jesus is also the crucified one. The Holy
Spirit is poured out from the side of the crucified Christ.
Therefore a powerful sign of the presence of the Holy Spirit is
resistance against the power of the realities that enslave man.
Moltmann insists that the remembrance of the crucified
Christ saves the church from succumbing to an exaggerated
enthusiasm of the Spirit. The criteria of the presence of the
Spirit cannot, therefore, be ecstasies, tongues, or mystical
flights of prayer. Since Christ died as one condemned by the
Jewish law, executed as a political threat and abandoned by the
God he called Father, the Spirit which he poured out must
always seek out the hopeless, the abandoned, and the Godforsaken of the earth. The real sign of the Holy Spirit in history
is this solidarity with the hopeless.[40]
We said that the resurrection of Jesus Christ contains a
promise which creates history. We said furthermore that this
history itself is the presence of the Holy Spirit. The man who is
caught up in this history is enabled to resist the powers of
bondage by actively taking upon himself the suffering of others.
By making a play on the Latin words, Moltmann can say that
the *pro-missio* of the kingdom contained in the resurrection
grounds the *missio* of the believer to the world, which is the work
of the Holy Spirit.[41] 'Thus the Spirit is the power to suffer in
participation in the mission and the love of Jesus Christ, and is
in this suffering the passion for what is possible, for what is

---

[40] Thus, for example, in *The Future of Creation (pp.* 53–4) Moltmann explains, 'The
notion of anticipation, through which here the future of God and the history of the
world are christologically mediated, remains vague and can lead us into illusion if we
do not say clearly enough where this divine anticipation of the future has taken place
and takes place. Here we shall have to turn back to a theology of the cross, away from
the "theology of hope" which understands the resurrection of Christ in its significance
for world history with the help of the idea of anticipation. The anticipation of the
coming kingdom of God has taken place in history in the crucified Jesus of Nazareth.
    What does that mean? It means . . . that it is manifest in the crucified Christ how the
future of God, and the future of freedom and righteousness, are mediated in this history
of ours; namely, through the representative suffering of Jesus Christ and, following
upon that, action in solidarity with those who suffer. The form which the anticipation of
the resurrection has permanently worn, through the crucified Christ, is his being
representative, his suffering and dying "for others". We do not need to go here into the
different ideas about Jesus Christ's "existence for others". What is important is to see
that the anticipation of Christian hope is living and effective only in representing those
who have no future. Hope is given us for the sake of the hopeless (W. Benjamin).'
[41] See Moltmann, *Theology of Hope*, p. 224.

coming and promised in the future of life, of freedom and of resurrection.'[42]

### v.   *Immanent and Economic Trinity*

In the classical Christian tradition theologians distinguished between the economic and the immanent Trinity, between the being of God for us and the being of God in himself. One can easily recognize the soteriological motives which lay behind such thinking. Only God has the power to save us. Therefore the believer wants the certainty that in the history of Jesus of Nazareth and in his presence in the church through the Holy Spirit one really has contact with God himself.

Yet theologians today have become ever more hesistant in their affirmations about the immanent Trinity. Several reasons have given rise to this reluctance. First of all, we have become more conscious of the limitations of human knowledge. Kant, for example, taught that we can know only how a thing appears in consciousness; what a thing is in itself, apart from consciousness, remains in principle unknowable. The question thus arises whether one can know anything about God apart from his revelation.

Even if we can say something about God's being in himself, there is the danger that we will be so carried away by our own speculations about the inner life of God that the doctrine of the Trinity becomes divorced from the concrete history of salvation. The doctrine then seems to have no relevance for the ordinary Christian, but rather appears reserved for the more subtle speculations of the theologian.

Another major difficulty which appears in regard to the doctrine of the immanent Trinity is the problem of dualism. The doctrine of the immanent Trinity has traditionally been linked to the problem of grace and the freedom of God. In order to safeguard the divine freedom and the totally free and undeserved gift of his grace, theologians have argued that God in himself has such a fullness of life that he could have refrained from creating the world and from offering himself as gift to that creation without diminishing his own happiness. God has concretely chosen to be a God of men but he could equally well

---

[42] Ibid., p. 212.

THE TRINITARIAN HISTORY OF GOD    125

have chosen otherwise. Such is the position of such modern theologians as Karl Barth and Karl Rahner.

This position, while correctly seeing the need to affirm the grace character of salvation, is involved in serious difficulties. For it is questionable whether we can affirm that God is essentially love, if he stands before a real either–or choice to create and redeem. Such a concept of God also lies at the base of various forms of modern protest atheism. Ernst Bloch, for example, finds the concept of God alienating precisely because God is 'an Above, where no man exists'.[43]

In the face of these problems, Moltmann develops the following doctrine of the immanent Trinity.[44] First of all, to meet the well-founded soteriological concern that in the cross of Christ God himself has acted, he affirms the intent of the hermeneutical principle of Karl Rahner, namely that the economic Trinity is the immanent Trinity. Thus, as we have seen, trinitarian thinking is not a type of divine geometry but rather the fullest and most adequate interpretation of the paschal mystery.

Secondly, in order to do away with any traces of dualism and in order to take the biblical affirmation 'God is love' as radically as possible, he abandons the whole scheme of economic and immanent Trinity and replaces it with the distinction between the 'Trinity in sending' and the 'Trinity in origin'. Moltmann writes,

As God appears in history as the sending Father and the sent Son, so he must earlier have been in himself. The relation of the one who sends to the one sent as it appears in the history of Jesus thus includes in itself an order of origin within the Trinity, and must be understood as that order's historical correspondence. Otherwise there would be no certainty that in the messianic message of Jesus we have to do with God himself.[45]

Moltmann makes an analogous reflection about the role of the Spirit. He writes,

[43] Eberhard Jüngel discusses the objection of Bloch in relation to the trinitarian theology of Barth in his essay 'Keine Menschlosigkeit Gottes, Zur Theologie Karl Barths zwischen Theismus und Atheismus', *Evangelische Theologie* 31 (1971) 376–90.

[44] See Jürgen Moltmann, *The Trinity and the Kingdom of God* (London: SCM Press, 1981), pp. 158–61.

[45] Moltmann, *The Church in the Power of the Spirit*, p. 54.

The same reasons which led from the concept of the history of Christ in the light of his sending to the eternal generation of the Son by the Father within the Trinity, lead here from the experience of the Spirit in the light of his divine sending to his eternal procession within the Trinity, from the Father, or from the Father and the Son. If this were not so, experience of the Spirit could not be termed experience of God; and fellowship with Jesus, the Son, and his Father could not be understood as fellowship with God.[46]

In replacing the scheme of economic and immanent Trinity with that of Trinity in sending and Trinity in origin, Moltmann hopes that he has avoided the cul-de-sac of a capricious God who creates and redeems merely by fiat. For according to this new model the Trinity is essentially an open mystery. From all eternity God is oriented outward. His inner life is itself open to creation and history. This in effect means that there is no possibility of a God who is 'an Above, where no man exists'. As Moltmann writes, 'The life of God within the Trinity cannot be conceived of as a closed circle — the symbol of perfection and self-sufficiency. A Christian doctrine of the Trinity which is bound to the history of Christ and the history of the Spirit must conceive the Trinity as the Trinity of the sending and seeking love of God which is open from its very origin. The triune God is the God who is open to man, open to the world and open to time.'[47]

Moltmann's account of the immanent Trinity makes minimal assertions about God in himself, but all that he says he can anchor firmly in the experience of salvation history. Therefore he is able to avoid a serious danger which he believes threatens to corrupt the Christian doctrine of God.

This danger arises from the influence of idealistic philosophy upon Christian theology. In modern theology, especially under the influence of Hegel, reality is understood to be spirit or subjectivity. Modern Christian theology has often appropriated this idea by regarding God as the absolute Subject. Distinctions within God are then seen to be necessary, for if God is an undifferentiated monad, he cannot go out of himself and yet remain himself. Under the influence of this type of thinking, the key to the doctrine of the Trinity is God's desire to share

[46] Ibid., p. 55.
[47] Ibid., pp. 55–6.

himself. Moltmann argues that the fundamental thrust of this whole approach to the doctrine of the Trinity is incorrect and leads to a concealed form of monotheism which is incompatible with the Christian faith. God is not a subject who wants to share himself. If we think in biblical terms, we must rather speak of the Father who wants to give us his Son.

Moltmann contends that when the doctrine of the Trinity is conceived within the perspective of a philosophy of absolute subjectivity, it degenerates into a modern form of modalism. He finds this tendency especially in the two most significant contemporary attempts to interpret the doctrine of the Trinity, namely those of Karl Barth and Karl Rahner.

In discussing the trinitarian theology of Barth, Moltmann points out that, given the modern bourgeois concept of personality, it is understandable that Barth would want to replace the ancient formulation *una substantia—tres personae* with the alternative expression, one subject—three modes of being. Nevertheless Moltmann contends that

viewed theologically, this is a late triumph for the Sabellian modalism which the early church condemned. The result would be to transfer the subjectivity of action to a deity concealed 'behind' the three persons. And the consequences of this would be a monotheism only fortuitously connected with Christianity in any way, a general transcendentality and a vague human religiosity which would simply swallow up the particular identity of the Christian faith.[48]

Moltmann makes the same critique of Rahner's trinitarian model, according to which the Father gives himself in absolute self-communication through the Son in the Holy Spirit. Moltmann writes,

It becomes clear that Rahner transforms the classicial doctrine of the Trinity into the reflection trinity of the absolute subject; and the way he does this is plain too. The 'self-communication' of the Absolute has that differentiated structure which seems so similar to the Christian doctrine of the Trinity. But in fact it makes the doctrine of the Trinity superfluous. The fact that God gives us himself in absolute self-communication *can* be associated with Father, Son and Spirit but it does not have to be. On the other hand what is stated biblically with the history of the Father, the Son and the Spirit is only vaguely paraphrased by the concept of God's self-communication.[49]

[48] Moltmann, *The Trinity and the Kingdom of God*, p. 139.
[49] Ibid., p. 147.

Moltmann argues on the contrary that in thinking through the doctrine of the Trinity it is critical to note that the relation of each person to the other persons of the Trinity is unique. One cannot employ a general concept of person and apply it univocally to Father, Son, and Spirit. A concrete instance would be, for example, the problem of the processions. We cannot treat the procession of the Son and the procession of the Spirit in an univocal fashion. Each procession is unique and cannot be subsumed under the general concept 'procession'. Moltmann summarizes his position in these words:

We have to conclude that no summing up, generic terms must be used at all in the doctrine of the Trinity. For in the life of the immanent Trinity everything is unique. It is only because everything in God's nature is unique that in the ways and works of God it can be recognized as the origin of other things. In considering the doctrine of the immanent Trinity, we can really only tell, relate, but not sum up. We have to remain concrete, for history shows us that it is in the abstractions that the heresies are hidden.[50]

### vi.  *The Filioque Controversy*

Having clarified Moltmann's position on the immanent Trinity, and having examined his understanding of the relations of the divine 'persons', we can explain briefly Moltmann's understanding of the relation of the Holy Spirit to the Son and to the Father. This issue is important for Moltmann not only for its own sake but also because of its relevance in the ongoing ecumenical dialogue.

Moltmann's initial reflection on this problem is the historical one that the 'filioque' clause in the Creed is a later addition to the Nicene-Constantinopolitan text of 381. The Fathers of the Council stressed the divinity of the Spirit without giving a theological interpretation of the relation of the Son and the Spirit. Moltmann argues then that it would be best to return to the original version of the text and to understand the 'filioque' as a later interpretation of this original text.

We are then left with two theological problems. First, the question of the procession of the Spirit. Does the Holy Spirit proceed from the Father alone or from the Father and the Son? Secondly, there is the problem of the relation of the Son to the Spirit.

[50] Ibid., p. 190.

In answering the first question, Moltmann reminds us that the Greek term *hypostasis* indicates the principle of independent existence. The question of the procession of the Spirit is therefore really the question of the Spirit's divine existence. Moltmann then argues that there is only one source of existence in God and that is God the Father. The Father's identity as sole source of origin and rule in the Trinity, which is so important in Eastern theology and which has never really been disputed in the West, leads to the conclusion that in regard to the divine existence the Holy Spirit proceeds from the Father alone. To this extent Moltmann believes that the position of the Orthodox Church has been substantially correct.

At the same time it would be an error to regard the Son as a stranger to the procession of the Holy Spirit. This is clear from the fact that the Father is always the Father of the Son. The Father has never been without the Son. Therefore the breathing of the Holy Spirit presupposes the existence of the Son. In regard to the procession of the Holy Spirit, then, Moltmann suggests that we speak of 'the Holy Spirit who proceeds from the Father of the Son'.

We come then to the further question of the relation of the Holy Spirit to the Son. Moltmann suggests that if the Holy Spirit receives his divine existence from the Father, he receives his form (*Gestalt*) from the Son. Moltmann is here developing an idea which he takes up from the Greek Father Epiphanius. According to Epiphanius the Holy Spirit proceeds from the Father and receives from the Son. Moltmann asks what the Holy Spirit receives from the Son. He argues that it cannot be his *hypostasis*, but rather it must be his *prosopon*, that is, his face (*Gesicht*) or his form (*Gestalt*). Moltmann writes, 'When we talk about the *form* of the Holy Spirit, we mean his face as it is manifested in his turning to the Father and to the Son, and in the turning of the Father and the Son to him. It is the Holy Spirit in the inner manifestation of glory.'[51]

Moltmann concludes that in the Filioque controversy both the Eastern church and the Western church had valid insights into the doctrine of the Trinity. In protesting against the Filioque clause the East rightly emphasized that the Father is

[51] Ibid., p. 187.

the sole cause of all relations in the Godhead. The West on the other hand correctly perceived that the Holy Spirit is always linked to the Son. Without this link between pneumatology and christology, the church is threatened by the excesses of misguided pentecostal enthusiasm. Moltmann tries to strike a balance. The Holy Spirit who was poured out upon the church on Pentecost is none other than the Spirit who was given on the cross of Calvary, i.e. the Spirit who proceeds from the Father *of* the Son and who receives his form from the Father *and* the Son.

### vii.   *God's Being is in His History*

We have already observed that in the course of Moltmann's development, history has always played a central and decisive role. We have also noted that a shift of emphasis has taken place from the early period of *Theology of Hope* to the later works *The Crucified God* and *The Church in the Power of the Spirit*. In the early period Moltmann emphasized revelation as promise. The resurrection of Christ is not an historical event in the empirically-verifiable sense, but it is a real event, in fact the eschatological event which sets history in motion. In the later period Moltmann speaks of history itself as God's own history. The real historical event of the cross is a trinitarian event, involving Father, Son, and Spirit. Moltmann thus speaks of the trinitarian history of God.

I would like to elucidate this point in more detail, for it touches the heart of our general problematic, namely the relation of God to temporality and becoming, and it shows the radicality and originality of Moltmann's thought over against the tradition and other contemporary philosophical and theological positions.

First, as to the radicality of Moltmann's position. We have already seen that Moltmann wants to do away altogether with the schema of economic–immanent Trinity. This means that it is impossible to conceive of God apart from his history. For Moltmann God is literally unthinkable apart from his relationship to his creation. Rather than speak of God as he is in himself and God as he is for us, we must speak of God in history and history in God. This implies that theology is ultimately not a speculative science but a narrative one, for history cannot be the product of pure reason. Moltmann thus draws the conclusion:

Whoever wants to speak about God in a Christian way must narrate and proclaim the history of Jesus as the history of God, i.e. as the history between the Father, the Son, and the Spirit, from which is constituted who God is; and this, to be sure, not only for men but also already in his existence itself. That means, on the other hand, that God's being is historical and indeed exists in this concrete history. 'God's history' is then the history of the history of man.[52]

He explains further what he means when he says, 'By "God" is not meant the "one divine nature" of the three persons nor is meant the one absolute subjectivity nor the Lord of one world monarchy, but rather that "history" of the Trinity which is open to the world and which redeems and unifies all that is.'[53]

Does this imply that God becomes, that God is in the process of realizing himself? Moltmann wishes to face this question squarely but he believes that an adequate answer can be offered only by making necessary distinctions.

First of all, over against the tradition, Moltmann argues that God does become in the sense that he is literally affected by the history of his creation. Through his history God acquires something new. He writes,

The incarnation of the Son therefore brings about something 'new' even within the Trinity, for God himself. After the Son's return the relationship between the Father and the Son is no longer entirely the same. The Father has become different through his surrender of the Son, and the Son too has become different through the experience of his passion in the world.[54]

Furthermore, the work of the Son is not yet complete. His mission will not be fulfilled until he hands over the kingdom to the Father. In this final act of obedience there will come to completion God's plan for his creation. This new creation is not merely a return to the beginning. It actually brings something new, both for the world and for God. Moltmann writes, 'The conception of the restoration of the old creation or the return of history to its point of origin is not depictable in the images of the new creation. Omega is more than alpha.'[55]

52 Moltmann, 'Der Gekreuzigte Gott, neuzeitliche Gottesfrage und trinitarische Gottesgeschichte', p. 412.
53 Moltmann, 'Das Neue Testament als Zeugnis der trinitarischen Geschichte Gottes', unpublished lecture notes, Tübingen, Winter Semester, 1978, p. 4.
54 Moltmann, The Future of Creation, p. 93.
55 Moltmann, Religion, Revolution and the Future, p. 36.

While willing to affirm that God becomes in the sense that he acquires something new in his ongoing relation to the world, Moltmann wishes to distinguish his position from that of the American process philosophers as well as from that of Ernst Bloch. Moltmann understands these philosophers as affirming that God's actual concreteness is inseparable from the process of the world's becoming.[56] Moltmann rejects all such philosophies as compromising the divine transcendence. He never surrenders his epistemological starting point, namely the cross and resurrection of Christ. On the basis of the resurrection one must believe in the God who can create out of nothing and raise the dead, the God who calls into existence the things that do not exist (Rom. 4:17). Moltmann writes,

God's being does not lie in the process of the world's becoming, so that he would be the unifiying goal of all tendencies and intentions of the transient things: *finis ultimus, point Omega.* God's being is coming. He is not a 'God with *futurum* as mode of being' (Bloch) but with the *Zukunft* (future) as his mode to act upon the present and the past.[57]

Finally then the question must be posed whether God needs the world. If it is impossible to think of God apart from his history, if this history actually brings something new for God, does God then stand in need of this creation in order to fulfil himself? If God and history are correlative terms, has Moltmann after all surrendered the divine transcendence, so that God becomes an Hegelian Absolute Spirit realizing itself

[56] In *Umkehr zur Zukunft* (pp. 156–7) Moltmann writes, 'So far as I see, process theology speaks of a "becoming God" in the perspective of the dynamic of world process. Eschatological theology, on the other hand, speaks of the "coming God" in the perspective of that dialectical dynamic which is designated by the symbols: creation out of nothing (*creatio ex nihilo*), justification of the godless (*justificatio impii*) and resurrection of the dead (*resurrectio mortuorum*).'

[57] Moltmann, 'Theology as Eschatology', in *The Future of Hope*, p. 13. Presupposed here is the distinction between *futurum* and *adventus.* Elsewhere Moltmann writes (*The Future of Creation*, p. 55) 'The history of language has meant that there are two different groups of words meaning future. For that which is going to be we have the Latin word *futurum* (the English "future"). For that which is going to come, we have the German word *Zunkunft* (the French *avenir*). The German word *Zukunft* is not an equivalent for the Latin word *futurum*; it is a translation of the Latin *adventus*, which is in its turn an equivalent for the Greek word *parousia*. The future in the sense of *futurum* can be extrapolated from the entrails of present history. It corresponds to the calculable future. But *adventus*, what is to come, can only be anticipated. Desirable future, hoped-for future, belongs to the realm of expectation of the parousia.' In this context one must say not that God is the *futurum* of the world but its *adventus*.

through the process of history? Moltmann answers these questions in the negative. He argues that if one speaks of God's abstract being in and for himself, then one must certainly say that God does not require history in order to realize himself. But if one understands by the term 'self-realization' what the bible speaks of as God's glory and his kingdom, then one would certainly have to say that God 'needs' the world in order to be glorified, though one could not understand this 'need' as an imperfection.[58] In fact it is due to the perfection of his love that God goes out of himself in creation in the first place. His love then consists of two movements, the searching love of creation, and the gathering love of redemption. Viewed protologically God's love creates, not because of a need but because of the overflowing goodness of his divinity. Were it otherwise, God would be the archetypal Narcissus. Viewed eschatologically, God's gathering love is incomplete, until all things are united in his kingdom and death shall be no more. Only then will he be fully God, when he is all in all, when his glory radiates throughout the creation and when the world corresponds to the intentions of his searching love.

viii.  *The Fulfilment of History: The Trinity in Glorification*

The question of how one understands the fulfilment of history is intimately linked to one's understanding of christology. Although theology since the end of the nineteenth century has become acutely aware of the eschatological message and mission of Jesus, Moltmann contends that we have not yet fully incorporated the eschatological perspective into our understanding of the significance of the Christ-event for the interpretation of history.

Thus, for example, although both Barth and Bultmann sought to give full weight to the eschatological character of Christian revelation, both according to Moltmann ultimately

[58] In his reply to Walter Kasper's critique, Moltmann asks whether God needs history in order to come to himself. He answers his question as follows: 'If one understands by "himself" his abstract being for and with himself, then one must deny this question. If by "himself" one understands what the bible calls his glory, his justice and his kingdom, then one must affirm this question, even if one will not want to pose the question in the sense of the "imperfection" of his love and the openness of his hope.' Moltmann, 'Dialektik, die umschlägt in Indentität—was ist das? Zu Befürchtigungen Walter Kaspers', in *Diskussion über Jürgen Moltmanns Buch 'Der Gekreuzigte Gott'*, p.155.

surrendered the God of the bible for the God of Greek metaphysics whose being is an eternal present. In this fashion Barth
interprets the meaning of the resurrection when he writes, 'Of
the *real* end of history it may be said at any time: the end is
near!'[59] Bultmann, writing in a more existentialist vein,
develops a similar perspective when he affirms that every
moment bears within it the unborn secret of revelation, which
the believer must awaken through faith.[60]

Lying behind such affirmations is the christological conviction that the work of Jesus is already complete. It must only
be appropriated. Moltmann, on the contrary, maintains that
the work of Jesus is not complete. Rather than look upon the
resurrection as the completion of Jesus's mission, we should see
it as pointing to his real future. Moltmann notes, 'The creed of
early Christian faith that "Jesus was raised *from* the dead"
expresses a certainty about the future of Jesus who was killed
and by his death was condemned to the past.'[61] For Moltmann
the death of Jesus and the ongoing suffering of the world are the
permanent challenges to Christian faith. Only the future
coming of Christ, his handing over of the kingdom to the Father
and the arrival of the new creation can decisively refute this
objection. Until then the faith of the believer is necessarily on
trial. He writes, 'Only the new creation in Christ and through
Christ will demonstrate the new element in the proclamation of
Jesus and the new element in his anticipated resurrection from
the dead.'[62]

Christ's work is therefore not complete. It continues through
the Holy Spirit which was poured out upon the world from the
cross. We have already seen that the Holy Spirit works by
creating anticipations of the coming kingdom and by resisting
the power of sin and death still prevalent in the world. Through
these functions the Spirit works for the uniting of all things in
God the Father.

Moltmann notes that in this uniting process we see clearly
the personality of the Spirit and the active role of the Spirit in

    [59] Karl Barth, *The Resurrection of the Dead*, 1933, p. 112, as cited by Moltmann,
*Theology of Hope*, p. 51.
    [60] Rudolf Bultmann, *History and Eschatology*, 1957, p. 155, as cited by Moltmann,
ibid., p. 51.
    [61] Moltmann, *The Crucified God*, p. 163.
    [62] Ibid., p. 173.

the Trinity. This dimension was often overlooked in the pneumatology of the patristic period. Augustine, for example, developed his theology of the Spirit as *vinculum amoris*. Impressive as this doctrine is, it leaves the Spirit without any personality of its own.[63] Moreover, as merely the *vinculum* between Father and Son, the Spirit's role is totally passive. The Father begets the Son and breathes the Spirit and, whereas the Son obeys the Father, the Spirit has no active role but is merely the uniting bond.[64]

Moltmann attributes this defect in part to the non-historical character of this trinitarian theology. If, on the contrary, we think of God in terms of his trinitarian history, we can develop a more adequate understanding of the Holy Spirit. For in the history of God there is the double movement of his searching love and his uniting love. In the outward movement the Spirit is passive, receiving his existence from the Father and his form from the Son. But in the return movement, the Spirit is active, carrying forward the mission of the Son and thus glorifying the Father. In the eschaton it is the Father who is passive, being glorified through the Son and the Spirit. Moltmann writes,

If we want to describe in pictorial terms the two orders of the Trinity which are to be found in the biblical testimony, we can say: In *the first order* the divine Trinity throws itself open in the sending of the Spirit. It is open for the world, open for time, open for the renewal and unification of the whole creation. In *the second order* the movement is reversed: in the transfiguration of the world through the Spirit all men turn to God and, moved by the Spirit, come to the Father through Christ the Son. In the glorification of the Spirit, world and times, people and things are gathered to the Father in order to become *his world*.[65]

[63] Moltmann, *The Trinity and the Kingdom of God*, pp. 143, 169.

[64] See Moltmann, 'Antwort', in *Diskussion über Jürgen Moltmanns Buch 'Der Gekreuzigte Gott'*, pp. 185–6. 'The other vivid example is derived from Augustine and Richard of St. Victor and since then has been used in the doctrine of the Trinity. It is the *Trinity of love*: Immo vero vides trinitatem si caritatem vides . . . Ecce tria sunt, amans et quod amatur et amor. The main proposition, which this doctrine of the Trinity develops, is this: "God is love". Because love is self-communication, it presupposes self-differentiation and is living and one in this self-differentiation: God is the lover, the beloved and the love. Therefore within the Trinity the Holy Spirit is nothing other than the "bond of love" which links the Father and the Son. It has always been difficult to posit personality for this bond of love, whose gender is neuter, for in this case the result would be the hypostazing of a relation rather than the discovery of a genuine personality.'

[65] Moltmann, *The Trinity and the Kingdom of God*, p. 127.

The goal of history then coincides with the completion of God's own history, that is, the eschatological glorification of the Trinity (*Trinität in Verherrlichung*). This will come to pass when the mission of the Son and the Spirit is accomplished and the kingdom is handed over to the Father. In this moment the seeking love of the Father which begot the replying love of the Son finds its completion in the replying love of the whole of creation through the Son and the Spirit. In this sense the fulfilment of the mission of the Trinity *ad extra* is not only a functional completion but the ontological completion of the persons of the Trinity themselves, and thus the completion of the life of the Trinity *ad intra* as well.[66]

### ix.  *From Theory to Praxis*

### (a)  *Political Theology of the Cross*

In the first half of this chapter we have tried to give an exposition of the principal points of Moltmann's trinitarian theology. Moltmann, however, has never intended to develop a theological system for its own sake. He always regarded his work as a stimulus to the church in the concrete as it tries to work out an authentic form of discipleship in the contemporary world. He writes,

[66] Thus Moltmann argues against such classical theologians as Calvin, and against such contemporary theologians as van Ruler and Sölle, that the soteriological role of Jesus is not merely functional, so that he becomes superfluous in the eschaton. Christ's mission to the world flows precisely from his Sonship, that is, from his ontological being as replying love. In gathering the creation in replying love before the Father, the Son does not make himself superfluous but rather fulfils his destiny as Son. His Sonship is not a functional capacity which he can subsequently dispense with but rather is the ontological relation which binds him to the Father. See, for example, *The Crucified God*, pp. 256–66.

Particularly noteworthy are Moltmann's reflections on the eschatological subordination of the Son in 1 Cor. 15:24–8 He writes, 'For Paul the title Son not only expresses a function of Jesus for men, but also denotes his whole being in relationship to the Father. . . . The relationships in the Trinity between Father and Son are not fixed in static terms once and for all, but are a living history. This history of God or this history in God begins with the sending and delivering up of the Son, continues with his resurrection and the transference of the rule of God to him, and only ends when the Son hands over this rule to the Father. The delivering up on the cross is the central point of this history of God, not its conclusion. Only with the handing over of rule to the Father is the obedience of the Son, and thus his Sonship, consummated.' Ibid., pp. 264–5.

In the same vein Moltmann notes, 'According to Paul, the whole Christian eschatology ends in this inner-trinitarian process, through which the kingdom passes from the Son to the Father. Eschatology accordingly is not simply what takes place in the Last Days in heaven and on earth; it is what takes place in God's essential nature.' *The Trinity and the Kingdom of God*, p. 92.

Finally, in the three books mentioned (*Theology of Hope*, *The Crucified God*, *The Church in the Power of the Spirit*), I have not attempted to write theological treatises—comprehensive in information, balanced in judgement and calming in their wisdom. With these three books I have wanted to do something specific in the respective intellectual, theological and political situation. They are written from their time for their time and therefore are to be understood as theology in the context of contemporary life. They have therefore been correctly characterized as more pastoral and prophetic than professorial and systematic.[67]

One of the functions of Moltmann's trinitarian theology is to lay the groundwork for a political theology which has as its focal point the cross of Christ. The political function of the Trinity is not an accidental one, as Moltmann tries to show in his dialogue with Karl Barth. Barth's central hermeneutical principle in developing his doctrine of God was the divine sovereignty. He insisted that to do full justice to the Lordship of God one must develop a trinitarian theology. The doctrine of the Trinity is a function of God's absolute sovereignty. Moltmann argues that this hermeneutical principle should be reversed and that we must interpret God's Lordship in terms of the doctrine of the Trinity. Otherwise we run the serious risk of bringing in a concept of Lordship which is fundamentally alien to Christian faith, which must revise all a priori concepts of Lordship in light of the experience of the cross. Moltmann writes,

We make the suggestion, to think the Trinity no longer for the sake of God's rule, neither immanently for the sake of the monarchy of the Father, nor economically for the sake of the sovereignty of the one God. The doctrine of the Trinity is not a key for interpreting the world-monarchy of God. It is to be applied precisely in the opposite way: the Lordship of the triune God reveals and opens the inner life of the Trinity for the creation, for history and for glory. Therefore God's rule interprets the Trinity.[68]

In the history of the West there have been several pre-dominant models of freedom.[69] Freedom has been interpreted,

[67] Moltmann, 'Antwort', in *Diskussion über Jürgen Moltmanns Buch 'Der Gekreuzigte Gott'*, pp. 166–7.

[68] Moltmann, 'Der Dreieinige Gott', p. 20. See also Moltmann's critique of Barth on this point, *The Trinity and The Kingdom of God*, pp. 139–44.

[69] Moltmann, *The Trinity and The Kingdom of God*, pp. 213–18.

for example, as power over another. In this sense freedom is contrasted to slavery. In Greek and Roman societies, only citizens were free. They could dispose of their own destiny in the *polis*. The slave, on the other hand, had no rights of his own. He was in no sense a master of his destiny.

A very different model of freedom is that of friendship. Here freedom isn't measured by one's ability to master the other. On the contrary, in friendship one grants the other a space in which he can grow and become himself. Moltmann notes that the two central characteristics of friendship are affection and respect.[70]

Jesus himself broke through the limited understanding of freedom in terms of a master–slave relationship, and offered his followers the new possibility of living with him and with one another in friendship. Key biblical texts which confirm this point of view are Mark 10:45 and John 15:15. Jesus says, 'The Son of Man came not to be served but to serve, and to give his life as a ransom for many.' And again he declares, 'No longer do I call you servants, for the servant does not know what his master is doing; but I have called you friends, for all that I have heard from my Father I have made known to you.'

In making this offer, Jesus breaks with the political categories that determined the Greek world. In Aristotle's treatment of friendship he notes that like goes with like. Thus, for example, the possibility of friendship between man and woman, or between free citizen and slave, was excluded. Jesus abandoned this principle and scandalized the Jews of his day by freely choosing to associate with tax-collectors and sinners. Even in his death he was surrounded by outcasts. He died as a political revolutionary, rejected as one who violated the Jewish law, and even abandoned by the God whom he called Father. None the less it was this Jesus and no other whom God raised from the dead. Because of God's identification with this man, a new hermeneutical principle is possible, namely like goes with unlike.[71]

[70] See Moltmann, *The Church in the Power of the Spirit*, p. 115.
[71] In *The Church in the Power of the Spirit* (p. 120) Moltmann writes, 'For Plato and Aristotle the reciprocal character of friendship is connected with the equality of the partners. It is true that wise men and heroes are called "the friends of God", but it is not really possible to talk about friendship with Zeus. It is true that a free man can be friends with a slave, but only insofar as he sees him as a man and not as a slave at all. Because of the principle of equality and rank, the Greek ideal of friendship tended to

Fundamentally this means that through the experience of the cross all hierarchical thinking has been overcome. We cannot think of ordering society from above to below in a monarchical or feudalistic structure. Rather, if we take the cross as our epistemological criterion, the ordering of human relations must be seen from below to above. We must read the world upside down from the perspective of the cross.[72] This is the meaning of Matt. 25. Jesus identifies himself with the poor of the earth, with the sick and imprisoned, with the naked and homeless. If one wants to live in friendship with Jesus, one must live in friendship with those on the fringes of society, for there Jesus has identified himself.

A trinitarian theology of the cross must be a political theology, for in the cross God identified himself with the politically powerless and poured out the Spirit which exalts the weak to confound the strong. If this is the only God there is, then Christian faith in the name of this God must play a critical role in society. This function consists in unmasking the ways in which a given society operates according to the master–slave model of human relationships. This model of Lordship must be constantly criticized in the light of the crucified God. The God who reveals himself on the cross demands the transvaluation of values.

Moltmann cites the work of E. Peterson to show that in the early history of Christianity the doctrine of the Trinity played a decisive political role. In the Constantinian period reality was interpreted in terms of political monotheism. The unity of God's Lordship over his creation had its counterpart in the unity of the Emperor's Lordship over his Reich. An undifferentiated monotheistic understanding of God proved to

---

conceive of it in exclusive terms. Jesus breaks through this closed circle of friendship, reaching out alike to God, the disciples, and the tax-collectors and sinners.

[72] In *The Future of Creation* (p. 57) Moltmann notes that the anticipation of the future of God took place on the cross. 'As a result it is not permissible for faith to develop society's future in an evolutionary way. It must develop it dialectically and in representation for those who have become, and are going to become, the victims of previous and present evolution. The future for which the Christian faith hopes does not begin "at the top", with the spearheads of evolution and in the advanced societies but—as we can see from the crucified Jesus—"below", among those who are without a future and without hope, the victims of world history. This reversal is brought about by the dialectic of the cross.'

be the Achilles' heel of this hierarchical model. Moltmann writes,

Political-religious monotheism was overcome by the development of the doctrine of the Trinity in the concept of God. The mystery of the Trinity is to be found only in God, and not by reflection, in creation. In the doctrine of the Trinity Christian theology describes the essential unity of God the Father with the incarnate, crucified Son in the Holy Spirit. So this concept of God cannot be used to develop the religious background to a divine emperor. The identification of the *Pax Romana* with the *Pax Christi* shatters on eschatology. No emperor can guarantee that peace of God which is past all understanding; only Christ can do this. The political consequence is a struggle for the freedom and independence of the church from the Christian emperor.[73]

Unfortunately this important breakthrough was all but lost in the course of the long history of the church and its relation to the secular political powers. Rather than maintain its independence as a critical force in society, the church for the most part accomodated itself to the prevailing ideologies, defended the status quo, and became a staunch resister against the movements of liberation that have shaped modern Western democracies. Moltmann maintains, moreover, that the church has hardly begun to acknowledge the consequences of the doctrine of the Trinity for the structuring of truly Christian relationships in the church. A practical acknowledgement of the trinitarian God revealed in the cross would require the removal of all hierarchical structures and the re-ordering of relations in the Christian community according to the model of friendship.[74]

[73] Moltmann, *The Crucified God*, pp. 325–26.

[74] Moltmann argues that a trinitarian understanding of God should lead necessarily to the abolition of the monarchical episcopate. In *The Church in the Power of the Spirit* he writes (p. 305), 'The monarchical justification of the ministry, which has been usual in the mainstream church since Ignatius of Antioch was: one God, one Christ, one bishop, one church. This may have had pragmatical reasons in its favour in its own time, but theologically it is wrong, and ecclesiologically it led to a false development. This unified hierarchy reflects a clerical monotheism which corresponded to contemporary "political monotheism", but which is in contradiction to the trinitarian understanding of God and his people.' Underlying Moltmann's argument is the presupposition that a hierarchical structure always implies a master–slave relation. It is interesting to note that among contemporary theologians Hans Urs von Balthasar, on the basis of his trinitarian understanding of God, has developed an ecclesiology which defends hierarchy in the church, though granting Moltmann's point that hierarchy ought not to function accordintg to the master–slave model of relations. Von Balthasar sees a

## (b) *Spirituality of Compassion*

In his introduction to Moltmann's book *The Open Church*,
Douglas Meeks notes, 'It may be said that one objective of
Moltmann's recent theology is to rehabilitate the word
"passion" for use in theology as well as everyday life in the
church.'[75]
Moltmann's thought is developed in the context of his
reading of the contemporary situation of man and his understanding of the trinitarian God. Moltmann believes the chief
god of our contemporary world to be success. How does a man
live who worships this God? Moltmann writes,

The man of success does not weep, and he keeps smiling only out of
courtesy. Coldness is his style. That which his activity demands he
calls 'good'; that which hinders his success is 'bad'. The other man is
simply his competitor in the struggle for existence. 'Survival of the
fittest' is his eschatology. Just as he wants to control the world, so he
holds himself under self-control. In short, he who believes in the God
of action and success becomes an apathetic man. He takes no more
notice of the world, of other men, or of his own emotions. He remains
oblivious to the suffering his actions cause. He does not want to know
about that and represses crucifying experiences from his life.[76]

In the stoic view of life apathy was considered the highest
virtue of gods and of men. Because of God's perfection, he is
sufficient unto himself. He stands in need of nothing. Therefore
he cannot suffer. The stoics advocated that human beings

masculine and a feminine dimension in the church. These two dimensions correspond
to the role of Peter and Mary. Both are ultimately grounded in the role of Christ. Christ
is receptive or feminine *vis-à-vis* the Father but he is masculine in his function before the
world; that is, he authoritatively represents the Father's design and purpose for his
creation. These two roles are subsequently embodied in the church. The role of Peter is
embodied in the hierarchical church (*Amtskirche*); the role of Mary in the church of love
(*Liebeskirche*). According to von Balthasar, these two cannot be played off against one
another. The hierarchical church has an authoritative role in the church. In this sense
the church is subordinate to Peter. But the hierarchical church exists for the sake of the
church of love. The hierarchical church has nothing of its own. It must receive
everything as gift from its Lord. In this sense it too is subordinate to Mary, existing
under the imperative to embody Mary's fiat. See Hans Urs von Balthasar, *Sponsa Verbi*,
*Skizzen zur Theologie* II (Einsiedeln: Johannes Verlag, 1961), pp. 164–74; *Spiritus Creator*,
*Skizzen zur Theologie* III (Einsiedeln: Johannes, 1967), pp. 215–17; *Theodramatik* II, 1
(Einsiedeln: Johannes, 1976), pp. 322–30.

[75] Jürgen Moltmann, *The Open Church, Invitation to a Messianic Life-Style* (London:
SCM Press, 1978), p. 16.
[76] Jürgen Moltmann, *The Experiment Hope*, p. 71.

should imitate the gods and seek to rid themselves of all desire. Only the man who stops wishing can become happy. That means that only as man becomes more apathetic does he become more godlike.

This vision of God and man radically contradicts what is at the heart of Christianity, namely the experience of the suffering of God in the cross.

Moltmann wants to redress the balance which has been lost in Christianity due to the influence of Greek conceptions of divinity and stoic philosophy. He finds a powerful impulse in the theology of Abraham Heschel.[77] In his study of the prophets Heschel developed what he called a theology of the divine pathos. The God of the Old Testament, the God of the covenant, was no stoic god detached from the events of the world. Rather God entered into the history of his people so fully that he actively suffered with them. The God of Israel made himself vulnerable.

Heschel's theology was dipolar. He stressed the dipolar relation between God and creation. Moltmann's theology is trinitarian, for the cross is an event involving Father, Son, and Spirit. From this event Moltmann draws the important conclusion that if man is to imitate the pattern of the divine life, he must live a spirituality not of apathy but of compassion. Christian faith gives man the courage to take an active stance toward the suffering of the world, in fact to take suffering upon oneself out of love. Moltmann aligns himself with Bonhoeffer in relating one's commitment to Christ with fidelity to the earth. He writes, 'The community with Christ always leads us deeper into suffering with humanity. The more intensely one loves the earth, the more acute is one's sensitivity to the injustice which human beings inflict on each other, to their forsakenness and self-destruction. Love makes the suffering of the other unbearable for one who loves.'[78]

## (c) *The Celebration of the Feast*

In this section we have been exploring the practical consequences of Moltmann's trinitarian theology. In concentrating thus far on Moltmann's political theology and on his

---

[77] See Moltmann, *The Trinity and The Kingdom of God*, pp. 25–30.
[78] Moltmann, *The Open Church*, p.. 42–3.

spirituality of compassion, we are also involved in the danger of one-sidedly stressing the active dimension of the response in faith to the trinitarian God. This could lead to the false conclusion that the ultimate response to Christ consists in ethical action. Such a theology would then have little place for the contemplative dimension of faith.

Moltmann makes it quite clear that in a Christian theological perspective the ultimate goal of history is an aesthetic one, that is, the enjoyment of God. The present atheistic situation is in large measure due to the mistaken notion that God has often been regarded only as a stop-gap or a problem-solver. What man couldn't solve on his own was left to God. God therefore had only functional validity.

Moltmann argues on the contrary that God exists not to be used but to be enjoyed. He writes, 'When we cease using God as *helper in need*, *stop-gap*, and *problem solver*, we are—according to Augustine—finally free for the *fruitio Dei et se invicem in Deo*, the joy of God and the enjoyment of each other in God. Purpose-free rejoicing in God may then take the place of uses and abuses of God.'[79]

One must, however, realize that this goal of the enjoyment of God is an eschatological one. It would be naive and irresponsible to think that this goal can be realized in the world as we know it. Still it is necessary to create anticipations of this eschatological goal. Such an anticipation exists in the celebration of the feast. Because Christian life is based on the resurrection of Christ, it must have the character of a feast. The new life under the influence of Christ, Moltmann writes,

cannot be understood merely as new obedience, as a reversal of life's direction and as an endeavour to change the world until it visibly becomes God's creation. It is also, and with equal emphasis, celebrated as the feast of freedom, as joy in existence and as the ecstacy of bliss. These aesthetic categories of the resurrection are part of the new life of faith; without them the imitation of Christ and the new obedience would become a joyless legalistic task. Easter begins with a feast, for Easter is a feast and that makes the life touched by Easter a festal life.[80]

It would be beyond the limits of our treatment of Moltmann's

[79] Jürgen Moltmann, *Theology and Joy*, (London: SCM Press, 1973), p. 80.
[80] Moltmann, *The Church in the Power of the Spirit*, p. 109.

trinitarian theology to develop the full implications of his understanding of the feast in its relation to his understanding of worship and sacramental theology. It might be worth mentioning in passing, however, that the notion of the feast plays a central role in his understanding of the Eucharist. The Eucharist as the meal in the presence of the risen Christ anticipates the eschatological banquet and renews the courage of the Christian to continue his efforts to alleviate the suffering he finds about him in the world.

There is thus a corresponding dialectic between cross and resurrection, anticipation and resistance. Christian faith is founded in the risen Christ who is none the less the Crucified. This dialectic has its counterpart in the Christian life through anticipation and resistance. Moltmann concludes,

The certainty of triumph celebrated in the Easter hymns will continue to rise above the bounds of our human life, because it cannot remain content with any victory. It works on the possibilities of the creative spirit in the world of death in a twofold way: it produces attitudes both of resistance and of consolation. Without resistance, consolation in suffering can decline into a mere injunction to patience. But without consolation in suffering, resistance to suffering can lead to suffering being repressed, pushed aside so that in the end it actually increases. In this double function of resistance and consolation the liberating feast becomes a 'messianic intermezzo' (A. A. van Ruler) on the risen Christ's way to the new creation of the world.[81]

### x.    *The Relation of Moltmann's Theology to the Patristic Doctrine of God*

Coming now toward the end of this chapter, I would like to relate briefly Moltmann's doctrine of God to the central conceptions of God developed during the patristic period.

In general one would have to say that Moltmann accepts all of the central affirmations of the ecumenical Councils during the patristic period up to the Council of Chalcedon. His difficulties arise not from the judgements of the early Councils but from the philosophical presuppositions which tended to undermine the doctrine of God which the Council Fathers wanted to affirm. The critical notions at stake are, for Moltmann, God's immutability, impassibility, and temporality. He writes,

[81] Ibid., p. 113.

We must drop the philosophical axioms about the nature of God. God is *not unchangeable*, if to be unchangeable means that he could not in the freedom of his love open himself to the changeable history of his creation. God is *not incapable of suffering* if this means that in the freedom of his love he would not be receptive to suffering over the contradiction of man and the self-destruction of his creation. God is *not invulnerable* if this means that he could not open himself to the pain of the cross. God is *not perfect* if this means that he did not in the craving of his love want his creation to be necessary to his perfection.[82]

The critical factor for Moltmann, which he believes was neglected in the middle ages, is history. The Christian doctrine of God, therefore, became detached from salvation history, and the working of the divine persons in that history received an ever greater modalistic interpretation.

By concentrating on the trinitarian history of God, Moltmann is able to pick up a number of elements that were either neglected or distorted in the patristic period. For example, by neglecting the historical dimension of the Christian understanding of God and by overemphasizing the divinity of Christ, the church almost totally lost its connection with Judaism and tended to absolutize itself, identifying its existence with that of the kingdom of God. If the church had more clearly maintained its historical perspective, it would have seen that the messianic hope of Judaism has been by no means superseded by the existence of the church, that the world is still visibly unredeemed, and that men's need for salvation cannot be answered by reference to Christ's existence alone but only by the future of Christ, his second coming to hand over the kingdom to his Father.[83]

If the church had thought out this problem more con-

---

[82] Ibid., p. 62.

[83] In *The Experiment Hope* (p. 66), Moltmann writes, 'The concrete existence of the Jews constantly raises the question of the messianic hope in Christianity. The existence of the Jews again and again forces Christians to the knowledge that they are not yet at the goal, that their church is itself not the goal, but that with eschatological provisionality and brotherly openness they remain on the way.

'Franz Rosenzweig was right when he said that the deepest reason for Christianity's hatred of Jews lay in its self-hatred, "in the hatred for its own unfulfillment, for its own not-yet". Ecclesiastical and political persecution of the Jews in Christian societies is always directed against the unstillable Jewish hope in the Messiah in view of the unredeemedness of the world.' On the role of Judaism in the theology of Moltmann, see also *The Crucified God*, pp. 100–2; *The Church in the Power of the Spirit*, pp. 136–50.

sistently, it would also have recognized that Arius's subordinationism was not utterly and irredeemably false. Both Arius
and orthodox Christianity suffered from the same defect.
Arius's ontological subordinationism resulted from his inability
to accept the Christian insight that God could freely enter into
history. This failure led to his conviction that Jesus Christ must
be a creature. Though orthodox Christianity correctly rejected
Arius's ontological subordinationism, its failure to understand
God's being historically led to a neglect of the authentic form of
subordinationism, namely the eschatological subordinationism
of the Son to the Father.

None the less a critical question remains to be asked of
Moltmann. In his emphasis on God's historicity to the point of
panentheism, according to which God suffers the death of his
Son, does Moltmann accept a patripassianism in the sense in
which it was so clearly rejected in the patristic period? To
answer this question adequately, one must make a number of
necessary distinctions. Although the theologians of the patristic
era assumed that the Father could not suffer and that God could
only suffer through his Son in the Son's human nature, what is
known as patripassianism refers to the monarchian modalism of
Praxeas and his followers, according to which the suffering of
the Son is identical with the suffering of the Father. For the
sake of the divine unity these theologians surrendered the real
distinctiveness of the three persons. Thus God is named Father
in his role as creator, Son in his incarnation and passion, and
Holy Spirit in his presence in the church. Moltmann's doctrine
makes precisely the opposite point. In the distinct suffering of
Father and Son in the cross, the two persons are both separated
and united, so that their tri-unity is preserved. Moltmann thus
prefers to speak of patricompassianism.[84] This distinction he
believes enables him to avoid the cul-de-sac of the death-of-God
theologians, who affirm that God as such died on Golgotha, as
well as the impasse of the classical theists, who affirm that God
cannot suffer and therefore cannot do justice to the event of the
cross. The way to pass through this Scylla and Charybdis is the
trinitarian understanding of the cross, which involves the
passion of the Son and the com-passion of the Father.

I would like to conclude this section by referring to the

[84] See, for example, Moltmann, *The Future of Creation*, p. 73.

objection which Maurice Wiles raises against the trinitarian thinking which developed in the patristic period.[85] Wiles, we recall, noted that an important impulse leading to the development of the doctrine of the Trinity was the Arian question. When that question was settled at Nicaea, it was an easy step to affirm the divinity of the Holy Spirit. Still the early patristic writers had accepted a fluidity between Logos and Spirit. But in the heat of later controversies patristic writers tended to give greater emphasis to the divine unity. This resulted in the principle: *opera trinitatis ad extra sunt indivisa*. Wiles then raises the critical question of how we are able to distinguish the persons from one another. He sees only two alternatives, neither of which is satisfactory. Either the distinction is the result of a direct propositional revelation, or revelation necessarily involves a three-foldness. In the last chapter we saw that Schubert Ogden opted for the second alternative, in effect making the doctrine of the Trinity a truth of philosophy as well as of Christian faith. Moltmann, on the other hand, opts for the first alternative. It has been objected that Moltmann's theology is a biblical fundamentalism. It is at least true that Moltmann's theology is a revelational fundamentalism and in this sense he remains true to the Protestant heritage extending from Luther to Barth. God is known where he makes himself known, that is, in the cross. The cross is a truth of history and not of pure reason. The doctrine of the Trinity is therefore not philosophical speculation but is rather the only adequate account of the event of the cross. It is there and there alone that one knows God to be Father, Son, and Holy Spirit.

xi. *Critical Questions for Moltmann's Theology*

(a) *Is God dissolved into history?*

There is no doubt that Moltmann's theology represents an impressive response to the God-question as it is raised in the face of the suffering of the world. The context of Moltmann's theology has consistently been the theodicy question, and his answer shows in large measure that God and humanity are not contradictories but complementaries. None the less significant issues have been raised in regard to this understanding of God.

[85] Maurice F. Wiles, 'Some Reflections on the Origins of the Doctrine of the Trinity', *Journal of Theological Studies* N.S. vol. viii (1957) 92–106.

First of all, there is the question whether God is dissolved into history. Why does this problem arise? The answer lies in the fact that Moltmann so identifies God with his trinitarian history that one is led to ask whether there is any remainder. Such formulations as the following give rise to this objection:

The nature of God thus does not stand behind the appearance of history and appearance in history as eternal, ideal being; it is that history itself.[86]

Doubts are further generated by Moltmann's abandonment of the distinction between the economic and the immanent Trinity. Moltmann's critics see in his rejection of this distinction a hidden form of Hegelianism. Thus, for example, Walter Kasper writes:

For all that is imposing in this dynamic-historical conception and actualization of the doctrine of the Trinity, yet there is the question how Moltmann can still preserve the freedom of God in this way. How does he safeguard himself from the (doubtless not desired) consequence, that God needs history, in order to come to himself? Does not the danger exist here, that the miracle of God's love, the cross, is dissolved in dialectic, which turns into identity?[87]

In so far as Moltmann has given an answer to this objection, he argues that the problem arises from a false dichotomy between freedom and necessity in God. God's relation to the world is not a matter of freedom of choice, as if it were an either–or choice whether God would create and redeem the world. Neither does God need the world to fulfil himself.[88] His

---

[86] Moltmann, *The Future of Creation*, p. 74.

[87] Walter Kasper, 'Revolution im Gottesverständnis? Zur Situation des ökumenischen Dialogs nach Jürgen Moltmanns *Der Gekreuzigte Gott*', in *Diskussion über Jürgen Moltmanns Buch 'Der Gekreuzigte Gott*', p. 146. See also Christolph Hinz, 'Feuer und Wolke im Exodus, Kritisch-assistierende Bemerkungen zu Jürgen Moltmanns *Theologie der Hoffnung*', in *Diskussion über die 'Theologie der Hoffnung*', pp. 141–2; also Peter Momose, *Kreuzestheologie*, p. 86.

[88] Moltmanm clearly makes this point in discussing the theology of Berdyaev. He writes that if God longs for the other, 'It is not out of *deficiency* of being; it is rather out of the superabundance of his creative fullness. If we talk about this divine longing, then we do not mean any "imperfection of the Absolute" when we transfer the principle of historical movement in this way. On the contrary, *the lack of any creative movement would mean an imperfection in the Absolute*. "For creative movement, indeed . . . is a characteristic of the perfection of being." God longs for his Other, in order that he may put his creative love into action. So the objection that any movement in God represents a deficiency of divine perfection falls to the ground. On the contrary, the drama of divine

relation to the world is not one of metaphysical necessity as in Hegel or process thought. The dichotomy between freedom and necessity is overcome in God in that God relates himself to the world in the overflowing of his love. In a recent attempt to meet this objection, Moltmann developed more fully his understanding of God's freedom:

Friedrich von Hügel has referred to the levels of freedom in the Augustinian doctrine of freedom, in order to say *by analogy*, that freedom of choice is in no way the highest level of freedom. The freedom to be able and to be required to choose between good and evil is a lesser freedom than the freedom to will and to do the good. In *not being able to sin*, man, by the power of grace, shares in the eternal freedom of God, which is freedom for the good. Therefore whoever is truly free, does not have to choose any longer. A proverb says, 'Whoever has a choice, has the torment of choice.' But true freedom is not a torment, but rather constant joy in the good. The truth of freedom is love, which is an overflowing of goodness. *Bonum est communicativum sui*: self-communication.[89]

(b) *Is Moltmann's doctrine of God tritheistic?*

The second objection which has been raised against Moltmann is tritheism. This objection arises first because Moltmann speaks more often not of the unity of God (*Einheit Gottes*) but of the unification of God (*Vereinigung Gottes*). Since the time of Augustine and the Cappadocians, Christian theology has emphasized the unity of the divine essence. For Thomas Aquinas, for example, the unity of God consists in the unity of the divine nature in abstraction from the three divine persons. Moltmann rejects this approach as leading inevitably to modalism. If one begins with a presupposed notion of unity, whether of one divine substance or of one divine subject, the three in God are reduced to modes of being.

Moltmann proposes a social doctrine of the Trinity which begins not with a preconceived idea of divine unity but with the concrete history of Father, Son, and Spirit. He writes,

After considering all this, it seems to make more sense theologically to love and human freedom, which begins in the innermost heart of the Godhead and constitutes its life, is the very proof of divine perfection.' *The Trinity and the Kingdom of God*, pp. 45–6.

[89] Moltmann, 'Antwort', in *Diskussion über Jürgen Moltmanns Buch 'Der Gekreuzigte Gott'*, p. 173. See also *The Trinity and The Kingdom of God*, pp. 52–6, especially p. 55.

start from the biblical history, and therefore to make the unity of the three divine Persons the problem, rather than to take the reverse method—to start from the philosophical postulate of absolute unity, in order then to find the problem in the biblical testimony. The unity of the Father, the Son, and the Spirit is then the eschatological question about the consummation of the trinitarian history of God.[90]

Given Moltmann's entire theological perspective, this approach has not only the advantage of beginning with revelation but of being ordered to history, the sphere where God makes himself known. The problem of God's unity is then also the problem of the unification of history, and since history is also the trinitarian history of God, the unification of history implies the unification of God. God's unity is not a presupposition of theology but God's unification is the goal of history.

This approach to the unity of God fits into Moltmann's eschatological conception of theology as a whole. Only when the Son hands over the kingdom to the Father is his mission complete, a mission which is being carried on in post-resurrection time through the Spirit. In completing his work, the Son fulfils his mission, and the unification of God is fulfilled in that there is a mutual indwelling of God and his redeemed creation. This is Moltmann's panentheistic vision of the end.

The tritheistic danger in this scheme is seen in Moltmann's reference to Father, Son, and Spirit as three subjects who work together in history. Classical trinitarian theology vigorously maintained that in God there is only one centre of consciousness and will. Moltmann implies that there are three. The ontological unity of one substance or subject seems to be replaced by a volitional unity of three subjects. Such fears of tritheism cannot help but be aroused when Moltmann speaks in the following way:

If the history of the kingdom is this history of God which is open and inviting in a trinitarian sense, how can we talk about God's *unity* (*Einheit*)? If the three divine subjects are co-active in this history, as we have shown they are, then the unity of the Trinity cannot be a monadic unity. The unity of the divine tri-unity lies in the *union* (*Einigkeit*) of the Father, the Son and the Spirit, not in their numerical unity. It lies in their *fellowship* (*Gemeinschaft*), not in the identity of a single subject.[91]

[90] Moltmann, *The Trinity and the Kingdom of God*, p. 149.
[91] Ibid., p. 95.

To be fair to Moltmann, one must acknowledge that he is aware of the danger and in his latest writing has gone some way to answering the charge of tritheism. His response is twofold. First, he argues that tritheism could only arise if one brings an individualistic understanding of 'person' to theology. It is precisely such an interpretation which Moltmann finds in modalistically-inclined theologians such as Rahner. This is a concept of person as 'a self-possessing, self-disposing centre of action which sets itself apart from other persons'.[92] Moltmann, on the other hand, drawing on the philosophical personalism of Hölderlin, Feuerbach, Buber, Ebner, and Rosenstock, wants to employ a genuinely social understanding of person according to which the 'I' can only be understood in relation to the 'Thou'.

Secondly, he brings in the traditional idea of the perichoresis to bolster his social understanding of the persons of the Trinity. This classical doctrine of trinitarian theology indicates that the persons of the Trinity are alive in one another and through one another. Moltmann writes,

In their perichoresis and because of it, the trinitarian persons are not to be understood as three different individuals, who only subsequently enter into relationship with one another (which is the customary approach, under the name of 'tritheism'). But they are not either, three modes of being or three repetitions of the One God, as the modalistic interpretation suggests. The doctrine of the perichoresis links together in a brilliant way the threeness and the unity, without reducing the threeness to the unity or dissolving the unity in the threeness.[93]

Whether or not Moltmann's reply to the charge of tritheism is adequate will no doubt be the subject of discussion among theologians for some time, and for the present the question remains an open one. What is important to observe, however, is how intimately the question of God's unity is linked to God's historicity. Thus the question of whether Moltmann's God is dissolved into history is interwoven with the question of tritheism. The close association of these two questions points to the consistency of Moltmann's attempt to revise classical trinitarian orthodoxy, but an affirmative answer to either question

[92] Ibid., p. 145.
[93] Ibid., p. 175.

may point to a key vulnerability in Moltmann's core conception.

(c)  *Does human action contribute anything to the kingdom of God?*

A third critical question which must be raised in regard to Moltmann's theology is the intrinsic worth of human activity for the building of the kingdom of God. Moltmann's early theological writings before *Theology of Hope* dealt with the thought of John Calvin.[94] Calvin's theology is well known for its emphasis on the sovereignty of God. For Calvin God is the ultimate actor in the human drama of salvation. Moltmann has clearly taken over this perspective. According to Moltmann's understanding of history the future creates the present. God's revelation of himself as future of the world in the resurrection of Christ sets history in motion and guarantees the ultimate coming of the kingdom, God's triumph over suffering and death. Moltmann stresses that in the resurrection of Christ God is known as the *creator ex nihilo.* Therefore on the basis of the resurrection a hope is enkindled which contradicts the present reality of the world.

To be sure, Moltmann argues that this hope is an impulse to action. One does not abandon the world but identifies with the poor and abandoned of the earth and struggles against the world as we know it. Still one does not base one's hope on these human activities. Hope is based solely on the event of the resurrection, an event which Moltmann consistently maintains is without analogy in human experience.[95]

Action is then created from the future. Rubem Alves notes that this is action which expresses obedience to the future but does not create the future. He then comments,

This concept of 'action which corresponds to' the future presented by revelation is very problematical. It seems to me that the only political attitude that would really 'correspond' to the future would be

---

[94] See, for example, Jürgen Moltmann, *Christoph Pezel (1539–1604) unde der Calvinismus in Bremen* (Bremen: Einkehr Verlag, 1958); *Prädestination und Perseveranz, Geschichte und Bedeutung der reformierten Lehre 'de perseverantia sanctorum'* (Neukirchen: Neukirchener Verlag, 1961).

[95] In *Theology of Hope* Moltmann writes (p. 180) 'The resurrection of Christ is without parallel in the history known to us. But it can for that very reason be regarded as a "history-making event" in the light of which all other history is illumined, called into question and transformed.'

pacifism. How to make room for conflict, struggle, if our action is to 'correspond' to the future which revelation bring to us?[96]

Peter Momose touches on the same point in his critique of Moltmann's theology of the cross. He asks if man's striving for a better world does not lose its basis if the promised future of the kingdom of God is totally independent of human effort. If human activity does not actually *contribute* something to the coming of God's kingdom, is not world history really just a stage on which human fate is ultimately decided by God alone?[97] Moltmann takes this objection seriously. He finds a clue for meeting it in 1 Cor. 15.[98] In verse 50 Paul writes, 'Flesh and blood cannot inherit the kingdom of God, nor does the perishable inherit the imperishable.' But then in verse 53 Paul goes on to say 'This perishable nature must put on the imperishable, and this mortal nature must put on immortality.' Moltmann understands this to mean that there is both continuity and discontinuity. There is continuity in that it is this world which God redeems. It is this world which will receive the kingdom. But the continuity is created from God's side. The critical caesura is death. This chasm can only be bridged from God's side. No human efforts are sufficient to cross this boundary. The relation of past, present, and future finds its critical instance in the dead. That the dead (those who are past) have a future can only be true if the future creates a new existence. For Moltmann all theologies of progress founder on the graves of the dead, especially the dead who were the victims of human hatred and cruelty. He writes, 'The symbol of hope of the resurrection of the dead means future for those who are past. This future results not *from* the past, but it is opened *for* those who are past. What other continuity should there be through the discontinuity of death?'[99]

(d) *Is God the executioner?*

In my opinion the most serious objection which has been raised against Moltmann's theology has been stated most precisely by Dorothee Sölle, in her claim that in the last analysis

[96] Rubem A. Alves, *A Theology of Human Hope* (New York and Cleveland: Corpus Books, 1971), p. 66.
[97] See Momose, *Kreuzestheologie*, p. 158.
[98] See 'Nachwort von Jürgen Moltmann', ibid., pp. 180–1.
[99] Ibid., p. 181.

Moltmann's God remains God the executioner and therefore
the threat to man which atheistic humanists perceive him to be.
She writes,

The author is fascinated by the brutality of his God. This kind of
'radicality' is certainly not verbally accepted by Moltmann, but in
substance it is retained and deepened. Of course he attributes the
death to the 'pain' of the Father who hands over the Son but it is the
'will' of the Father not to spare the Son, and thus the Trinity is so
constituted, that the first person 'annihilates' the second. The story of
the sacrifice of Isaac is then not the human overcoming of an earlier
level of religiosity, which could satisfy the divinity only with human
sacrifices, but the unfulfilled first stage, in which the full severity of
this theology of the cross was not yet reached. Only the Trinity brings
God to his concept: that of the annihilator.[100]

It is clear that there is some evidence for this objection in
Moltmann's writings. The clearest text occurs in *The Crucified
God* in Moltmann's treatment of the Father's 'delivering up' of
his Son. Citing the research of W. Popkes on the concept
'Dahingabe' in the New Testament, Moltmann writes,

That God delivers up his Son is one of the most unheard-of statements
in the New Testament. We must understand 'deliver up' in its full
sense and not water it down to mean 'send' or 'give'. What happened
here is what Abraham did not need to do to Isaac; Christ was quite
deliberately abandoned by the Father to the fate of death; God
subjected him to the power of corruption, whether this be called man
or death . . . God made Christ sin (2 Cor. 5:21), Christ is the accursed
of God. A theology of the cross cannot be expressed more radically
than it is here.[101]

I find it disappointing that in his reply to the critique of his
theology of the cross Moltmann fails to give any serious
response to this objection, which strikes at the heart of his entire
theological project.[102] For it seems to me that there are
resources in Moltmann's theology for meeting this objection.

---

[100] Dorothee Sölle, 'Gott und das Leiden', in *Diskussion über Jürgen Moltmanns Buch
'Der Gekreuzigte Gott'*, p. 115.

[101] W. Popkes, op. cit., pp. 286 f., as cited by Moltmann, *The Crucified God*, p. 191.

[102] Although Sölle's critique is included in *Diskussion über Jürgen Moltmanns Buch 'Der
Gekreuzigte Gott'*, Moltmann mentions her only in passing and fails to develop a
response to her objections in his 'Antwort' to his critics.

These resources lie in a fuller trinitarian development of the double surrender of Father and Son.[103] It is interesting, for example, that Hans Urs von Balthasar moves in this direction in his theology of the paschal mystery. He too, for example, cites the identical passage of Popkes in his lengthy article 'Mysterium Paschale'. But he notes that the handing over of the Father can be properly interpreted only in a trinitarian context. This implies that the 'delivering up' of the Father must be complemented by the self-surrender of the Son.[104] According to von Balthasar it would be a mistake to see the Father's will as something imposed upon the Son, as something

---

[103] That the resources for meeting this objection are seminally present in Moltmann's trinitarian theology is clear from the following cryptic and suggestive remarks: 'Paul certainly takes over from the tradition the conception that Jesus was constituted Son of God by his resurrection from the dead, but he sees it at work in the sending of Jesus by God and in his being given up by the Father, which is at the same time his own self-surrender.' (p. 192. *The Crucified God*) 'In Gal. 2:20 the "delivering up" formula also occurs with Christ as its subject: "the Son of God, who loved me and gave himself for me". According to this, it is not just the Father who delivers Jesus up to die godforsaken on the cross, but the Son who gives himself up. This corresponds to the synoptic account of the passion story according to which Jesus consciously and willingly walked the way of the cross and was not overtaken by death as by an evil, unfortunate fate. It is theologically important to note that the formula in Paul occurs with both Father and Son as subject, since it expresses a deep conformity between the will of the Father and the will of the Son in the event of the cross, as the Gethsemane narrative also records.' (ibid., p. 243.) See also *The Future of Creation*, p. 73.

[104] Commenting on the text of Popkes, von Balthasar writes, 'But this aspect is only a properly New Testament one, if it is complemented by the active self-surrender of Christ, which again cannot be isolated to an independent moment, because otherwise there is the danger of forfeiting the eschatological horizon and of drifting into a mere theology of the martyrs. Christ must be God, in order so to make himself available for the event of love, which proceeds from the Father and wants to reconcile the world to itself, that in him the entire darkness of all that resists God is judged and suffered to the end. The human action of surrendering can only be subordinated in this event, and the contradiction between the human betrayal and the surrendering love of God must be bound together and therefore disentangled in the "contradiction of the cross". But for that purpose the handing over and taking captive, the binding in chains and abduction by the guard must be of absolute historical seriousness.' *Mysterium Salutis, Grundriß heilsgeschichtlicher Dogmatik.* Herausgegeben von Johannes Feiner und Magnus Löhrer (Einsiedeln, Zürich, Köln: Benziger, 1969), vol. iii, part 2, p. 202. See also *Herrlichkeit* III, 2, teil 2 (Einsiedeln: Johannes Verlag, 1969), pp. 196–211, where the trinitarian dimension of the cross event is stressed, On p. 208, von Balthasar writes, 'The entire thought can only be sustained in a trinitarian way, so that the entire action of judgement remains included between the love of the surrendering Father (John 3:16) and the love of the Son who lets himself be disposed of: within this bracket lies the entire force of the curse of the sin of the world which crashes down upon the one who bears it (Gal. 3:13).'

alien to him. The obedience of the Son is in fact the a priori of his human existence. His incarnation and correlative divesting of his divine form are already the expression of his obedience of Sonship. And, as Moltmann would argue, this Sonship must be interpreted not in a functional way but in an ontological one. The Son's being consists in his obedience.

Jesus's obedience of Sonship plays a critical role in the question of his being handed over to death. Seen in the perspective of the New Testament, this 'delivering up' cannot be the 'handing over' of an executioner. Jesus freely lays down his life.

Thus, for example, in the scene of Jesus's arrest as narrated in the gospel of Matthew, Jesus asks rhetorically: Do you think that I cannot appeal to my Father and he will at once send me more than twelve legions of angels?' But he adds immediately, 'But how then should the scriptures be fulfilled, that it must be so?' Matt. 26:53f.) In commenting on this text, von Balthasar notes, 'This "can" in the spirit of Jesus is just as unreal as, for instance, the consent to the enticements of Satan in the temptation in the desert. What could be *"de potentia absoluta"* is not possible *"de potentia trinitaria"*: namely, that the Son transgress the realm of his mission.'[105]

I would suggest then that the answer to Sölle's objection lies not in the abandonment of Moltmann's trinitarian understanding of God but rather in deepening it, by developing more fully the doctrine of the double surrender, the eternal obedience of the Son, and the joint action of Father and Son in the divine plan for the liberation of this world. This is not a decree of execution but the Father's readiness to suffer the loss of his Son (in the sense of Luke 20)[106] and the Son's readiness to lay down his life for his friends (in the sense of John 15).[107]

### xii.   *Conclusion: Theism, A-theism, and Trinity*

From the beginning of Moltmann's theological career, he has developed his thought in the context of the atheist critique of

---

[105] Von Balthasar, *Theodramatik* II, 1, p. 270.
[106] See the parable of the vineyard, Luke 20:9–19, especially v. 13 'The the owner of the vineyard said, "What shall I do? I will send my beloved son; it may be they will respect him."'
[107] See John 15:13 'Greater love has no man than this, that a man lay down his life for his friends.'

classical philosophical theism and has sought to find an alternative that is both consistent with Christian revelation and adequate to meet the objections of protest atheists. From the early days of his dialogue with Ernst Bloch, Moltmann has not hesitated to refer to himself as an a-theist. In response to Bloch's assertion that only an atheist can be a good Christian, Moltmann offered the rejoinder that only a Christian can be a good atheist.[108] How seriously should we take this counter-claim of Moltmann? Obviously the critic must proceed here with some caution. For it is clear that Moltmann's a-theism cannot be identified *tout court* with unbelief. Moltmann's position resembles that of Bonhoeffer who wrote that we have to live in the world *etsi deus non daretur*. Yet Bonhoeffer, as a believer, felt himself constrained to add the qualifier, 'And this is just what we do see—before God!'[109] Nevertheless, though I would not want to question that Moltmann's theology is written from the commitment of faith, it still remains true that in the fifteen years since the appearance of *Theology of Hope* Moltmann has remained basically consistent in his rejection of theism. If in his early works Moltmann appeared as an a-theist in rejecting the eternally present God for the sake of a God whose mode of being is future, he has emerged as an a-theist in his later works in his vehement critique of monotheism. He expresses this conviction in an oft-repeated polemic against H. Richard Niebuhr's thesis that Christianity is radical monotheism.[110]

Why does Moltmann stress this point so vehemently? The answer lies in the identification that Moltmann finds between monotheism and monarchy. One God implies for him one world-ruler. Moltmann draws the conclusion that, if God is the

[108] In *The Crucified God* (p. 195) Moltmann writes, '"Without Jesus I would be an atheist", remarked Gottschick. But "atheist" is a relative term and a polemical expression. We must therefore use a more pointed expression and say, "For Christ's sake I am an atheist", an atheist in respect of the gods of the world and world history, the Caesars and the political demigods who follow them. "Only a Christian can be a good atheist", I once remarked to Ernst Bloch, turning round his remark "Only an atheist can be a good Christian". He accepted this offering.'

[109] See Dietrich Bonhoeffer, *Letters and Papers from Prison* (Collins: Fontana Books, 1959), pp. 121–22.

[110] See, for example, *The Crucified God*, p. 215; also Johann Baptist Metz, Jürgen Moltmann, Willi Oelmüller, *Kirche im Prozeß der Aufklärung, Aspekte einer neuen 'politischen Theologie'* (München-Mainz: Kaiser-Grünewald, 1970), p. 26; *The Trinity and The Kingdom of God*, pp. 191 ff.

supreme world-ruler, then the God–world relationship must be a master–slave relationship.

By substituting a trinitarian history for a monotheistic God Moltmann believes that he can find a way out of the master–slave model and substitute instead a model of friendship. God's goal for the world is the kingdom of freedom, freedom being understood not as power over another but as mutual relations of affection and respect.

The word 'God' has always had a performative function in Moltmann's theology. In his earliest works God and resurrection were practically synonymous terms.[111] In the course of time Moltmann's usage has shifted. The more recent writings tend to identify 'God' and 'kingdom'. The doctrine of the kingdom and the doctrine of the Trinity mutually interpret one another, for the history of the coming of the kingdom is God's own history. In this sense, Moltmann continues to adhere to the a-theism of his early period, for God and his kingdom cannot be thought of apart fron one another. God will be fully God only when his kingdom comes. And until that day our knowledge of God remains a hoping knowledge, which must acknowledge the element of truth in the atheist's claim that God does not exist.

[111] See *The Crucified God*, p. 218.

# V

## THE GOD OF PROCESS AND THE
## GOD OF HOPE:
## THE CRITICAL ISSUES

i. *Introduction: The Points of Agreement*

IN the last two chapters we have taken a fully detailed look at
two recent attempts in Christian theology to re-think the
doctrine of God in such a way that the specifically Christian
revelation of God becomes apparent and that God's link with
temporal process and history is affirmed.

When seen in the light of the modern problematic and when
viewed in the context of their critical reception of the tradition,
several obvious similarities become clear.

First, both Ogden and Moltmann develop their doctrine of
God with a constant eye to the atheistic critique of theism in
general and of Christian faith in particular. For both of these
theologians it is true to say that faith itself stands or falls with
the ability of Christian theology to articulate a reasonable
account of its doctrine of God.

Thus, for example, Moltmann in his inaugural lecture in
Tübingen in 1968 stated that belief in God can no longer be the
presupposition of Christian faith. Faith in God and faith in
Jesus Christ are inextricably linked together. He writes,

Once it was maintained that even without a Christ, a mediator and
saviour, God exists. For Christians also the existence of God was not
in doubt. But under the influence of the history of Christian culture,
relations have been so altered that now what is at stake in the question
of faith in Christ is faith in God; yes, God himself is ever more the issue
of faith and is no longer its generally provable presupposition.[1]

Although the points of emphasis in the theologies of Ogden
and Moltmann are not absolutely identical, Ogden being more
conversant with the English philosophical tradition and more
preoccupied with the claim of the logical positivists that God
language is meaningless, none the less a large portion of their

[1] Jürgen Moltmann, *Perspektiven der Theologie* (München-Mainz: Kaiser-Mathias
Grünewald, 1968), pp. 36–7.

writings is devoted to showing that belief in God still makes sense, even in the face of the suffering of the world. For both writers the theodicy question is the one which a Christian doctrine of God, rooted as it is in the cross, must address.

From its inception process philosophy has been interested in the problem of evil. Whitehead in his small book *Religion in the Making* expressed the dilemma of the believer most starkly when he wrote 'All simplifications of religious dogma are shipwrecked upon the rock of the problem of evil',[2] and he saw his vast metaphysical system as an attempt to add one more speaker to Hume's *Dialogues Concerning Natural Religion*.[3] One could even say that process philosophy is an attempt to develop a philosophical eschatology, for Whitehead defines the ultimate philosophical problem as that of 'perpetual perishing'.[4]

Ogden is keenly aware that no theology has a chance of survival today unless it takes into account the problem of evil. Whether his opponent is a Camus or a Flew, Ogden is thoroughly conscious of the vulnerable point of any doctrine of God. The alternative is this: either we are not free and God is all-powerful and responsible for evil. Or we are free and responsible but God is not all-powerful. This conundrum is the impulse which drives Ogden to re-think the doctrine of God along new metaphysical lines.[5]

Although Moltmann's solution is less metaphysical in character, the impulse behind it is precisely the same. In the same inaugural lecture mentioned above he sounds a theme which is a leitmotiv of his work, namely that the God-problem is

[2] Alfred North Whitehead, *Religion in the Making* (Cambridge University Press, 1926), p. 77.

[3] Alfred North Whitehead, *Process and Reality*, p. 521.

[4] Ibid., p. 517.

[5] In his lecture notes 'The Problem of God: A Discussion with Langdon Gilkey' (p. 14) Ogden writes, 'In no other way, I think, can we possibly break out of the impasse into which secularist critics of Christian theism again and again try to force us—as Camus does, for example, when he confidently asserts in *The Myth of Sisyphus*, "You know the alternative: either we are not free and God the all-powerful is responsible for evil. Or we are free and responsible but God is not all-powerful. All the scholastic subtleties have neither added anything to nor subtracted anything from the acuteness of this paradox." So far as I have been able to learn, "the acuteness of this paradox" is due entirely to certain—to my mind, dubious—assumptions of classical Christian theism.' See also Ogden's reply to Antony Flew in 'God and Philosophy: A Discussion with Antony Flew', *Journal of Religion* 48 (1968) 161–88.

not a theoretical question but rather the practical one of man's suffering. He writes,

Georg Büchner said, 'Why do I suffer? That is the rock of atheism.' And precisely in this experience of pain there lies a deep solidarity between Christians and atheists. In it faith suffers the absent God. In it unbelief hungers for present meaning. Behind the various forms of enlightenment and post-enlightenment atheism stands that suffering, which expresses itself in the theodicy question which can neither be dismissed nor settled.[6]

Futhermore the theme of human suffering might be seen as a specification of the larger issue which dominates the thinking of both men, namely the compatibility between belief in God and the realization of a genuine humanity. The systematic goal of both theologians is to demonstrate that Christian faith leads to the full humanization of man.

Ogden, for example, in the first pages of his book *The Reality of God* clearly sets himself the task of developing an apologetic theology. Placing himself in the tradition of such theologians as Bultmann and Tillich, Ogden defines an apologetic theology as one based upon the insistence 'that Christian faith is not utterly alien to man, whatever his historical situation, but rather is his own most proper possibility of existence, which can and should be understandable to him, provided it is so expressed as to take his situation into account'.[7]

Moltmann speaks in analogous terms when he locates his understanding of God in the historical experience of the delivery of Israel out of bondage in Egypt. The divinity of God and the humanity of man are not contradictories. On the contrary God reveals himself to be God precisely in bringing man the authentic experience of liberation. Writing of the contradiction between God and man, which he sees to lie at the base of both theism and atheism,[8] he says

[6] Moltmann, *Perspektiven der Theologie*, p. 37. See also *The Crucified God*, pp. 175, 219–20; *The Experiment Hope*, p. 50; *Umkehr zur Zukunft*, p. 19; 'The Crucified God: a Trinitarian Theology of the Cross', *Interpretation* 26 (1972) 281; 'Der Gekreuzigte Gott, neuzeitliche Gottesfrage und trinitarische Gottesgeschichte', *Concilium* (1972), p. 408; 'Theology as Eschatology', in J. Moltmann and Frederick Herzog, *The Future of Hope: Theology as Eschatology*, p. 4.

[7] Ogden, *The Reality of God, p.* 6.

[8] Moltmann writes, 'In their struggle against each other, theism and atheism begin from the presupposition that God and man are fundamentally one being. Therefore

Over against this alternative, which measures God and man with the same standard, Jews and Christians are a third classification. Already the Old Testament histories speak of God in a different way. They speak of Jahweh neither atheistically by way of negation nor theistically by way of eminence but by way of history. What is fundamental are not pre-temporal myths but rather the historical event of the exodus. The 'character' of God is inseparably bound in this event to the freedom of the people. The God, who 'leads his people out of Egypt, out of the house of slavery', is the 'God of freedom', and from their side 'freedom' is life in the covenant of this God and a march forward into the free land of the promise.[9]

For Moltmann then the clue to overcoming the apparent dilemma of having to choose either God or man but not both lies in history. A God who is wholly removed from history, uninvolved in the struggles of his world, must be either useless or inimical to man. This fundamental stance is another one of the major areas of agreement with process thinkers. Both Moltmann and Ogden agree in tracing much of protest atheism to a rejection of what we termed in earlier chapters of our study classical philosophical theism. Only by rejecting the God of classical philosophical theism is there any chance of meeting the critique levelled against believers. The God of Greek metaphysics, a-temporal, unchanging, incapable of suffering, must be rejected in favour of a God who is more intimately related to process, temporality, and history. In both these traditions then there is the conviction that the key to re-thinking the doctrine of God lies in the divine temporality or historicity. Thus, for example, Langdon Gilkey in his critical assessment of process theology locates the central nerve of the process re-interpretation of Christianity in its rejection of ideas of deity alien to Christianity's understanding of God as one essentially involved in the affairs of men. He writes, 'When process theologians read the history of Christianity or of Christian doctrine, they find as the cause of most of Christianity's errors of theology and of life the false ontology of Absoluteness, the concept of the unchanging, a-temporal, unrelated, impassible, omnipotent, omniscient Deity.'[10]

what is ascribed to God must be taken from man and what is ascribed to man must have been taken from God.' *The Crucified God*, p. 249.

[9] Moltmann, *Perspektiven der Theologie*, pp. 190–1.
[10] Langdon Gilkey, 'Process Theology', *Vox Theologica* 43 (1973) 7.

Moltmann comes to the same conclusions not from a metaphysical reflection upon the antinomies of classical philosophical theism but from a prolonged relfection upon the implications of the cross for the Christian doctrine of God. He writes,

In the metaphysical concept of God from ancient cosmology and the modern psychological concept of God, the being of the Godhead, of the origin of all things or the unconditioned mover, as the zone of the impossibility of death, stands in juxtaposition to human being as the zone of the necessity of death. If this concept of God is applied to Christ's death on the cross, the cross must be 'evacuated' of deity, for by definition God cannot suffer and die. He is pure causality. But Christian theology must think of God's being in suffering and dying and finally in the death of Jesus, if it is not to surrender itself and lose its identity.[11]

This leads us to the final consideration in our introductory section on crucial points of agreement between process theolgy and Moltmann's theology of hope. Although process theology relies more heavily on a philosophy than does Moltmann's it none the less, even as a philosophy, has strong historical roots in the Christian faith. Whitehead once remarked that Christianity was a religion seeking a metaphysics,[12] and it can be argued, I think, that Whitehead's metaphysical system essentially springs from a vision which he received from Christianity. In *Adventures of Ideas* he wrote, 'The essence of Christianity is the appeal to the life of Christ as a revelation of the nature of God and of his agency in the world.'[13] In *Process and Reality* he spoke of this revelation as the Galilean vision. In Christ the humility of God was clearly perceived. Unfortunately the Christian tradition by and large surrendered this original vision and re-fashioned God in the image of Egyptian, Persian and Roman imperial rulers. Dubious metaphysical compliments were paid to God. The Church gave unto God the attributes which belonged exclusively to Caesar.[14]

In one sense then one could say that even process philosophy

[11] Moltmann, *The Crucified God*, p. 214. See also *The Future of Creation*, pp. 68–9, 93; also *The Church in the Power of the Spirit*, p. 62.
[12] Whitehead, *Religion in the Making*, p. 50.
[13] Alfred North Whitehead, *Adventures of Ideas* (New York: Macmillan, 1933), p. 170.
[14] Whitehead, *Process and Reality*, p. 520.

is based on a christology. The determinative experience is the
suffering of God. And certainly that is the guiding thought of
Moltmann's theology. To think of the event of the cross as a
God-event implies a revolution in our concept of God.[15]
Moltmann's entire theological project is an effort to work out
the implications of that revolution. It could be said of his
theology that it has taken up the task proposed by his Tübingen
colleague Eberhard Jüngel as the decisive one for Christian
reflection today. Jüngel writes,

In our debate with the traditional doctrine of God, we stand today
before the task of understanding God's Being from that event which
has forced us to keep our metaphysical conception of God separate
from our understanding of him until such time as traditional metaphysical conceptions are conceived anew and metaphysical con-
ceptualizing is overcome. That event is the death of Jesus.[16]

   In summary then, we can see that there are critical areas of
agreement between process thinkers and eschatological theologians. They are both motivated to address the protest
atheisms of our time. They both find an essential part of the
answer to the atheistic critique to be a rejection of the absolute
God of classical metaphysics and a closer alignment of God with
temporal process and history. They both identify their conception of the God–world relation as panentheistic. They both
take as their starting point the God who suffers with man, who
identifies himself with human history in the event of Jesus
Christ. Nevertheless despite these profound areas of agreement,
they have produced radically different theologies. It will be the
task of the remaining part of this concluding chapter to examine
some of the significant areas of divergence and disagreement
between them and to offer a critical assessment of the issues
with a view to the ongoing effort of constructing a contemporary
systematic theology.

## ii. *Methodology*

The divergence between these two schools of theology becomes

[15] Moltmann writes, 'The more one understands the whole event of the cross as an
event of God, the more any simple concept of God fails apart. In epistemological terms
it takes so to speak trinitarian form. One moves from the exterior of the mystery which
is called "God" to the interior, which is trinitarian. This is the "revolution in the
concept of God" which is manifested by the crucified Christ.' The Crucified God, p. 204.
[16] Eberhard Jüngel, 'Vom Tod des lebendigen Gottes', in Unterwegs zur Sache
(München: Kaiser, 1972), p. 117.

clear as soon as one looks at the methodological presuppositions underlying their understanding of theology. Let us begin with a consideration of Ogden's methodology. Ogden specifically lays down two criteria for the truth of theological statements.[17] First, they must be appropriate, that is, they must express the same understanding as expressed by the primary symbols of the witness of faith. But for Ogden this can only be the first step, for nothing has yet been said about the truth value of such statements. The second criterion is therefore said to be understandability. Theological statements must meet the relevant conditions of meaning and truth universally established with human existence.

In this second criterion lies the unique dimension of Ogden's methodology. Understandability for Ogden as a criterion of true theological assertions implies in effect the establishment of a valid metaphysics. Without such a metaphysics theology can establish that its statements agree with the symbols of the primary witness of faith, but it cannot be established that these assertions are either meaningful or true. Only a fully developed metaphysics could do this.

There is thus an intrinsic and inseparable connection between theology and metaphysics. In fact one could even say that the goal of both disciplines is the same. In his essay 'The Task of Philosophical Theology', Ogden explains his position as follows:

Christian theology necessarily presupposes philosophy and that not simply in general or in any of philosophy's widely different forms, but in the quite particular form of philosophical theology or theistic metaphysics. Because theology and philosophy by their very natures finally lay claim to the same basic ground, appeal to the same evidence—in short, serve an identical ultimate truth—their material conclusions must be in the last analysis mutually confirming, if either is to sustain its essential claim.[18]

If then one wanted to make an assertion such as 'Jesus is the Lord' or 'Jesus is the absolute bearer of salvation' one would not only have to show that this statement conforms to the primary symbols of the witness of faith but one would also have to prove

[17] See Ogden's essay, 'What is Theology?', *Journal of Religion* 52 (1972) 22–40.
[18] Schubert Ogden, 'The Task of Philosophical Theology', in *The Future of Philosophical Theology*, pp. 76–7.

that this statement is meaningful and true on the basis of metaphysics, that is, as Ogden says, on the conditions of meaning and truth universally established with human existence itself.

Such a methodology clearly determines from the outset a number of theological issues. For example it would be impossible on methodological grounds to say that Jesus Christ is the incarnation of God in a way uniquely different from other revelatory events, since that would be a priori impossible to establish on metaphysical grounds. The same could be said of such soteriological statements as 'salvation is found in Jesus Christ and no other'.

Ogden's methodology commits him then to the position that the truth of Christian faith and the truth of metaphysics are identical. For him the two stand or fall together. We might then ask whether Christian revelation is in any way necessary or even useful. Ogden maintains that it certainly is not absolutely necessary but it is useful or relatively necessary in that it re-presents the truth of human existence which can also be demonstrated by a valid metaphysics.[19] Commenting on the commitment of process philosophers to metaphysicize the truths of Christian faith, Langdon Gilkey notes, 'Jesus (and the entire panoply of *Heilsgeschichte events*) is simply a concrete symbol or illustration of wider universal truths about God, rather than an *einmalig*, once-for-all, unique manifestation about God that could not otherwise be known at all.'[20]

This is certainly true for Ogden except that he would reject the idea that the truths of Christian faith are reduced to universal propositions of reason.[21] He would rather insist that God is revealed in every moment, that he is always and everywhere accessible to human beings through his primordial revelation. So-called special revelation merely re-presents this primordial revelation.

[19] See Ogden's essay 'On Revelation' in *Our Common History as Christians: Essays in Honor of Albert C. Outler*, edd. John Deschner, Leroy T. Howe, and Klaus Penzel (New York: Oxford University Press, 1975), pp. 261–92.

[20] Gilkey, 'Process Theology', p. 9.

[21] For Ogden, revelation does not consist in the unveiling of universal truths of reason. Rather, it is an event happening in every moment. For Ogden's notion of revelation in relation to Kierkegaard's famous alternative of understanding revelation either as a Socratic reminiscence of eternal truths or as a unique, unrepeatable event, see chapter 3, note 28.

None the less it is clear that Ogden's methodology is a theological rationalism, a term which Ogden would gladly accept, so long as one added the proviso that the ultimate criterion of truth is not reason but experience, of which reason is a part. Still it is this universal human experience, whose necessary conditions of possibility metaphysics must establish, which has the last word as to the truth and meaningfulness of theological assertions.

Turning now to the methodology of Jürgen Moltmann, we note first of all his kinship with the neo-orthodox theology of Barth. This implies that theological reflection takes its origin from the Word of God, from the revelatory event which is Jesus Christ. Philosophy cannot demonstrate the truths of faith, for philosophy deals with universal necessary propositions, whereas Christian faith is rooted in a particular history-making event. The theologian then lets revelation itself pose the problem. He does not come with a preconceived world-view or philosophical stance. Thus in his early work *Theology of Hope* Moltmann could write, 'It is essential to let the Old Testament itself not only provide the answers, but also pose the problem of revelation, before we draw systematic conclusions.'[22]

Moltmann then clearly believes that it is possible to accept the Christian faith and to do theology without establishing an ontology. He gladly accepts help from philosophers and his work has been consistently influenced by them. He borrows freely from the philosophy of Bloch and from the critical theory of the Frankfurter school. At the same time the thought of Hegel is always in the background. None the less he does not hesitate to reject key points of the doctrines of each of the schools mentioned above, and on the cardinal point of the resurrection he has consistently maintained that this is an event without analogy. This position would seem to make Moltmann in the last analysis and in the critical instance a neo-orthodox theologian.

We could say then that philosophy has a limited role to play in this type of theology. It can offer help in understanding or conceptual categories but finally it can make no ultimate claim to truth. One reason for this is that for Moltmann reality is essentially broken. This means that in regard to man's ultimate

22 Moltmann, *Theology of Hope*, p. 95.

questions reason can offer no speculative solution. The world as we know it does not correspond to God and therefore Kierkegaard's critique of Hegel, that he created castles while men lived outside in a hovel, will always be true so long as history continues. The basic hope of metaphysics, to show the rationality of experience, is fundamentally doomed. Moltmann then rejects the conviction of process philosophy that a speculative solution to the problem of evil can be found. Whereas Ogden argues that an account of experience can be given according to which no event could in principle contradict the certitude of God's existence, Moltmann maintains that such an account could be given only in the eschaton when reality corresponds to God. Moltmann hopes not on the basis of a philosophical system but on the basis of a unique, unrepeatable event which sets history in motion toward that correspondence which this event promises and which will be a reality only in the eschaton. To sum up the positions in other words, Ogden is committed to the principal of analogy and Moltmann to that of dialectics. For Ogden God is revealed in every event. For Moltmann, God is revealed in one event which makes possible the hope that he will be revealed in every event.

When we look at these two methodologies, which contain already in embryo a number of conclusions for systematic theology, we notice that the differences between Ogden and Moltmann revolve around that ancient tension in Christianity between particularly and universality. To speak in the language of Langdon Gilkey, it is the tension between the language of story and the language of ontology. As Gilkey tries to show, both are essential to Christianity.

Gilkey maintains, correctly in my opinion, that Christian theology cannot without fatal results be reduced to purely metaphysical or ontological assertions. The reason is that while God is dynamically related to all experience, he is nevertheless known most clearly and decisively in certain places and through certain events and persons. Thus he argues.

This essential relation of Christian theology to a particular history inevitably implies that God acts differently or uniquely in certain times and places, that certain events and sections of history are for us more revelatory than others of the depths of his divine being and the mystery of his divine purposes. Thus for any Christian theology there are *uniquely* unique events, qualitatively different from other events, and thus by implication ontologically different, in relation to the divine activity.[23]

It seems to me the strength of Moltmann's theology over against Ogden's to recognize this fact and to build his theology upon it.

On the other hand, though Christianity must always have story or narration as its primary language, since the encounter between God and man is essentially dramatic, it cannot dispense with the task of *thinking* the divine–human relation. Both Ogden and Gilkey agree that the Christian witness of faith uses symbolic language. But symbols, as Ricoeur points out, invite thought. Thinking, however, cannot exist in a vacuum. Christians can think only in the conceptual tools of their age. This means that we can think our faith only in terms of our understanding of ourselves, of our world, and of our history. Such an understanding is exactly what we mean by ontology. Therefore, as Gilkey argues 'Constructive theology requires for its completion the conceptuality of a modern ontology, given to it by loan from some example of contemporary philosophy.'[24] On this second point, Ogden's theology clearly has the advantage, for it aims at being thoroughly metaphysical. Moltmann, while being open to philosophical dialogue partners, retains an essentially loose connection with ontology. Because of his neo-orthodox background, he has resisted metaphysicizing the mythological language of scripture. Thus certain critical points, such as the meaning of the resurrection or history, the final fulfilment, God as future, remain without conceptual clarity. To quote Gilkey once again, we might summarize this discussion by saying that one of the fundamental differences between the process school of theology and that of the eschatological theologians is 'that the process God is ontologically conceived in terms of the categories of process philosophy, whereas the God of dialectical and eschatological theology is *ontically* conceived in the personalistic or "mythical" categories derived directly from Scripture.'[25]

This difference is obviously not only one of method but, as we

[23] Langdon Gilkey, *Catholicism Confronts Modernity, A Protestant View*, pp. 91–2.
[24] Ibid., p. 123.
[25] Gilkey, 'Process Theology', p. 15.

have seen above, has profound consequences for the content of systematic theology as well. For lying beneath the surface of the methodological question is an implicit resolution of the tension between the particular revelation of God in Jesus Christ and his universal presence in creation and history. The different stances taken by our two representative thinkers on this question effect two profoundly different christologies, and it is to this topic that we should now direct our attention.

### iii.    *Christology*

The critical points in Ogden's christology are the following. First, Ogden rejects any unique act of God as a mythological account of faith. The most stringent formulation of this position, I believe, can be found in his critique of Bultmann. Over against Bultmann's conviction, that the possibility of authentic existence becomes real in fact for the first time in Jesus Christ, Ogden states, 'There is not the slightest evidence that God has acted in Christ in any way different from the way in which he primordially acts in every other event.'[26]

Secondly, Ogden is not interested in the historical Jesus but in the historic, apostolic Christ, i.e. the witness of the Christ of the kerygma. Ogden pushes this position so far that even if the historical Jesus could be shown (*per impossibile*) not to have existed, this truth would not affect the truth of Christian faith. Therefore, Christian faith in no way affirms that Jesus actualized the possibility of authentic existence but only that he re-presents it.

Finally, Ogden insists that the Christ-event is not the constitutive event of God's love but rather the re-presentative event of this love. This means that it would be impossible to say that without the Christ-event God would not be gracious. We must rather say that always and everywhere God is the God of grace. The decisive re-presentation of his graciousness is the Christ-event.

The christology of Moltmann moves in precisely the opposite direction. First, Moltmann wants to define God in terms of the event of the cross. God *is* this trinitarian event, this event between the Father who 'delivers up', the Son who is

[26] Schubert Ogden, 'Bultmann's Project of Demythologizing and the Problem of Theology and Philosophy', *Journal of Religion* 37 (1957) 169.

abandoned, and the Spirit who is the bond of union between them. According to Moltmann, when the Christian says 'God', he means this event, an event which is at one and the same time particular and universal, for the particularity of the cross-event opens up to embrace the whole world because of the Spirit which is poured out.

Secondly, Moltmann rejects any discontinuity between the Jesus of history and the Christ of faith. The apostolic Christ is this Jesus in his particularity who has been raised and now has universal significance. In *Theology of Hope* he writes,

The sole bridge of continuity between the primitive Christian proclamation and the history and proclamation of Jesus is *via* the raising of the one who was crucified. This is a continuity in radical discontinuity, or an identity in total contradiction. The engima of this mysterious identity between the crucified and risen Christ is manifestly the driving force in the christological controversies of primitive Christianity.[27]

For Moltmann then the choice between a 'Jesuology' and a christology is a false one.

Finally, Moltmann insists that this Jesus who has been raised has a future. His mission does not come to an end with his resurrection. Rather his resurrection points to and guarantees the completion of his work in the handing over of the kingdom to his Father in the eschaton. As he says in his essay 'The End of History', 'The primitive Christian Easter faith teaches us that Jesus is always intelligible only in the relationship to his future.'[28] Or as he puts it in *The Crucified God*, 'This question of Christ (Who do you say that I am?) can only be answered by a new creation, in which the novel which is Jesus is no longer a novelty, and his cross is no longer a scandal and in which they have become the basis and the light of the kingdom. By con-

[27] Moltmann, *Theology of Hope*, p. 199; see also *The Crucified God*, p. 22. There Moltmann, speaking of false alternatives in interpreting Christian faith, writes: 'In Christian terms evangelization and humanization are not alternatives. Nor are inner repentance and a change in situations and circumstances. Nor are the "vertical dimension" of faith and the "horizontal dimension" of love for one's neighbour and political change. Nor are "Jesuology" and christology, the humanity and the divinity of Jesus. Both coincide in his death on the cross. Anyone who makes distinctions here, enforces alternatives and calls for a parting of the ways, in dividing the unity of God and man in the person, the imitation and the future of Christ.'

[28] Moltmann, 'The End of History', in *Hope and Planning* (London: SCM Press, 1971), p. 171.

fessing Jesus as the Christ, faith also confesses that this future of
his is real.'[29]

Moltmann is here making two significant points. First, the
present experience of salvation and grace which we experience
in Christ is not complete in itself. It is always promissory and
points beyond itself. Thus the eschaton is not experienced when
the kerygma is proclaimed and accepted. For the eschaton
consists in more than the living out of authentic existence. The
eschaton includes the overcoming of death, the elimination of
suffering and injustice, in short the new creation. Secondly, this
future of Jesus is more than just a restoration of what was lost by
sin. The future which Christ brings is something that has not
yet happened. If one were to ask what this future of Christ will
bring, Moltmann would reply

> Not a mere repetition of his history, and not only an unveiling of it,
> but something which has so far not yet happened through Christ. The
> Christian expectation is directed to no other than the Christ who has
> come, but it expects something new from him, something that has not
> yet happened so far: it awaits the fulfillment of the promised
> righteousness of God in all things, the fulfillment of the resurrection of
> the dead that is promised in his resurrection, the fulfilment of the
> lordship of the crucified one over all things that is promised in his
> exaltation.[30]

In evaluating these two christologies, although one would no
doubt want to question aspects of Moltmann's thought, one
would probably find the greater difficulties with Ogden's
christological ideas since he deals with the tension between
universality and particularity by virtually dissolving the pole of
particularity. It seems difficult to see how Ogden can affirm the
New Testament doctrine that Christ is the eschatological event.

More interesting than what a theolgian says is often what lies
behind his theological assertions, his motivations, the positions
which his theological statements are meant to safeguard.
Certainly one of the motives behind Ogden's christology is his
conviction that the New Testament itself affirms that God
reveals himself to men outside of the Christ-event. Moreover
the New Testament holds all men responsible for their sin, a

---

[29] Moltmann, *The Crucified God*, p. 106.
[30] Moltmann, *Theology of Hope*, pp. 228–9.

fact which would be unintelligible if God did not also universally bestow his grace upon them.[31]

A second factor influencing Ogden is his correct concern to
think through radically the New Testament doctrine that God
is love. This leads him to reject what he terms a constitutive
christology. By this term he understands the doctrine that
maintains that God in his sovereign freedom was free either to
create or not to create and later to redeem or not to redeem,
once man fell into sin. God is in fact the God of grace. He is
constituted as such by the event of Jesus Christ. But he could
have been otherwise.

Ogden seems to connect these two propositions: the constitutive christology outlined in the last paragraph and the unique,
particular eschatological event of Jesus Christ. By affirming the
latter, Ogden seems to believe that he must also affirm the
former.

Yet it seems to me that it is possible to detach these two
positions from one another. If one truly thinks historically, then
it is possible to conceive of God acting differently in different
times and places. Moreover it is possible to understand the
Christ-event as the unique, unrepeatable, eschatological event
of God. This would not imply that without the Christ-event
God would not be gracious, but rather that the always gracious
God achieves his purposes for history in Jesus Christ, so that in
him history reaches its God-given destiny.

Such is in fact the substance of the view proposed by Karl
Rahner. According to Rahner, Christ is the eschatological act of
God by being the final end of history. Let me cite briefly from
Rahner's *Foundations of Christian Faith* in which he explains the
relationship of the Christ-event to the history of the human
race. He writes,

If we understand the whole realm of time up to now which we call
'historically accessible' history, as a relatively brief transition, then
the place of Christ, in this secular history of the world, and of course
all the more so in the history of religion which is co-extensive with this
realm of time, becomes intelligible and becomes correlative to the
caesura which has lasted several thousand years. After an almost
incalculable sojourn in an almost natural existence, in this caesura

---

[31] See, for example, Schubert Ogden, 'Present Prospects for Empirical Theology', in
*The Future of Empirical Theology*, pp. 73 ff.

mankind becomes conscious of itself, and not only in introverted reflection, art and philosophy, but also in an art and reflection which turns out to the world around it. And at the same time as the history of the human race enters into this period it reaches the God–Man, the absolute historical objectification of its transcendental understanding of God. In this objectification, namely, in Jesus Christ, the God who communicates himself and the man who accepts God's self-communication become irrevocably one, and the history of revelation and salvation of the whole human race reaches its goal. This does not, however, decide the question of individual salvation.

Now man no longer moves toward his goal only transcendentally but rather this history of mankind also reaches its very goal categorically, and within this goal it actively directs itself toward the final goal. for in this history and within the period of this caesura there is already present the very thing toward which mankind is moving: the God-humanity of mankind in the one God-Man Jesus Christ.[32]

Rahner deals with the tension between particularity and universality by seeing creation and incarnation not as two separate and juxtaposed acts of God but rather as two moments or phases of God's self-giving and self-expression. It is true that Rahner likewise goes on to affirm just such a supernaturalist position as I outlined above. He writes, 'Such an understanding in no way denies that God could also have created a world without an incarnation, that is, that he could have denied to the self-transcendence of matter that ultimate culmination which takes place in grace and in incarnation.'[33] It is this doctrine which Ogden rejects. I would only like to add here that in my judgement this supernaturalist position of Rahner need not follow logically from his understanding of the eschatological act of God and of its relation to the history of mankind. I want to affirm that one can adopt this position without interpreting it in the supernaturalist way that Rahner does. If God's being itself is revealed in this event, then we can say with full logical rigour that God is love. Thinking this through in trinitarian terms would mean that God from all eternity is ordered to creation and incarnation. We could then say, as Moltmann and Jüngel do, that God's being is in coming. There is no other God except the God who wants to give himself away in creation and incar-

[32] Karl Rahner, *Foundations of Christian Faith, An Introduction to the Idea of Christianity*, trans. William V. Dych (New York: Seabury Press, 1978), pp. 169–70.
[33] Ibid., p. 197.

nation, a God therefore ordered to history. Rahner uses the categories of nature and supernature because he wants to preserve the divine freedom and the grace character of salvation. We shall come back to this problem later in this chapter when we discuss the nature of God's freedom. I will there try to show that God's freedom, the freedom of his self-possession, is deeper than freedom of choice. If this is true, it would seem to be possible to accept Moltmann's insistence on Jesus as the eschatological event without falling into a kind of particularism which denies the universality of grace or which in any way compromises the radicality of the New Testament assertion 'God is love'. We would only have to say that God's love, freedom, and grace have themselves a history, the history of God's dealings with men, a history which reaches its definitive, irreversible and thus eschatological turning point in the event which bears the name Jesus Christ.

iv. *The End of History—God's Immanence and Transcendence*

From the question of christology, we turn to that of eschatology. The transition is a natural one, for eschatological assertions can be understood as christological statements from the point of view of their fulfilment.[34]

If we were to ask of the future of Jesus in Ogden's process theology, we would have to say that he has no future in the sense of subjective immortality. But he has the same future which any other actual entity or personally-ordered series of actual entities has, namely to be redeemed by God, to be taken up into God's everlasting life. In accordance with the process doctrine that nothing is ultimately lost, we can say that God uses all that Jesus has been in his ongoing creative interaction with the world. Process theologians would interpret the resurrection along these lines.

Moreover, process theologians are not interested in the future of Jesus as such nor in the subjective immortality of any other person. This is true, first of all, because as Ogden stresses, the *theological* significance of eschatological statements is the

---

[34] See, for example, Karl Rahner, 'The Hermeneutics of Eschatological Assertions', *Theological Investigations* IV (London: Darton, Longman and Todd, 1966), pp. 323–46. On p. 346 Rahner writes, 'Eschatological assertions of scripture are and intend to be . . . no more than such assertions of christology and anthropology in terms of their fulfilment.'

meaning of events, persons, the world, for God. The eschatological dimension of faith grounds the worthwhileness of human
life and action in the face of the perpetual perishing of all
temporal events. Everything temporal is shown to be
worthwhile because all temporal events are received
everlastingly into God. Process theology can meaningfully
assert this, since according to this doctrine God is not only
eminent cause but also eminent effect. Thus the real point of
eschatological assertions is to affirm that 'because God not only
*affects*, but is also *affected by* whatever exists, all things are in
every present quite literally resurrected or restored in his own
everlasting life, from which they can nevermore be cast out'.[35]

The process doctrine of eschatology follows secondly from the
principles of process metaphysics. According to this system
God is not the ultimate source of our metaphysical situation.
The most radical source of our metaphysical situation is
creativity itself, the ultimately inexplicable fact that the many
become one and are increased by one. The metaphysical
principles are basically the most generalized description of this
situation. And God is not an exception to them but, as Whitehead observes, their chief exemplification.[36]

If creativity is the irreducible, aboriginal ground of experience, then it follows, as process philosophers assert, that there
can be in principle no completion to temporal process. In
Whitehead's striking words, 'Neither God, nor the World,
reaches static completion. Both are in the grip of the ultimate
metaphysical ground, the creative advance into novelty. Either
of them, God and the World, is the instrument of novelty for the
other.'[37]

Clearly then within this context it is impossible to speak of a
final or transcendent end to history. Thus Ogden notes that the
belief that God is the ground or end of whatever is or is even
possible in no way requires 'that there sometime will be, nay
even must be, a last stage of the cosmic process. To suppose that
the promise of faith in itself requires us to make any such claim
is as wrong as to hold that faith in God as the creator implies

---

[35] Ogden, *The Reality of God*, p. 226.
[36] Whitehead writes, 'God is not to be treated as an exception to all metaphysical
principles, invoked to save their collapse. He is their chief exemplification.' *Process and
Reality*, p. 521.
[37] Ibid., p. 529.

that the world process sometime had a first stage.'[38] But particularly interesting here is that Ogden's position is derived not only from theological considerations but, in accordance with his metaphysicizing of faith, from the ontological limits of what Christian faith *could* meaningfully assert. As Daniel Day Williams comments, for process philosophers a final event is in principle impossible, because these philosophers envision a loosely organized universe in which there is an endless pluralty of events. In such a world there can be no final event that consummates the unity of the whole. Therefore while God himself can be said to be the future of every becoming and while it can even be affirmed that he himself has a future, God cannot be said to be the Absolute Future of the world in the stronger sense which eschatological theologians such as Moltmann want to affirm.[39]

How then could we summarize the principle tenets of Moltmann's eschatological doctrine? First of all, taking our clue from christology, we note that Jesus of Nazareth, risen from the dead, has a real future in his handing over of the kingdom to his Father in the eschaton. In this act his mission to the world is completed and he fulfils his ontological role as Son in his obedience to the Father.

This implies an eschatological event in which history reaches its completion. From the perspective of our present history, this eschatological event is future. But we must be careful to affirm that this future event is not an inner-worldly historical event. Moltmann clearly distinguishes the future of history from future history. He writes, 'Only a future which transcends the experiment of history itself can become the paradigm of transcendence and give meaning to the experiment "history".'[40]

To speak in language of the kingdom, this means that no future event within history as we know it can realize the kingdom of God. Nevertheless the kingdom of God has an intrinsic relation to present history. The relation of the kingdom to history is the relation of transcendence to immanence which

---

[38] Ogden, *The Reality of God*, p. 213.

[39] See Daniel Day Williams, 'Response to Wolfhart Pannenberg', in *Hope and the Future of Man*, ed. Ewert H. Cousins (Philadelphia: Fortress Press, 1972), pp. 83–8.

[40] Jürgen Moltmann, 'The Future as New Paradigm of Transcendence', in *Religion, Revolution and the Future* (New York: Charles Scribner's Sons, 1968), p. 196.

Moltmann understands as the relation of future to present.
Moltmann explains what this means when he writes,

In history God rules in a disputed and hidden way. That is why his
liberating rule in history points towards its own fulfilment in the
coming kingdom, just as, conversely, the coming kingdom already
casts its light on the conflicts of history. The liberating rule of God can
thus be understood as the immanence of the eschatological kingdom,
and the coming kingdom can be interpreted as the transcendence of
the believed and experienced rule of God in the present. This understanding forbids us to banish the lordship of God to a future world
totally unrelated to our earthly, historical life. But it also forbids us to
identify the kingdom of God with conditions in history, whether they
be already existing or desired.[41]

Moltmann then adopts the same view of the possibility of
realizing an historical utopia as that taken by Karl Rahner who
writes

All utopian conceptions of salvation-in-the-world are to be rejected as
doctrines meriting condemnation. History is by this fact declared to
be the realm of the provisional, the unfinished, the ambiguous, the
dialectical—and any attempt to seize salvation in this world and to
find completion in the history of the world as such would itself remain
a moment in history—part of what is evil, godless and vain in
history—and would itself give way to other history coming after it.[42]

Underlying these two different views of eschatology, we can

---

[41] Moltmann, *The Church in the Power of the Spirit*, p. 190. In a similar way Langdon
Gilkey notes the necessity for Christian theology to affirm the transcendent end of
history when he writes: 'The eschatological symbols of the kingdom and its glory,
representing the *ultimate* goal of providence, must, we said, have a double reference.
First and foremost, the eschatological symbol of the kingdom has an *immediate* and
*immanent* reference to the new possibilities of social betterment in the immediate future
as defining those possibilities indicating the ultimate goal of God's hidden providential
working—namely, being, participation, community and self-actualization—and so
guiding political action for the future . . .

'Secondly, however, the eschatological symbols must have as well a *transcendent*
reference beyond every historical possibility, even the one that lures us now, and
beyond even what providence and human freedom can together produce in history—
lest our historical program and action claim to achieve and represent that ultimate
goal. The judgment of God on what is alien to himself will be an essential part of the
relation of the rule of God to *every* social achievement and so to *every* period of history.
For no society in history *is* the kingdom, and realization of this is one essential part of
every society's health.' *Reaping the Whirlwind*, p. 292.

[42] Karl Rahner, 'History of the World and Salvation-History', *Theological Investigations* V (London: Darton, Longman and Todd, 1966), pp. 97–8.

discern at least three central theological and philosophical principles upon which Ogden and Moltmann disagree. The first we might call the difference of tense. For Ogden, all eschatological assertions refer to the present tense. He writes,

Being really and truly *last* things, that is, *ultimate* things, things constituting the most essential reality of *all* places on the time-line, they are always and only matters of the present—though, of course, of *every* present. Just as the reality of God as the creator is not something belonging to the past of nature and history, but is their ever-present primordial ground, so the reality of God as a judge and redeemer is not a particular event of the future, but the ever-present final consequence of each passing moment in the stream of time.[43]

It is against this view of eschatology that Moltmann directed his polemic in *Theology of Hope*. What he wrote there against Bultmann's realized eschatology could equally be said in reference to Ogden, Bultmann's disciple. Moltmann finds this view ultimately a-historical. Hidden beneath this view lies the God of Greek metaphysics, the eternally present God, not the God of the bible, the God of history and of promise. Summing up his critique of this reduction of eschatological assertions to present realities, Moltmann writes

The theological question arises whether it is really true that in the event of revelation in proclamation and faith man already comes 'to himself' in that authenticity which is at once both original and final. In that case faith would itself be the practical end of history and the believer would himself already be perfected. There would be nothing more that still awaits him, and nothing more towards which he is on his way in the world in the body and in history. God's 'futurity' would be 'constant' and man's openness in his 'wayfaring' would likewise be 'constant' and 'never-ending'. This, however, is just what would cause believing existence, understood in an 'eschatological' sense of this sort, to turn into a new form of the 'epiphany of the eternal present'.[44]

Moltmann then wants to assert that eschatological statements do truly refer to the future, both to the future of the individual and of the cosmos. He admits that the epistemological foundation for such assertions is the present, namely our

[43] Ogden, *The Reality of God*, p. 210.
[44] Moltmann, *Theology of Hope*, pp. 67–68.

experience of the death and resurrection of Christ.[45] Without this foundation, our statements about the future become either extrapolation from present secular experience or wildly fantastic projections of the imagination. But on the basis of the paschal mystery, one can truly affirm the consummation of history in the handing over of the kingdom by the Son to the Father. Faith points to a real future event and as such is hoping knowledge. Verification can only take place in the eschaton.

Our previous discussion leads us to the second principle of disagreement among process thinkers and eschatological theologians. This is the question of how we are to conceive the relation of future to present. In discussing this point we are really elaborating on the previous one, for as John Cobb writes, 'Whitehead agrees with Bultman that if meaning is to be found anywhere, it must be found immediately in each moment.'[46] In Whitehead's philosophy every moment is a moment of decision. The decision lies between the two alternatives of repetition of the past and response to new possibility. Whitehead locates the realm of possibility in God. From the infinite number of possibilities in God's primordial nature, he offers to every occasion the novel possibility that can maximize the potentiality of that occasion. This is the ideal aim for this occasion. The future is then a moment in the becoming of every occasion.

This view of the relation of future to present involves both continuity and discontiunity with the past. For Whitehead it is the nature of reality to be open. There is no occasion which does not have an element of freedom. Every occasion has the possibility of real novelty, of a genuine future. The future does not have to conform to the past. God's function is precisely to be the lure of freedom, to open up a new possibility for each occasion. But God must work within the limits of what is presented to

<hr>

[45] In *The Future of Creation* (p. 44) Moltmann writes, 'I must express my criticism of Rahner here. He has rightly pointed to the fact that the basis of our knowledge of eschatology lies in the present experience of salvation, as this is christologically and · anthropologically determined. Berkhof, better than Rahner, defines the basis of our knowledge christologically and pneumatologically; for in Christian terms the experience of the Spirit precedes the person's experience of himself. The basis of our knowledge of eschatology lies here, and this is disputed neither by me not by anyone else.'

[46] John Cobb, 'What is the Future? A Process Perspective', in *Hope and the Future of Man*, p. 4. This essay provides a good summary of the Whiteheadian view of the future which I am trying to outline in this paragraph.

him. God and the world both have their freedom of interaction. God cannot radically overcome the false alternatives of the past. Rather, presented with a finite world, with its history, its previous decisions, its limitations, he can draw it beyond itself into a new future which is still possible given its past.

For Moltmann too the future comes to the present from God. The future is not merely an extrapolation of the present. But although Moltmann and Ogden both agree that the future is a genuine novelty and not a mere repetition of the past, they have a radically different conception of the relation of future to past. And the difference seems to me to lie precisely in this question of contunuity. Ogden's God, the God of process, works within limitations. He offers a new possibility to the world which is presented to him. This possibility must be consonant with the history of freedom up to that point. Moltmann's God, on the other hand, is not limited by the past. He can create a world out of nothing; he can raise the dead. He can therefore create possibilities where none exist. Even the dead, the victims of Auschwitz and Hiroshima, have a future because of this God. In *Religion, Revolution and the Future* Moltmann sums up his position when he asks

Is there thus for Paul no continuity between history and this new future? Yes, even for him there is continuity. But it does not consist in some human or immanent factor in perpetual process; it is, rather, the faithfulness of God, who, in creating the new, remembers and brings back the old, which has turned away from him and been lost. The expression 'resurrection of the dead' means that God brings back the dead in his new creation and gathers up the lost. The new creation therefore takes up the old creation in itself, just as all historical continuity is created by the future which takes up into itself what has been lost. Thus historical continuity distinguishes itself in principle from an organic or ontological continuity. If God creates a quali- tatively new future, then he is not only the future of the present, but also the future *of* the past and *for* the past.[47]

This citation from Moltmann brings me to the third principle of disagreement underlying these two eschatologies and this is the decisive one which leads to such radically different theologies, namely the conception of God himself. For at the

[47] Moltmann, 'What is "New" in Christianity: The Category Novum in Christian Theology', in *Religion, Revolution and the Future*, pp. 12–13.

heart of these two theologies are two different understandings of God which we could perhaps conveniently describe by saying that the God of process theology is a God who becomes whereas the God of eschatological theology is a God who comes. In one formulation Moltmann sums up the difference this way: 'The German word *Zukunft* translates not the Latin word *futurum* but the Latin word *adventus*, whose Greek equivalent is *parousia*. *Adventus* designates *that which is coming*. If we apply this to theology, we are not able to speak of a "becoming God" but only of the "coming God". This is the difference between eschatology and process philosophy.'[48] Elsewhere Moltmann expands this comment explaining in more detail what he means when the writes

There remains a difference beteen eschatological theology which speaks of the 'coming God', and teleological metaphysics and process philosophy, which speaks of the 'becoming God' or of God as the *finis ultimus* ('the final end') of all things. As far as I can tell, process theology, on the one hand, speaks of the 'becoming God' in the context of the dynamics of world process. Eschatological theology, on the other hand, speaks of the 'coming God' in the context of the dialectical dynamics, circumscribed by the symbols of *creatio ex nihilo*, *justificatio impii*, and *resurrectio mortuorum*.[49]

The fundamental difference then seems to be that of creativity itself. For Moltmann, God is the source of creativity. For Whitehead, God is the aboriginal instance of creativity. For process philosophy creativity or the fact that things exist in a dynamic interaction is an ultimate for which no explanation can be given and for which no one is responsible. The ultimate issue between process theolgians and eschatological theolgians is whether this account of our metaphysical situation with all its consequences for the doctrine of God is to be accepted. Is God the lure of freedom, the source of possibilities, the fellow-sufferer who understands or is he the source of creativity, the God who creates out of nothing and who raises the dead, the God who can make all things new?

### v.  *Nature and History*

Ogden and Moltmann both agree that the exploitative attitude

[48] Moltmann, *The Experiment Hope*, p. 52.
[49] Moltmann, 'Hope and History', in *Religion, Revolution and the Future*, p. 210.

toward nature which has been characteristic of Western culture since the rise of modern science, and which is partly due to a prevalent interpretation of the biblical doctrine of man as lord over nature, must be overcome if man is to survive. Ogden writes for example,

The sharp separation Christianity especially has traditionally made between man and nature, on the one hand, and God and nature, on the other, along with its understanding of God's mandate to man to dominate the rest of creation, are the fundamental presuppositions behind the modern development of science and technology and their use to exploit the natural environment for the sake of human ends.[50]

Moltmann writes in a similar vein,

The ecological crisis caused by the progressive destruction of nature was brought about by Christianity and science together; and if man and nature want to win a chance to survive, then Christianity and science must together revise both the picture of man found in the traditional belief in creation ('subdue the earth,' Gen. 1:28) and the picture of men reflected in Cartesian science (*'Maître et possesseur de la nature'*).[51]

Nevertheless in spite of this superficial agreement as to the necessity of a changed attitude toward nature, there are profound philosophical differences in their understanding of nature and of the relation of nature to history.

We could begin describing the process position by remarking that these theologians are sympathetic to philosophical naturalism, although a version of naturalism open to the transcendent. Daniel Day Williams succinctly sums up the meaning of naturalism as a philosophical position when he writes, 'Naturalism sees nature-history as one continuous order, with a direction in which time is meaningful both to the "natural" processes, that is, the physical and biological processes, and to historical process.'[52]

In understanding the relation of history to nature, process philosophers tend to assimilate history to nature. Thus, for example, Ogden explains,

[50] Schubert Ogden, 'Prolegomena to a Christian Theology of Nature', Honors Day Convocation Address, Perkins School of Theology, 24 April 1974, p. 1.
[51] Moltmann, *The Future of Creation*, p. 115.
[52] Daniel Day Williams, 'Christianity and Naturalism: An Informal Statement', *Union Seminary Quarterly Review* 12 (1956–7) 48.

The *absolute* distinctions between man and nature, or history and nature, all become merely *relative* distinctions. . . . Even nonhuman nature is, in its way, or at its various levels, historical. Indeed, reality as such, or, in principle, is interpreted in *historical* terms, it being the metaphysical nature of things that, as Whitehead puts it in defining his basic concept 'creativity', 'the many become one and are increased by one'.[53]

Moltmann approaches the problem in exactly the opposite way, namely, by assimilating nature to history. This tendency is seen in his early work *Theology of Hope* in the section in which Moltmann discusses apocalyptic. Moltmann asks whether apocalyptic thinking is not ultimately non-historic thinking.[54] Does not apocalyptic, for example, apply cosmological patterns to history? Although a superficial reading of apocalyptic may indicate this, Moltmann judges that such a reading is ultimately false. Apocalyptic does not mean a cosmological interpretation of eschatological history, but rather an eschatological and historic interpretation of the cosmos. In other words the cosmos itself is taken up into the process of eschatological history. This is the groaning of all creation spoken of by St. Paul in Rom. 8:22.

Moltmann comes back to this perspective in his second major book *The Crucified God*. There he speaks of the cosmological dimension of the cross. He writes,

Nevertheless, the theology of the cross also has cosmological dimensions, because it sees the cosmos in the eschatological history of God. For the 'history of God', whose nucleus is the event of the cross, cannot be thought of as history in the world, but on the contrary makes it necessary to understand the world in this history. . . . The history of God is then to be thought of as the horizon of the world; the world is not to be thought of as the horizon of this history.[55]

[53] Ogden, 'Prolegomena to a Christian Theology of Nature', p. 5. Elsewhere Ogden explains 'The dualism of history and nature presupposed by such homocentrism is both theoretically false and practically vicious . . . To continue to speak, therefore, as some theologians do, of "nature's hostile territory", and thus to claim that "man is emancipated *from* nature *for* history", is to foster the very attitudes toward our natural environment that have already driven us to the brink of historical catastrophe, whether through the exhaustion of nonrenewable resources upon which any progress in history is dependent or through so polluting our natural home that it is no longer humanly habitable.' *Faith and Freedom, Toward a Theology of Liberation*, pp. 108–9.
[54] See *Theology of Hope*, pp. 133–8.
[55] Moltmann, *The Crucified God*, pp. 218–9.

If one understands the cosmos in the eschatological process of history, then one can say that nature, or at least humanized nature, does not yet exist. Rather nature is the final goal of history. In one of his essays Moltmann puts it this way, ' "Human nature", or that which makes men men, is not given at the beginning of their history and does not exist as idea behind the multiplicity of man's appearances. If it exists at all, it stands at the goal and end of his history and its conflicts. "Man has no nature; he has only history" (Ortega y Gasset).'[56]

Looking at these two conceptions of the relation of man and his history to nature, we find two divergent philosophical positions, the one based on the Anglo-American empirical naturalistic tradition which seeks to understand man as a part of nature, however developed his capacities in regard to it, and the other based on the tradition of German idealism, according to which spirit is the ultimate reality and nature is spirit's own self-objectification. If for idealism nature exists for spirit, for naturalism man is so inextricably bound up with the processes of nature, that all talk of resurrection from the dead and transcendent future for history must be ruled out. Thus although Ogden and Moltmann are both committed to the overcoming of the Greek idea of God as a-temporal and although they both agree that the atheistic critique of Christianity can hardly be met unless God is brought into closer contact with temporal process, none the less on their fundamental understanding of what time and history are, they so seriously disagree that it was inevitable from the outset that they should have produced the radically different doctrines of God and eschatology as we have previously sketched in this chapter.

## vi.   *The Value of the Secular*

One of the motivations of Ogden's theology has been to show that Christian faith is compatible with an affirmation of the secular. He has tried to show that Christian theology must rethink its doctrine of God to demonstrate the compatibility between belief in God and affirmation of the world, for in Ogden's opinion these two are contradictories in classical philosophical theism. The reason is that the God of classical

---

[56] Jürgen Moltmann, 'Man and the Son of Man', in *No Man Is Alien, Essays on the Unity of Mankind*, ed. J. Robert Nelson (Leiden: E. J. Brill, 1971), p. 208.

philosophical theism is impassible and therefore is metaphysically incapable of being affected by his creatures. Ogden
contends that this position undermines our commitment to
secular reality, since in the last analysis whatever we do is
indifferent to him whom we take to be the ultimate. He writes,

Supernaturalists have traditionally maintained that the end of man is
to serve or glorify God through obedience to his will and command-
ments. And yet the God whom we are thus summoned to serve is, in
the last analysis, so conceived that he can be as little affected by our
best actions as by our worst. As *actus purus*, and thus a statically
complete perfection incapable in any respect of further self-
realization, God can be neither increased nor diminished by what we
do, and our action, like our suffering, must be in the strictest sense
wholly indifferent to him.[57]

For this reason Ogden rejects the God of classical philosophical theism but he also rejects a God such as that of
Moltmann who promises that in spite of suffering and death, his
purposes for the world will certainly triumph. Ogden asks: if
faith is given this guarantee, can it really enter into the risks of
freedom? Is such a faith capable of hope or is hope reduced to
confidence, as Ernst Bloch alleges?[58] Daniel Day Williams has
most cogently expressed this objection when he asked: 'How
can life be serious if in a final event it will all be one absolute
good, no matter what has happened?' He continues,

Love does not ask for guarantees. Why should love demand final
completion when its very joy is participation in the task yet to be done,
the anticipation of the community yet to be created? Of course there is
rest, rest in every glimpse of fulfillment and every moment of
communion. The intrinsic logic of love is not that of identity but that
of creative community in which real suffering and loss are risked.[59]

Certainly a theologian such as Moltmann is aware of this
difficulty, and especially in his early work *Theology of Hope* he
seems to leave little scope for the place of human efforts to bring
about the kingdom. Thus, for example, speaking of God's

[57] Ogden, *The Reality of God*, pp. 17–18.
[58] See 'Kann Hoffnung enttäuscht werden?' in *Ernst Bloch, Auswahl aus seinen Schriften.*
zusammengestellt und eingeleitet von Hans Heinz Holz (Frankfurt: Fischer Bücherei,
1967), pp. 175–81.
[59] Daniel Day Williams, 'Response to Wolfhart Pannenberg', in *Hope and the Future of
Man*, pp. 87–8.

promises, he unequivocally maintained, 'If they are God's promises, then God must be regarded as the subject of their fulfilment.'[60] Such statements do seem to confirm the objection raised by Williams and other process thinkers against eschatological theology. Even a sympathetic reader such as Peter Momose is led to object:

One must ask whether the partial fulfilment, which Moltmann certainly does not want to deprecate, but which because of the *novum ultimum* he believes he must leave behind him, contributes anything to the coming of this *novum ultimum*, i.e. whether world-history is fundamentally nothing other than a stage, on which, hope, as the formal structure of man, finds its expression, but whose fate is finally decided by God alone.[61]

Part of Moltmann's answer lies in his rejection of an either–or solution. He rejects the dilemma: either man is subject to the risk of history and has a free choice in regard to his co-operation with God's purposes, with the result that God's promise of the kingdom is conditioned, or God alone brings the kingdom about, with the result that human action is ultimately irrelevant. He proposes instead a dialectical understanding of the relation of future to present. The future of the kingdom revealed in the resurrection of the crucified one is both the unshakable ground of hope and the impetus to action. In view of the future revealed in the face of the risen but crucified Jesus the present is criticized and concrete steps are taken to make the present conform to the promised future. Moltmann writes:

The Christian faith does not supplant history so that history would become an indifferent matter to believers. Because the Christian can hope in the new future through faith in Christ, he begins to suffer in the unredeemedness of the present and realize solidarity with all who suffer consciously or unconsciously in this unredeemedness. But neither does he become absorbed into history so that the future would become indifferent to faith. Because he can hope in this future, he begins to oppose the 'scheme of this world' and the systems of the present to change them.[62]

From what we have seen, both thinkers are committed to the

---

[60] Moltmann, *Theology of Hope*, p. 104.

[61] Momose, *Kreuzestheologie*, p. 158.

[62] Moltmann, 'The Future as New Paradigm of Transcendence', in *Religion, Revolution and the Future*, p. 198.

value of secular activity. They are also both committed to the idea that our actions make a difference to God, for both reject the tenets of classical philosophical theism. They further agree that whatever continuity exists between human achievements and the kingdom of God must be created from God's side. Thus, for example, in Ogden's Perkins lectures on systematic theology, in his treatment of eschatology, he writes, 'The continuity that the Christian witness undoubtedly affirms between present and future is the continuity established by *God's* subjectivity, not by ours, by his redemption and judgment of the world, and, in the human case, by his universal offer of salvation to all men and women—not by our continued subjective existence beyond the limit of our death.'[63]

Writing in a similar vein, Moltmann notes, 'What unites the present with the past is the future of God whose present form receives the future of the past into itself. For the past changes from within the coming of the future. Christ is not only the hope of the present, but also the hope of the past. If he is raised into the future of God, he also becomes the future of the past.'[64]

Both thinkers then agree that our world and all our human efforts are embraced by God and in this sense a final meaning is given to human activity. The critical difference lies in the power which God has to transform what is given to him. For process thinkers, God can use anything that is given to him in furthering his purposes for the world. In one sense then even tragedy is not final, for there remains the *possibility* that some good can be drawn out of it. There remain eternal resources in God for overcoming evil.[65] In another sense, however, one could say that for process thinkers tragedy is irrevocable. Even God cannot overcome the past. What has been is part of the unalterable record of man's history and freedom. Because Moltmann's God, on the other hand, is the creator *ex nihilo*, he not only has resources for drawing good out of the past; he can even re-create the past. For Moltmann the key discontinuity is death. For him too the real issue is the perpetual perishing.

---

[63] Schubert Ogden, 'On the Last Things', (Unpublished Lecture Series, Perkins School of Theology, 1975–6), p. 13.

[64] Moltmann, 'Theology as Eschatology', in *The Future of Hope: Theology as Eschatology*, p. 22.

[65] See Daniel Day Williams, 'Tragedy and the Christian Eschatology', *Encounter* 24 (1963) 61–76, especially pp. 74–6.

Therefore he hopes in the God of the resurrection. He writes, 'The symbol of hope of the resurrection of the dead means future for those who are past. This future results not *from* the past, but it is opened *for* those who are past. What other continuity should there be through the discontinuity of death?'[66]

In the last analysis then, faced with the final enemy death, the Christian must live by grace. No human effort can bridge this chasm. Ogden's eschatology, so radically demythologized, is an attempt to think through the doctrine of grace to the end. For he finds in man's persistent request for subjective immortality a last refusal to let go and live solely by and for God's pure unbounded love. He writes, 'The usual arguments for subjective immortality appear, however unintentionally, to be witnesses more to man's persistent sin than to God's abiding love.'[67]

As Ogden's remarks on immortality make clear, the real issue underlying the question of the significance of our commitment to the secular is the issue of grace and works. Granted that Ogden is right in affirming that a God unable to be affected in any way by what we do would undermine our commitment to this world, does it follow that unless the future is really uncertain, that unless success or failure in establishing the kingdom genuinely lies in the balance, then our real involvement in the risks and struggles of history is ultimately not serious? I think not. So long as God invites us to share with him the task of building the kingdom, so long as he assures us that he will not establish the kingdom without our efforts, then we can enter into the struggles of our world, fully aware of the risks involved. And indeed we have no assurance that all our efforts will not fail. Moreover we know that even with our best efforts we cannot bring about the kingdom, for we cannot on our own cross the unbridgable gulf of death. But this does not destroy our hope, because on the basis of the death and resurrection of Christ, we await the transcendent fulfilment of every life and of the cosmos itself, trusting that God will bridge the gap that we of ourselves are unable to cross. A theology of

---

[66] 'Nachwort von Jürgen Moltmann', in Momose, *Kreuzestheologie*, p. 181.
[67] Schubert Ogden, 'The Meaning of Christian Hope', in *Religious Experience and Process Theology*, p. 210.

the paschal mystery, with its belief in the transcendent end of history, requires us then at one and the same time to relativize (not abandon) all human activity and at the same time to radicalize it in view of God's identification with the suffering of the world in the event of the cross and in view of his word of promise in the event of the resurrection.[68]

### vii.  *The Divine Freedom*

In turning now to the topic of the divine freedom, we are dealing with a variation of the recurring theme of our study, namely God's relation to the world. For at the heart of the problem of God's freedom is his relation to creation and redemption. Does God, for example, have the freedom of choice to create a world or not, and later to redeem that fallen world or not?

Process theologians reject such a freedom of choice in God. For them 'to be is to be related', and therefore it is impossible for God to exist in isolation. He is God precisely by being in relation to a world. William Christian in his commentary on Whitehead's philosophy summarizes this point as follows. He writes:

A second criticism is leveled against the doctrine that God is absolutely complete and self-sufficient. This doctrine belongs to a more reflective phase of traditional theology. For the early Christian theologians, 'He was internally complete' (AI 217; see RM 70). In the words of Descartes, God was 'absolutely self-sustaining' (RM 106). God's existence required 'no relations to anything beyond himself' (AI 217). This last phrase carries the main point of the doctrine Whitehead is attacking.[69]

Although this classical position as understood by Whitehead

---

[68] The Second Vatican Council speaks along similar lines in its *Pastoral Constitution on the Church in the Modern World* when it declares, 'While we are warned that it profits a man nothing if he gain the whole world and lose himself, the expectation of a new earth must not weaken but rather stimulate our concern for cultivating this one. For here grows the body of a new human family, a body which even now is able to give some kind of foreshadowing of the new age.

'Earthly progress must be carefully distiguished from the growth of Christ's kingdom. Nevertheless, to the extent that the former can contribute to the better ordering of human society, it is of vital concern to the kingdom of God.' See *Pastoral Constitution on the Church in the Modern World*, in *The Documents of Vatican II* ed. Walter M. Abbot, S. J. (London-Dublin: Geoffrey Chapman, 1966), p. 237.

[69] William A. Christian, *An Interpretation of Whitehead's Metaphysics* pp. 386–7. [RM: *Religion in the Making*; AI: *Adventures of Ideas*].

must be judged at least inadequate and failing to give full weight to the New Testamant affirmation that God is love, Whitehead's position, from the point of view of Christian theology, is also inadequate, for it puts God in metaphysical dependenence upon the world, thereby preserving his freedom at the cost of his transcendence.

The key to understanding God's freedom then will be a deeper probing into the meaning of love. Ogden, taking his starting point from Wesley's notion that God is pure unbounded love, develops the idea of positive and negative freedom. By negative freedom Ogden means the freedom to do nothing at all. By positive freedom he means the freedom to do this or that. Ogden rejects the concept of negative freedom in the case of God. If the New Testament doctrine of God is true, then we must say that God cannot be himself without loving his creation. Ogden distinguishes his conception of the divine freedom from the classical understanding as follows. On the neoclassical construction

God's grace toward man is free in the sense that he can love man in this way rather than that . . . even though, given the existence of man, God would not and *could* not [italics mine] be himself without loving man in *some* unsurpassably appropriate way. On the classical construction, by contrast, God could and would be himself even though, despite the fact of man's existence, he were not to show his grace toward man *at all*. Even though the existence of man necessarily implies the existence of God, it in no way implies the love of God for man beyond such love as may be said to be expressed by the sheer fact of man's existence, i.e., it in no way implies God's grace. Clearly, the difference between these views is the difference between views for which God's gracious action toward man is respectively God's only way of dealing with him who is made in God's image and but one of the ways in which God may deal with man consistently both with his own essential nature as God and with the fact of his having created man *imago Dei*.[70]

The problem then is clearly one of understanding the relation of God's freedom *vis-à-vis* the world in such a way that God is not affirmed to 'need' the world in order to be God nor is the

[70] Schubert Ogden, Unpublished notes 'On the Concept of God's Freedom', pp. 1–2. Although, in the passage quoted, Ogden discusses negative and positive freedom in relation to the question of grace, the same argument could be developed in relation to the doctrine of creation.

world reduced to being merely an accident of his freedom of choice.[71]

This is the very dilemma which confronts Moltmann. Moltmann, like Ogden, wants to think radically the meaning of the New Testament affirmation that God is love. This affirmation he can accept on the basis of the event of the cross. God has so identified himself with this event that we can say that God is this event. But this event opens out to embrace all history. Moltmann is led then to see history itself as the trinitarian history of God, God in his seeking and gathering love. Moltmann writes,

The life of God within the Trinity cannot be conceived as a closed circle—the symbol of perfection and self-sufficiency. A Christian doctrine of the Trinity which is bound to the history of Christ and the history of the Spirit must conceive the Trinity as the Trinity of the sending and seeking love of God which is open from its very origin. The triune God is the God who is open to man, open to the world and open to time.[72]

But then the question arises: has Moltmann fallen into the same trap as Whitehead—has he made the world metaphysically necessary for God? Moltmann's answer is twofold. First, we cannot say that God relates himself to the world out of need. He writes,

We cannot talk about God's love being open to the world and time out of deficiency of being. God's love is open because of the divine abundance and superabundance of being. When, therefore, we talk about a 'history' of the Trinity, we do not mean the time of deficiency, imperfection, sin and death; we mean the eternity of overflowing abundance, of perfection that communicates itself, of ever-increasing grace and of life-creating life.[73]

[71] Among modern thinkers Hegel has pointed the way in suggesting that the God–world relationship can be properly understood only when we think through the meaning of God as subject. In his lectures on the philosophy of religion, Hegel writes, 'For love implies a distinguishing between two, and yet these two are, as a matter of fact, not distinguished from one another.' *Lectures on the Philosophy of Religion*, trans. from the second German edition by the Rev. E. B. Speirs, B. D. and J. Burdon Sanderson (London and New York: Routledge and Kegan Paul and Humanities Press, 1971), vol. iii. p. 10. In one sense then God is independent of the world. But in another sense, since God is loving subject, the world is not accidental or even extrinsic to God, since he loves it and to this extent, in the logic of love, it becomes necessary to him.

[72] Moltmann, *The Church in the Power of the Spirit*, pp. 55–6.

[73] Moltmann, *The Future of Creation*, p. 86.

Secondly, Moltmann argues that the alternative between
freedom and necessity in God is a false one. Such an alternative
is only valid in the case of alienated existence, not for the
existence of God whose essence is love. Moltmann writes,

The compulsion to think within the alternative, either God is absolutely free and sovereign or he is his own prisoner and therefore a
controllable idol in our hands, leads one astray. The oppressed
thinking of the slave questions in this way: either God has control over
me or I over him. But that is not the free thinking of the truth, a
thinking liberated from the categories of domination and slavery. The
'truth, which makes free,' can be comprehended only in a thinking
which is free both from the purposes of domination and from slavish
obedience. The objectivizing alternative of controllable/uncontroll-
able is not true even for the community of human persons; how much
less is it 'appropriate for God'! According to the biblical witness God
is, to be sure, all-powerful but he is not power as such. He *is* love.[74]

The question of God's freedom *vis à vis* the world is therefore
ultimately the question of God's love. Moltmann cannot understand love as anything other than goodness overflowing itself.
'The truth of freedom is the love which is an "overflowing of
goodness". *Bonum est communicativum sui*: self-communication.'[75]

This seems to me to be the correct solution. God's essence is
love and if this is so, then we can even speak of a primordial
decision in God, not an either–or decision, but a decision
identical with God's essence. If we take seriously the unity of
God's being, then his primordial decision is only rationally
distinct from his being. Jüngel speaks of the primordial decision
by which God decides to be/is himself. But in the unity of his
essence as love, this decision is at the same time his decision to
be for man. He writes,

Revelation, however, resolves the tautology 'God is God' in such a
way that God's own decision is to be understood not only for *God*, but
precisely as a decision for God, which is also a decision for *man*. . . . He
does not will to be *himself* in any other way than he is in this *relationship*.
God's setting-himself-in-relation (being as event) to us qualifies
God's act of revelation as *love*.[76]

[74] Moltmann, 'Antwort', in *Diskussion über Jürgen Moltmanns Buch 'Der Gekreuzigte Gott'*, pp. 170–1.
[75] Ibid., p. 173.
[76] Eberhard Jüngel, *The Doctrine of the Trinity, God's Being Is in Becoming*, p. 67.

194    THE GOD OF PROCESS AND THE GOD OF HOPE

We could end this section by referring to Jüngel's definition of love. Love is a being-related to oneself, but in such a way that this self-possession exists within a greater self-gift. God then does not exist in a metaphysically dependent relationship to his creation. He does not need the world to be himself. Rather, being what he is, he is already beyond himself in his desire to be for and with the other. His essence is already a going-out-of-himself.[77] Human reflection can go no further than to express this paradox. Let us give Jüngel the last word, for with his characteristic love of paradox, he sums up the meaning of God's freedom in this way:

> In the midst of so great—and rightly so great—a self-relatedness, it is still an even greater selflessness, that is to say, it is nothing other than a self-relation—in freedom going out beyond itself, pouring itself out and giving itself away: pure overflow, Being gushing over—for the sake of another and only to this extent for its own sake.[78]

## viii.  *The Doctrine of the Trinity*

Throughout our study we have taken the position that the Christian doctrine of God is the doctrine of the Trinity and vice versa. In this sense then these final remarks on the differences between Ogden and Moltmann on trinitarian questions are subsidiary. The more fundamental issues have already been discussed. None the less a few concluding remarks on trinitarian theology as such seem to be in order.

The origin of this study lies partially in Moltmann's contention that process theology, while rightly grasping God's relation to time, fails to be an adequate Christian theology because it is not trinitarian. In *The Experiment Hope* he writes, 'Christian

---

[77] 'We bring these theological reflections now to their ontological *concept*, when we comprhend the Being of God as Going-out-of-himself-into-Nothing.' *Gott als Geheimnis der Welt, Zur Begründung der Theologie des Gekreuzigten im Streit zwischen Theismus und Atheismus* (Tübingen: J. C. B. Mohr, 1978), p. 303. The 'Nichts' refers both to God's *creatio ex nihilo* and his encounter with death on the cross. On the cross God takes the *Nichts* into his own life. Jüngel argues that the appropriate locus for speech about the death of God is not atheistic philosophy but Christian theology.

[78] Jüngel, ibid., p. 506. In order to grasp the full paradoxical flavour of Jüngel's definition, it is useful to cite the original German text, the force of which is difficult to capture in an English translation. 'Es ist aber "eine inmitten noch so größer—und mit Recht noch so größer—Selbstbezogenheit immer noch größere Selbstlosigkeit" nichts anderes als ein in Freiheit über sich selbst hinausgehendes, sich verströmendes und verschenkendes Selbstverhältnis: reiner Überfluß, überströmendes—zugunsten eines anderen und nur insofern zugunsten seiner selbst überströmendes—Sein.'

theology cannot develop (as is often done in process theology) a bipolar theology of interaction between God and the Spirit in man. It must, for the sake of the crucified one, intentionally become a trinitarian theology.[79] In chapter three, I tried to show that this objection does not hold. Process theology can also be trinitarian. None the less in these concluding remarks I would like to call attention to a significant difference in approach between Moltmann and Ogden. If, as Piet Schoonenberg asserts, there are two basic models for trinitarian thinking today, the modalistic model and the communitarian one,[80] then certainly Ogden is in the modalistic school and Moltmann in the communitarian one.

Given the basic philosophical convictions of process philosophy, it is difficult for a process theologian to adopt any other model for trinitarian thinking than the modalistic one. In an article entitled 'Process Trinitarianism' Lewis Ford explains why process thinkers reject the communitarian model. He writes,

This latter, social interpretation is precluded in terms of Whitehead's categories because of the intrinsic connection forged between substantial unity and subjectivity. The denial of vacuous actuality entails that every substantial unity enjoys its own subjectivity, and no meaning can be attached to a subjective process of becoming which does not terminate in some sort of substantial unity. Thus while 'person' as 'center of subjectivity' may be distinguished from 'substance' as 'substantial unity', the two are in strict correlation. Three persons entails three substances, while one substance entails a single person. Moreover, substance in the sense of a divine substratum in which the three persons inhere is just that sort of vacuous actuality devoid of its own subjectivity which Whitehead rejects. 'Person' in trinitarian formulations must mean rather a formally distinct aspect or principle or mode of functioning for a single, unitary actuality, that which Whitehead termed a 'nature' when speaking of the primordial and consequent natures of God.[81]

[79] Moltmann, The Experiment Hope, p. 78.

[80] Schoonenberg stressed this point in his lecture 'Modalistic and Personalistic Views of the Trinity', delivered in Oxford, 5 May 1977. By modalism Schoonenberg does not mean the ancient heresy of Sabellianism, but such modern attempts to interpret the doctrine of the Trinity as those of Barth and Rahner. Among representatives of the communitarion school are Leonard Hodgson (The Doctrine of the Trinity (London, 1944)) and Heribert Mühlen (Der Heilige Geist als Person, 2nd edn. (Münster, 1966)).

[81] Lewis Ford, 'Process Trinitarianism', Journal of the American Academy of Religion 43, 2 (June 1975) 207.

On the other hand it is precisely this modalistic approach of process thinkers which Moltmann cannot accept. Although he directs his polemic against Rahner and Barth, he could have written the same against process theologians. He writes, 'Because Rahner's "self-communication of God" just as Barth's "self-revelation of God" can be completed by only one transcendent subject, he must reduce the three divine persons to "three distinct ways of subsistence." '[82] Moltmann wants us to take this word 'reduce' with full seriousness. As he says in another place, such an understanding of the three persons is not an interpretation of the Trinity but rather its modalistic dissolution.[83]

Without repeating what I already said about Moltmann's understanding of the persons of the Trinity in chapter four, I can merely recall here that he views them as three persons in the modern sense of the term. Thus he does not have so much a theory of the divine unity as a doctrine of the divine uniting.[84] The distinction is nicely connoted in the German by the two words *Einheit* and *Vereinigung*. On strictly linguistic grounds the latter term has a more active connotation. For Moltmann then the divine unity is the eschatological goal of God's own history.

But in maintaining that God's unity is the goal of God's history, Moltmann comes full circle again and joins the process theologians. For in spite of the crucial difference between them in their interpretation of the three persons, there is a deeper bond which unites them. And that is their common conviction that God's being lies in his becoming/history. And for both Moltmann and process thinkers one could say that the one God, Father, Son, and Holy Spirit, is both absolute and relative, eternal and temporal. The critical question then which eschato-

---

[82] Jürgen Moltmann, 'Der Dreieinige Gott', Unpublished Lecture Notes on the Trinity, p. 26.

[83] Moltmann writes, 'The reflection-Trinity of the absolute subject has only the appearance of a doctrine of the Trinity in itself, but in fact this doctrine is the monotheistic dissolution of the Trinity. This happens—as always—by the introduction of *modalism* (the three persons are three ways of the appearance of the being of the one God).' 'Das Neue Testament als Zeugnis der trinitarischen Geschichte Gottes', unpublished Lecture Notes, Tübingen, Winter Semester, 1978, p. 2. This point of view is developed at length in *The Trinity and the Kingdom of God* (London: SCM Press, 1981). See especially V, 1, 'A Criticism of Christian Monotheism', pp. 129–50.

[84] See Moltmann, *The Church in the Power of the Spirit*, Chapter II, 4 (iv), 'The "union" of God', pp. 60–2.

logical thinkers such as Moltmann and process theologians such as Ogden address to us is this: how do we think God's transcendence in such a way as to include his immanence? Both theologians whom we have examined in this study have adopted radical stances in regard to this question, and their systems are no doubt impressive. Yet for many critics there are lingering doubts that something essential in the Christian understanding about God has been threatened. In a seminar of the Catholic Theological Society of America entitled 'Trinity and World Process' the leaders of the seminar expressed their consensus about this in a statement addressed to Moltmann's theology. But remarkably the point of their questioning concerned precisely the area of agreement between Moltmann and process thinkers. They summarize the results of their discussion in these words, 'It was agreed that Moltmann's thesis of the suffering God has to be more carefully nuanced. Is divine suffering truly compatible with everything else we believe about God, e.g. his transcendence, immutability, infinity? Or does it compel acceptance of a finite God, as so many of the process thinkers, notably Alfred North Whitehead, concede?'[85] These unresolved questions lead me to conclude that a significant task for contemporary theology lies precisely in the direction of 'nuancing' the meaning of the divine suffering, both by building upon the critique of classical philosophical theism articulated in the writings of Ogden and Moltmann and by seeking to integrate the experience of the cross with the Christian conviction of God's transcendence.[86]

[85] Joseph Bracken, S. J., Robert Sears, S. J., William Hill, O. P., 'Seminar on Trinity and World Process', *Proceedings of the Catholic Theological Society of America* 33 (1978) 244.

[86] Langdon Gilkey argues that part of the answer to the challenge of classical philosophical theism by such thinkers as Ogden and Moltmann lies in the notion of God's self-limitation in his relation to finite being. Such a self-limitation would make God vulnerable without compromising his transcendence. God becomes vulnerable because of his self-*limitation*. But he remains transcendent because it is a *self*-limitation. Gilkey writes, 'God alone does not create the present. The divine creativity out of which the present arises from its past establishes a *self-creative* process: God creates by giving each occasion the power of self-creation out of its destiny. Thus each event actualizes itself in freedom out of its destiny and out of the possibilities relevant to that destiny. We do not create ourselves in whole, *ex nihilo*, for freedom always is polar to a destiny we have not created, and clearly, we are not the cause of the power to be self-determinative. Our freedom does not arise from our freedom, and we are self-determinative through a power of self-determination given to us. But we do shape what is given to us into what we are. Thus do men and women help to shape historical process into what it is. The

ix.   *The Significance of the Doctrine of the Trinity for Understanding God's Relation to the World*

In our first chapter we suggested that one reason for contemporary atheism lies in the idea of God developed by classical philosophical theism, and we argued that in the light of the critique of atheism Christian theology must christianize its doctrine of God, i.e. think through the meaning of God radically in the light of Jesus Christ. Both Ogden and Moltmann contend that classical philosophical theism is a failure because it cannot express the radical Christian assertion: God is love. For both thinkers the truth of this assertion can be grounded in the Christ-event, although Moltmann would see this event in a more restricted sense than Ogden.

In this concluding section I would like to indicate that it is the event of Jesus Christ which logically compels the Christian believer to think in trinitarian terms, and that by thinking through the meaning of this event in terms of the Trinity one finds in embryo the key to the solution of God's relation to the world.

If the event of Jesus Christ is the event of revelation, if God defines himself by this event, then God's being is in this event. It is impossible to think of God without this event. Jesus Christ belongs to the very being of God. Classical trinitarian theology in its language about the pre-existence of the Son is, in my judgement, trying to express this insight.

But if Jesus Christ belongs to the very being of God, then God is in his very being a movement outward to creation and to incarnation. From the historical event of Jesus Christ in which God defines himself we must think the historicality of God's being itself. Eberhard Jüngel in his study of Karl Barth's trinitarian theology puts it this way:

If revelation as God's *being*-for-us is to be taken seriously, then in Jesus Christ God's being must *become* visible and *be able* to become

---

limitation on God's sovereignty in history is achieved, therefore, not through the notion of the finitude of God as one factor in the process balanced by other factors. Nor is God "in the grip" of a process which transcends and so makes him possible, since as the power alike of being, of freedom and of possibility, he is the ground of process. The limitation on God's sovereignty is understood as the self-limitation of God in creating and preserving a finitude characterized by freedom and so by self-actualization.'
*Reaping the Whirlwind*, p. 307.

visible. This means, however, that both this becoming as well as this being-able to become must be understood from God's being itself, if indeed it is really true that *God* has revealed *himself*. Thus the historicality of God must be formulated *from God*. And on the other side, God's being must be formulated in view of this becoming and of this being-able to become if indeed it is really true that God has *revealed* himself. Thus at all cost we must formulate God's *historicality*.[87]

The move then is from the historical event of God's self-identification in Jesus Christ to the condition of possibility of that self-identification. To quote Jüngel once again, 'If the doctrine of the economic Trinity speaks of God's *history* with man, then the doctrine of the immanent Trinity has to speak of God's *historicality*. God's history is his coming to man. *God's historicality* is his Being-in-coming.'[88]

Creation, man, incarnation are then not afterthoughts on God's part. The church's formulation of the doctrine of the Trinity preserves this truth. For through this doctrine the church affirms the historicality of God's Being. In Jüngel's words, 'God comes from God; but he does not want to come to himself without coming to us. God comes to God—but with man. Therefore humanity belongs already to God's divinity.'[89]

If this understanding of God prevents us from thinking of humanity as extrinsic and accidental to God, it also prevents us from compromising God's transcendence and making him metaphysically dependent upon time. For according to this understanding of God, time and history are grounded in God's being which is already in motion. It is not time that makes possible God's self-communication but it is God's being as self-communicating love that makes time and history possible. In Jüngel's words,

So long as the becoming in which God's being is, is understood as the becoming *proper* to God's being, the statement 'God's being is in becoming' remains from the first guarded from the misunderstanding that God *would* first *become* that which he is, through his relationship to an other than himself. God therefore does not first become in the faith which he grants. But certainly God chooses to become in faith what he

[87] Jüngel, *The Doctrine of the Trinity*, p. 94.
[88] Jüngel, *Gott als Geheimnis der Welt*, p. 475.
[89] Ibid., p. 47.

*already is.* And in so far God, in the self-relatedness of his being in becoming, is already ours in advance.[90]

If this understanding of the Trinity is correct, then a resolution of the problematic outlined in chapter one can be found. The Christian God is not the absolute, impassible God of classical philosophical theism, rightly rejected by atheists. The Christian God is the God who suffers in time, who enters our history in the event of Jesus Christ. To think God in the light of this event is to think of a God whose being is in coming. God's coming to man proceeds from his sovereign freedom of overflowing love. In this sense God's coming is grounded in his transcendence. But since God's being itself is his coming, we cannot think of God without his creation or without man. Man is not accidental or external to God but through the unfathomable mystery of his love part of God's own self-definition.

### x.   *Postscript: The Limits of a Speculative Solution*

A central problematic which has occupied the two thinkers whom we have examined in this study is the theodicy question: how can one continue to believe in the face of the enormous suffering of human beings over the centuries continuing up to the present day?

Whitehead saw his entire philosophical system as an attempt to throw new light on this question.[91] And process philosophy and theology is convinced that a rational explanation can be given to the problem. But the question arises whether such thinkers as Ogden do not solve the problem by dis-solving it. For as Ogden once remarked, 'As for the so-called problem of evil, I can say only that I incline to regard it as a pseudo-problem, in that it only arises given certain premises of classical Christian theism, which are in themselves incoherent quite aside from the fact of evil.'[92] Without repeating here the solution Ogden proposes for the problem of evil, we should note that, according to his view of metaphysics, philosophy can reach universal and necessary propositions which no empirical

---

[90] Jüngel, *The Doctrine of the Trinity*, pp. 100–1, n. 152.

[91] This is seen, for example, in Whitehead's remark that *Process and Reality* is meant to add another speaker to Hume's *Dialogues Concerning Natural Religion*. See *Process and Reality*, p. 521.

[92] Schubert Ogden, 'On Creation and Man', Unpublished Lecture Series, Perkins School of Theology 1975–6, p. 6.

assertion can falsify.[93] That means that metaphysics can construct a doctrine of God which no account of human suffering can contradict.

Obviously Ogden's system is a version of philosophical and theological rationalism against which the usual criticisms of rationalism could be directed. The question which the Christian theologian is left with is whether the brokenness of human life and history can really be healed by pure reason.

With this problem in mind, Bernard Meland, a sympathetic reader of Ogden, offers him this advice. 'The correlative I would like to urge upon Schubert Ogden, then, is not that he abandon his method of process theology based upon analogical thinking, but that he consider some means by which he might avoid the inevitable drift of such thinking toward a closed rationalism, in which only man and his formulations speak forth.'[94]

Turning to the theology of Moltmann, we must admit that his thought is less rationalistic, since it is so firmly anchored in the concrete event of the cross. Moltmann admits that the present experience of the world is in large measure godless, that faith must await an eschatological verification, and that meanwhile our confidence is based upon the knowledge that God is with us in suffering.

Nevertheless there is some tendency toward rationalism in Moltmann as well, in so far as he wishes to use the cross as the foundation upon which to build a system. The cross is, as it were, the epistemological key to understanding the ways of God in dealing with the world. Given this key, one can construct a theological ontology. The history of the world which is the history of suffering equals the history of God.

Johannes Metz criticizes the impressive system of Moltmann in that it is in the last analysis a subtle form of rationalism which subsumes individual suffering under the idea of universal history.[95] Metz contends that this is precisely what Christian

[93] See Schubert Ogden, 'Falsification and Belief', *Religious Studies* 10 (1974) 21–43.
[94] Bernard Meland, 'Analogy and Myth in Postliberal Theology', *Perkins School of Theology Journal* (Winter 1962) 27.
[95] J. B. Metz writes, 'Among the universally historical approaches that are described (critically) in this chapter as "idealistic" are not only Wolfhart Pannenberg's influential ontology of history and meaning that is strongly orientated towards Hegel and in which the idea of a meaning of history is not a category of practical reason, but

theology cannot do. Suffering cannot be reduced to a concept.
He writes,

> A purely conceptual reconciliation between the history of the
> redemption accomplished in Jesus Christ and the history of man's
> suffering is, in my opinion, not possible, because it can only lead
> either to a dualistic gnostic perpetuation of suffering in God or to a
> reduction of suffering to the level of a concept. This dilemma cannot
> be resolved by any more subtle speculative reason. It can only be
> resolved if salvation and redemption in the non-identity of the history
> of suffering are approached in a different way.[96]

What then is this different way? I would suggest that it
involves two elements. The first is the way of narration. The
Christian does not have a speculative solution to the problem of
suffering. What he does have is a story to relate, a gospel about
how God came to us in our suffering. In the words of the
opening verses of the First Letter of John, 'That which was from
the beginning, which we have heard, which we have seen with
our eyes, which we have looked upon and touched with our
hands . . . we proclaim to you.' (1 John 1:1-3.) Of such story-
telling Metz observes, 'Narrative is unpretentious in its effect.
It does not have, even from God, the dialectical key which will
open every door and throw light in the dark passages of history
before they have been trodden. It is not, however, without light
itself.'[97]

The second dimension of this different way is that of praxis.
This means that the problematic of the unanswered cries of
suffering men and women cannot admit of a speculative
solution but only of a practical one, that of discipleship itself.
Again Metz says, 'The salvation that is founded "for all men" in
Christ does not become universal via an idea, but via the
intelligible power of a praxis, the praxis of following Christ.'[98]

(following idealistic traditions) a category of reflection. A universally historical and
idealistic conception—in the sense of a stage in the history of human freedom that can
be eschatologically and messianically integrated into Christianity—has, I believe, been
provided by Jürgen Moltmann, in his impressive attempt to interpret the present
situation of Christianity in the light of the revolutionary history of freedom.' *Faith in
History and Society: Toward a Practical Fundamental Theology* (New York: Seabury Press,
1980), p. 157.
[96] J. B. Metz, 'A Short Apology of Narrative', *Concilium* vol. v. 9 (1973), p. 92.
[97] Ibid.
[98] Metz, *Faith in History and Society*, p. 165.

A striking feature of the two theologians that we have examined in this study is that they have become apologetic theologians by becoming systematic theologians. They have sought to reply to the critique of the non-believer not so much by showing that he is wrong but by thinking through in as radical and consistent a way as possible what the Christian claims in fact are.

This final paragraph has the modest aim of suggesting that any speculative solution can go only so far, for the history of the suffering of the world goes on and refutes all our systems. Beyond all our reasons, however, lies another argument, that of our discipleship itself. Moltmann speaks of this discipleship in terms of taking upon ourselves the suffering of others. Ogden speaks in more biblical terms of our witness of 'faith working through love'. Though their language is different, the praxis would seem to be the same. It is my conviction that such praxis will be in the final analysis the most convincing argument, for our age or any other, of the truth of the Christian experience of God.

# SELECT BIBLIOGRAPHY

THIS bibliography seeks to be as complete as possible in citing the works of Schubert Ogden and Jürgen Moltmann, the principal authors studied in this book. Extensive bibliographies of process philosophers and theologians can be found in Delwin Brown, Ralph E. James and Gene Reeves (edd.), *Process Philosophy and Christian Thought*, Indianapolis and New York: Bobbs-Merrill, 1971; also in Ewert H. Cousins (ed.), *Process Theology, Basic Writings*, New York: Newman Press, 1971. A thorough bibliography of the writings of Charles Hartshorne can be found in Colin E. Gunton, *Becoming and Being, The Doctrine of God in Charles Hartshorne and Karl Barth*, Oxford University Press, 1978.

## I  GENERAL WORKS ON CHRISTIAN DOCTRINE OF GOD

FEINER, JOHANNES and LÖHRER, MAGNUS. *Mysterium Salutis, Grundriss heilsgeschichtlicher Dogmatik*, 5 vol. (Einsiedeln: Benziger, 1965–76); especially vol. 2 and vol. 3, part 2.

GRILLMEIER, ALOYS. *Christ in the Christian Tradition*, vol. 1, *From the Apostolic Age to Chalcedon* (AD 451). Oxford: Mowbrays, 1975.

JOHNSON, AUBREY R. *The One and the Many in the Israelite Conception of God*, Cardiff: University of Wales Press, 1942.

JÜNGEL, EBERHARD. *The Doctrine of the Trinity, God's Being Is in Becoming*, Edinburgh and London: Scottish Academic Press, 1976.

—— *Gott als Geheimnis der Welt. Zur Begründung der Theologie des Gekreuzigten im Streit zwischen Theismus und Atheismus*, Tübingen: J. C. B. Mohr, 1977.

KELLY, J. N. D. *The Athanasian Creed*, London: Adam and Charles Black, 1964.

—— *Early Christian Creeds*, London: Longmans, 1972.

—— *Early Christian Doctrines*, London: Black, 1977.

KNIGHT, G. A. F. *A Biblical Approach to the Doctrine of the Trinity*, Scottish Journal of Theology Occasional Papers, No. 1, Edinburgh: Oliver and Boyd Ltd., 1953.

LONERGAN, BERNARD J. F. *The Way to Nicaea, The Dialectical Development of Trinitarian Theology*, London: Darton, Longman and Todd, 1976.

MOULE, C. F. D. *The Origin of Christology*, Cambridge University Press, 1977.

O'DONNELL, JOHN J. 'The Doctrine of the Trinity in Recent German Theology', *Heythrop Journal* 23, no. 2 (April, 1982), 153–67.

PANNENBERG, WOLFHART. 'The Appropriation of the Philosophical Concept of God as a Dogmatic problem of Early Christian Theology', in *Basic Questions in Theology*, vol. 2, London: SCM Press, 1971, pp. 119–183.

PELIKAN, JAROSLAV. *The Christian Tradition, A History of the Development of Doctrine*. vol. 1, *The Emergence of the Catholic Tradition (100–600)*, Chicago: University of Chicago Press, 1971.

—— vol. 2, *The Spirit of Eastern Christendom (600–1700)*, Chicago: University of

Chicago Press, 1974.

PRESTIGE, G. L. *God in Patristic Thought*, London: SPCK, 1952.

RAHNER, KARL. *Foundations of Christian Faith, An Introduction to the Idea of Christianity*, London: Darton, Longman and Todd, 1978.

—— *The Trinity*, London: Herder and Herder, 1970.

RICHARDSON, CYRIL. *The Doctrine of the Trinity*, New York and Nashville: Abingdon Press, 1958.

WAINWRIGHT, ARTHUR W. *The Trinity in the New Testament*, London: SPCK, 1962.

WILES, MAURICE. *The Making of Christian Doctrine, A Study in the Principles of Early Doctrinal Development*, Cambridge University Press, 1967.

—— *The Remaking of Christian Doctrine*, London: SCM Press, 1974.

—— 'Some Reflections on the Origins of the Doctrine of the Trinity', *Journal of Theological Studies* n.s. 8 (1957), pp. 92–106. Reprinted in *Working Papers in Doctrine*, London: SCM Press, 1976.

II THE THEOLOGY OF SCHUBERT OGDEN

OGDEN, SCHUBERT. *Christ Without Myth, A Study Based on the Theology of Rudolf Bultmann*, London: Collins, 1962.

—— *Faith and Freedom: Toward a Theology of Liberation*, Belfast-Dublin-Ottawa: Christian Journals Limited, 1979.

—— *The Point of Christology, The Sarum Lectures 1980*, London: SCM Press, 1982.

—— *The Reality of God and Other Essays*, London: SCM Press, 1967.

—— 'The Authority of Scripture for Theology', *Interpretation* 30 (1976), 242–61.

—— 'Beyond Supernaturalism', *Religion in Life* 33 (1963–4), pp. 7–18.

—— 'Bultmann and the "New Quest"', *Journal of Bible and Religion* 30 (1962), pp. 209–18.

—— 'Bultmann's Demythologizing and Hartshorne's Dipolar Theism', in *The Hartshorne Festschrift, Process and Divinity, Philosophical Essays Presented to Charles Hartshorne*, edd. William L. Reese and Eugene Freeman. La Salle, Ill.: Open Court, 1964, pp. 493–513.

—— 'Bultmann's Project of Demythologizing and the Problem of Philosophy and Theology', *Journal of Religion* 37 (1957), 156–173.

—— 'The Challenge to Protestant Thought', *Continuum* 6, 2 (Summer 1968), 236–240.

—— 'The Christian and Unbelievers', in *Motive* 25, 8 (May 1965), 21–3.

—— 'The Christian Proclamation of God to Men of the So-Called "Atheistic Age"', in *Concilium*, vol. 6: *Church and World: Christian Faith and Modern Atheism*. London: Burns and Oates, 1966, pp. 46–50.

—— 'Christliche Theologie und die neue Religiosität', in *Chancen der Religion*, ed. by Rainer Volp. Gütersloh: Gütersloher Verlagshaus Gerd Mohn, 1975, pp. 157–74.

—— 'Christology Reconsidered: John Cobb's *Christ in a Pluralistic Age*', *Process Studies* 6 (1976), 116–22.

—— 'The Concern of the Theologian', in *Christianity and Communism* ed. Merrimon Cuninggim, Dallas: Southern Methodist University Press, 1958,

pp. 58–74.
—— 'The Criterion of Metaphysical Truth and the Senses of "Metaphysics"', *Process Studies* 5, 1 (Spring 1975), 47–8.
—— 'The Debate of Demythologizing', *Journal of Bible and Religion* 27 (1959), 17–27.
—— 'Doctrinal Standards in the United Methodist Church', *Perkins School of Theology Journal* 28 (Fall 1974), 19–27.
—— 'Faith and Secularity', in *God, Secularization and History: Essays in Memory of Ronald Gregor Smith* edited by Eugene Thomas Long, Columbia, South Carolina: University of South Carolina Press, 1974, pp. 26–43.
—— 'Faith and Truth', in *Frontline Theology*, ed. by Dean Peerman, Richmond: John Knox Press, 1967, pp. 126–33.
—— 'Falsification and Belief', *Religious Studies* 10 (1974), 21–43.
—— 'God and Philosophy: A Discussion with Antony Flew', *Journal of Religion* 48, 2 (April 1968), 161–81.
—— 'How Does God Function in Human Life?', *Christianity and Crisis*, 27, 8 (15 May 1967), 105–08.
—— Introduction to *Existence and Faith, Shorter Writings of Rudolf Bultmann*, London: Hodder and Stoughton, 1961, pp. 9–21.
—— 'Karl Rahner: Theologian of Open Catholicism', *Christian Advocate* II, 17 (7 Sept. 1967), 11–13.
—— 'Lonergan and the Subjectivist Principle', *Journal of Religion* 51, 3 (July 1971), 155–72.
—— '"Love Divine, All Loves Excelling": Theological Reflections', *United Methodists Today* 1, 9 (Sept. 1974), pp. 68–71; 10 (Oct. 1974), pp. 84 f.
—— 'Love Unbounded: The Doctrine of God', *Perkins School of Theology Journal* 19, 3 (Spring 1966), 5–17.
—— 'The Meaning of Christian Hope', in *Religious Experience and Process Theology: The Pastoral Implications of a Major Modern Movement*, edd. Harry James Cargas and Bernard Lee, New York: Paulist Press, 1976, pp. 195–212.
—— 'On Demythologizing', *Pittsburgh Perspective* 8, 2 (June 1967), 27–35.
—— 'On Revelation' in *Our Common History as Christians: Essays in Honor of Albert C. Outler*, edd. John Deschner, Leroy T. Howe, and Klaus Penzel, New York: Oxford University Press, 1975, pp. 261–92.
—— 'On the Trinity', *Theology* 83 (Mar. 1980), 97–102.
—— 'The Point of Christology', *Journal of Religion* 55, 4 (Oct. 1975), 375–95.
—— 'The Possibility and Task of Philosophical Theology', *Union Seminary Quarterly Review* 20, 3 (Mar. 1965), 271–79.
—— 'Present Prospects for Empirical Theology', in *The Future of Empirical Theology*, ed. Bernard E. Meland, Chicago: University of Chicago Press, 1969, pp. 65–88.
—— 'The Reformation That We Want', *Anglican Theological Review* 54, 4 (Oct. 1972), 260–73.
—— 'Response to Jürgen Moltmann', in *Hope and the Future of Man*, ed. Ewert H. Cousins, Philadelphia: Fortress Press, 1972, pp. 109–16.
—— 'The Significance of Rudolf Bultmann for Contemporary Theology', in *The Theology of Rudolf Bultmann*, ed. Charles W. Kegley, New York: Harper

and Row, 1966, pp. 104–26.

—— 'The Situation in Contemporary Protestant Theology, IV: Systematic Theology', *Perkins School of Theology Journal* 12, 2 (Winter 1959), 13–20.

—— 'Sources of Religious Authority in Liberal Protestantism', *Journal of the American Academy of Religion* 44, 3 (1976), 403–16.

—— 'The Task of Philosophical Theology', in *The Future of Philosophical Theology*, ed. Robert H. Evans, Philadelphia: The Westminster Press, 1971, pp. 55–84.

—— '"Theology and Falsification" in Retrospect: A Reply', in *The Logic of God: Theology and Verification*, edd. Malcolm L. Diamond and Thomas V. Litzenburg, Jr., Indianapolis: Bobbs-Merrill, 1975, pp. 290–7.

—— 'Theology and Metaphysics', *Criterion* 9, 1 (Autumn 1969), 15–18.

—— 'Theology and Philosophy: A New Phase of the Discussion', *Journal of Religion* 44 (1964), 1–16.

—— 'Truth, Truthfulness and Secularity', in *Christianity and Crisis* 31, 5 (5 April 1971), 56–60.

—— 'The Understanding of Theology in Ott and Bultmann', in *New Frontiers in Theology*, vol. 1: *The Later Heidegger and Theology*, edd. James M. Robinson and John B. Cobb, New York: Harper and Row, 1963, pp. 157–73.

—— 'What is Theology?' *Journal of Religion* 52, 1 (Jan. 1972), 22–40.

—— and Van A. Harvey, 'How New is the "New Quest of the Historical Jesus"?' in *The Historical Jesus and the Kerygmatic Christ*, edd. Carl E. Braaten and Roy A. Harrisville, New York: Abingdon Press, 1964, pp. 197–242.

## III    SECONDARY LITERATURE ON THE THEOLOGY OF SCHUBERT OGDEN

BAKER, ROBERT J. 'Symbol in the Thought of Schubert M. Ogden.' Dissertation: Rome, Pontifical Gregorian University, 1976.

BERGER, PETER L. 'Secular Theology and the Rejection of the Supernatural: Reflections on Recent Trends', *Theological Studies* 38 (1977), 39–56.

BROWN, DELWIN. 'God's Reality and Life's Meaning: A Critique of Schubert Ogden', *Encounter* 28 (1967), 256–62.

BURI, FRITZ. *How Can We Still Speak Responsibly of God?* Philadelphia: Fortress Press, 1968.

COBURN, ROBERT C. 'A Budget of Theological Puzzles', *Journal of Religion* 43 (1963), 83–92.

DIAMOND, MALCOLM L. 'Contemporary Analysis: The Metaphysical Target and the Theological Victim', *Journal of Religion* 47 (1967), 210–32.

FENTON, J. Y. 'The Post-Liberal Theology of Christ without Myth', *Journal of Religion* 43 (1963), 93–104.

FLEW, ANTONY. 'Reflections on *The Reality of God*', *Journal of Religion* 48 (1968), 150–61.

GILKEY, LANGDON. 'A Theology in Process: Schubert Ogden's Developing Theology', *Interpretation* 21 (1967), 447–59.

GRAY, JOHN A. 'Always and Everywhere: The Reality of God and Man, A Study of Schubert Ogden's Christian Theologizing.' Dissertation: Catholic University of America, 1969.

GRIFFIN, DAVID. 'Schubert Ogden's Christology and the Possibilities of Process Theology', *The Christian Scholar* 50 (1967). Reprinted in *Process Philosophy and Christian Thought*, edd. by Delwin Brown, Ralph E. James, Jr., and Gene Reeves, Indianapolis and New York: Bobbs-Merrill, 1971, pp. 347–61.

HART, RAY L. 'Schubert Ogden on the Reality of God', *Religion in Life* 36, no. 4 (1967) 506–15.

MELAND, BERNARD. 'Analogy and Myth in Postliberal Theology', *Perkins School of Theology Journal* 15, 2 (Winter 1962), 19–27.

NEVILLE, ROBERT C. 'Neoclassical Metaphysics and Christianity: A Critical Study of Ogden's *Reality of God*', *International Philosophical Quarterly* 9 (1969), 605–24.

ODEN, THOMAS, C. 'The Alleged Structural Inconsistency in Bultmann', *Journal of Religion* 44 (1964), 193–200.

PREGEANT, WILLIAM RUSSELL. 'The Meaning of Matthew's Christology: A Hermeneutical Investigation in Conversation with the Theology of Schubert Ogden.' Dissertation: Vanderbilt University, 1970.

RICHARDSON, HERBERT W. *Toward an American Theology*, New York: Harper and Row, 1967.

ROBERTSON, JOHN C. 'Rahner and Ogden: Man's Knowledge of God', *Harvard Theological Review* 63 (1970), 377–407.

SCHMIDT, LAWRENCE E. 'Historical Process and Hermeneutical Method in the Theologies of John Macquarrie, Schubert Ogden and Wolfhart Pannenberg.' Dissertation: St. Michael's College, University of Toronto, 1975.

## IV THE THEOLOGY OF JÜRGEN MOLTMANN

MOLTMANN, JÜRGEN. *The Church in the Power of the Spirit, A Contribution to Messianic Ecclesiology*, London: SCM Press, 1977.

—— *The Crucified God, The Cross of Christ as the Foundation and Criticism of Christian Theology*, London: SCM Press, 1974.

—— *The Experiment Hope*, London: SCM Press, 1975.

—— *The Future of Creation*, London: SCM Press, 1979.

—— *Herrschaft Christi und Soziale Wirklichkeit nach Dietrich Bonhoeffer*, Munich: Kaiser, 1959.

—— *Hope and Planning*, London: SCM Press, 1971.

—— *Im Gespräch mit Ernst Bloch, Eine theologische Wegbegleitung*, Munich: Kaiser, 1976.

—— *Man, Christian Anthropology in the Conflicts of the Present*, London: SPCK, 1971.

—— *The Open Church, Invitation to a Messianic Life-Style*, London: SCM Press, 1978.

—— *Perspektiven der Theologie, Gesammelte Aufsätze*. Munich and Mainz: Kaiser und Grünewald, 1968.

—— *Prädestination und Perseveranz*, Neukirchener Verlag, 1961.

—— *Religion, Revolution and the Future*, New York: Charles Scribner's Sons, 1968.

—— *Die Sprache der Befreiung—Predigten und Besinnungen*, Munich: Kaiser, 1972.

—— *Theology and Joy*, London: SCM Press, 1973.

—— *Theology of Hope, On the Ground and the Implications of a Christian Eschatology*, London: SCM Press, 1967.

—— *The Trinity and the Kingdom of God, The Doctrine of God*, London: SCM Press, 1981.

—— *Umkehr zur Zukunft*, Munich and Hamburg: Siebenstern Taschenbuch, 1970.

—— and Herzog, Frederick, *The Future of Hope: Theology as Eschatology*, New York: Herder and Herder, 1970.

—— 'Das befreiende Fest', *Concilium* (1974), pp. 118–23.

—— 'The Crucified God: A Trinitarian Theology of the Cross', *Interpretation* 26 (1972) 278–99.

—— 'Der gekreuzigte Gott, Neuzeitliche Gottesfrage und trinitarische Gottesgeschichte', *Concilium* (1972), pp. 407–13.

—— 'Gemeinschaft in einer geteilten Welt', *Evangelische Kommentare* (1972), pp. 524–8.

—— 'Glaube im Kampf um Befreiung,' *Evangelische Kommentare* (1977), pp. 651–5.

—— 'Der Gott der Hoffnung' in *Gott heute, Fünfzehn Beiträge zur Gottesfrage*, Herausgegeben von Norbert Kutschki. Mainz and Munich: Grünewald und Kaiser, 1967, pp. 116–26.

—— 'Gott versöhnt und macht frei', *Evangelische Kommentare* (1970), pp. 515–20.

—— 'Jesus und die Kirche', in J. Moltmann und W. Kasper, *Jesus Ja—Kirche Nein?* Zürich, Einsiedeln, Cologne: Benziger, 1973, pp. 37–63.

—— 'Das Leiden des Menschensohnes und Ruf in die Nachfolge', in Jürgen Moltmann und Johann Baptist Metz, *Leidensgeschichte, Zwei Meditationen zu Mk 8, 31–38*, Freiburg, Basel, Vienna: Herder, 1973, pp. 13–35.

—— 'Man and the Son of Man', in *No Man is Alien*, ed. J. Robert Nelson, Leiden: E. J. Brill, 1971, pp. 203–24.

—— 'Die messianische Hoffnung im Christentum', *Concilium* (1974), pp. 592–6.

—— 'Die politische Relevanz der christlichen Hoffnung, Eine politisch— philosophisch—theologische Thesenreihe', in *Christliche Freiheit im Dienst am Menschen*, ed. K. Herbert, Frankfurt: Otto Lembeck, 1972, pp. 153–62.

—— 'Politische Theologie als Dialog', in *Neue Generation und alte Strukturen der Macht*, Herausgegeben von Erich Kellner, Vienna: Europa Verlag, 1973, pp. 119–38.

—— 'Theologische Kritik der politischen Religion', in Johann Baptist Metz, Jürgen Moltmann, Willi Oelmüller, *Kirche im Prozeß der Aufklärung, Aspekte einer neuen 'politischen Theologie'*, Munich-Mainz: Kaiser-Grünewald, 1970, pp. 11–51.

—— 'Versöhnung und Befreiung: der Beitrag der Christenheit zum Frieden', in *Begegnung mit Polen, Evangelische Kirchen und die Herausforderung durch Geschichte und Politik*, Herausgegeben von J. Moltmann und M. Stöhr, Munich: Kaiser, 1974, pp. 165–82.

——— 'Die Verwandlung des Leidens, Der dreieinige Gott und das Kreuz', *Evangelische Kommentare* (1972) pp. 713–17.

——— 'Das Ziel der Mission', *Evangelische Missionszeitschrift* 22 (1965), 1–14.

## V   CRITICAL LITERATURE ON MOLTMANN AND THE 'THEOLOGY OF HOPE' MOVEMENT

BRAATEN, CARL E. 'Trinitarian Theology of the Cross', *Journal of Religion* 56 (1976), 113–21.

CAPPS, WALTER H. *Time Invades the Cathedral, Tensions in the School of Hope*, Philadelphia: Fortress Press, 1972.

FIORENZA, FRANCIS P. 'Dialectical Theology and Hope', I, *Heythrop Journal* 9 (1968), 143–63; II (1968), 384–99; III, *Heythrop Journal* 10 (1969), 26–42.

HUNSINGER, GEORGE. 'The Crucified God and the Political Theology of Violence: A Critical Survey of Jürgen Moltmann's Recent Thought', *Heythrop Journal* 14 (1973), 266–79, 379–95.

MARSCH, WOLF-DIETER (ed.). *Diskussion über die 'Theologie der Hoffnung' von Jürgen Moltmann*, Munich: Kaiser, 1967.

MEEKS, M. DOUGLAS. *Origins of the Theology of Hope*, Philadelphia: Fortress Press, 1974.

METZ, JOHANN BAPTIST. 'A Short Apology of Narrative', *Concilium*, vol. 5, no. 9 (1973), pp. 84–96.

MOMOSE, PETER F. *Kreuzestheologie, Eine Auseinandersetzung mit Jürgen Moltmann*, Freiburg: Herder, 1978.

MORSE, CHRISTOPHER. *The Logic of Promise in Moltmann's Theology*, Philadelphia: Fortress Press, 1979.

TRIPOLE, MARTIN R. 'Ecclesiological Developments in Moltmann's Theology of Hope', *Theological Studies* 34 (1973), 19–35.

WELKER, MICHAEL. (ed.) *Diskussion über Jürgen Moltmanns Buch 'Der gekreuzigte Gott'*, Munich: Kaiser, 1979.

# INDEX